A BORN AGAIN EPISCOPALIAN

Thomas Garrett Isham, career journalist and independent scholar, is a native of lower Michigan. A licensed lay preacher of the Diocese of Western Michigan, he is a conservative Episcopalian active in a variety of church-related causes. A graduate of Michigan State University, he is author of *The Geography of the Soul, A Christian Spiritual Psychology*, and other books.

A
BORN AGAIN
EPISCOPALIAN

*The Evangelical Witness
of
Charles Petit McIlvaine*

Thomas Garrett Isham

SOLID GROUND CHRISTIAN BOOKS
BIRMINGHAM, ALABAMA USA

Solid Ground Christian Books
PO Box 660132
Vestavia Hills AL 35266
205-443-0311
mike.sgcb@gmail.com
www.solid-ground-books.com

A BORN AGAIN EPISCOPALIAN
The Evangelical Witness of Charles Petit McIlvaine

Thomas Garrett Isham

First Solid Ground Edition October 2011

Cover design by Borgo Design
Contact them at borgogirl@bellsouth.net

ISBN- 978-159925-266-7

To James Cracraft, mentor and friend, with appreciation.

TABLE OF CONTENTS

PREFACE

Charles Pettit McIlvaine, who lived from 1799-1873, embodied the evangelical creed of the nineteenth century. A clear-thinking, intellectually rigorous Episcopalian, he exemplified the deep emotional currents of revival and rebirth, of the "conviction of sin," of the need to be born again into new life. An aristocrat by birth and bearing and a bishop by consecration of the Episcopal Church, he knew himself to be a common sinner in God's sight, as much in need of rescue as the folk to whom he ministered.

McIlvaine united character and creed in a remarkable witness. Both his strengths and his weaknesses equipped him to be a peerless propagator of evangelical faith, even as they alerted him to the spiritual medicine he himself needed. "Just as I Am" was his favorite hymn and it summed up his faith. He had no illusions about himself, as an individual or as a member of what he held to be a fallen race. He believed that "all is grace" and that self-rescue was out of the question, for him or anyone else. He threw himself "on the mercies," a sick soul in need of healing, a divided soul in need of unification, a sinning soul in need of forgiveness.

McIlvaine deserves to be better known. He deserves to be known for his doctrine, for his character, and for the compelling manner in which his doctrine and character expressed the evangelical paradigm in a liturgical church. To be sure, he may appear at first glance to be of little current interest. The movement he led so ably ended in apparent failure; his name is largely forgotten; his evangelical religion is little heeded—indeed, little known until recently—within The Episcopal Church. Yet he is not in fact the ambassador of a failed and forgotten movement. Rather, he may be heard as the perennial voice of a tradition that finds rebirth again and again in the ongoing life of the Christian. As preacher, polemicist, and bishop, McIlvaine vigorously critiqued the themes and thoughts that inspired emerging trends in nineteenth-century churchmanship. A prolific writer, he smote hip and thigh the advocates of the Anglo-Catholic movement, kept traditional High Churchmen off balance, and challenged the scholarship of the new schools of biblical criticism, schools which drew inspiration from German academic theologians and their English followers. In doing so, he fashioned a cogent statement of what many conservative Christians to this day regard as the enduring verities.

To be sure, McIlvaine witnessed ardently for a movement that has been largely forgotten by the intellectual elites of the Protestant mainstream. In the case of The Episcopal Church of the United States, it is a movement that was eclipsed by the Anglo-Catholic (or Ritualist) and liberal theologies that were in the ascendance in his day and that continue in their evolved forms to dominate church discourse, though not without challenge. Such neglect needs to be addressed. At a time when there is a resurgent evangelical movement in The Episcopal Church, as well as in much of the worldwide Anglican Communion, thoughtful Christians—both evangelical and otherwise—might wish to learn about McIlvaine and his work and their possible relevance for today. He raised and answered in a distinctly evangelical way perennial questions of spiritual and theological moment.

The following book is the first since the nineteenth century devoted solely to McIlvaine and his witness. I wish to acknowledge with gratitude Dr. James Cracraft, Professor of History and University Scholar, University of Illinois at Chicago, for his keen interest in this project. His encouragement, scholarly acumen, and friendship have played equal parts in turning this project from an idea into a reality. I wish to acknowledge also the late Dr. Peter Toon, president of the Prayer Book Society of the USA, for suggestions that balanced and deepened my discussion of the doctrinal issues of McIlvaine's day. Further thanks are due to Carol Marshall, Special Collections Reading Room coordinator, and Tom House, librarian and technology consultant, both of Library and Information Services, Kenyon College, for providing copious amounts of archival materials about and by Charles Pettit McIlvaine. Many thanks are owed also to Sharon Fitzpatrick, library assistant, Library Company of Burlington, New Jersey; Laura Chace, curator of rare books for the Cincinnati Historical Society Library; Phil Nuxhall, historian, Spring Grove Cemetery and Arboretum, Cincinnati, Ohio; Glenn Metzdorf, archivist, Christ Church Georgetown; Don Wilcox, curator of books, William L. Clements Library, University of Michigan, Ann Arbor, and the late John Harriman, supervisor of the William L. Clements Library; Clare Brown, Lambeth Palace Library, London, and Gary Hood, Curator of Art, West Point Museum, the United States Military Academy, West Point, New York.

I am indebted as well to historian Diana Hochstedt Butler, whose Standing Against the Whirlwind: Evangelical Episcopalians in Nineteenth Century America, admirably chronicles McIlvaine's role in the religious movement he led, and to Loren Dale Pugh, whose dissertation, Bishop Charles Pettit McIlvaine: The Faithful Evangel, judiciously examines McIlvaine's life and work in the context of early American political and church history. I wish to thank as well Nancy Cracraft, Brooks and Wanza Grantier, Dr. Frank Burris and Hugh Welsh, friends all who encouraged me by their enthusiasm for and comments on my project. Lastly, I wish to thank my wife, Nancy, for both her assistance in research and her patience as a traveling companion in quest of McIlvainia.

A note on terminology: The word "evangelical" will be used with both a small e and a large E. In lower case, it will refer to a Protestant of pietistic, revivalist, and conversionist convictions; in upper case, it will refer to the party in the Episcopal Church led by McIlvaine.

INTRODUCTION

The Church of the Holy Spirit stands at the very center of the Kenyon College campus, in an open space bordered by the lawns of academic buildings both larger and smaller than itself. The college, carved from the wilderness early in the nineteenth century as a training ground for Episcopal clergy, stands on a hill amidst the rolling woodlands of central Ohio. Today, in the early years of the twenty-first century, young men and women clad in jeans or sweatpants, wearing running shoes, and equipped with backpacks and iPods, pass the venerable church on their way to class in the early morning hush. They walk in silence but for the occasional bit of cell phone chat, preoccupied with personal matters or maybe with the state of the world, oblivious one suspects to the significance of the church they pass. Yet that stately edifice, consecrated on Ascension Day 1871, stands as an enduring witness to the Evangelical movement in the Episcopal Church of the nineteenth century and to the bishop who led that movement, Charles Pettit McIlvaine. Consecrated less than two years before McIlvaine's death, it memorializes in stone and slate, oak and pine the long and distinguished career of a man who was at once a natural leader, a brilliant preacher, an ardent revivalist, and a born-again saint.

Architecturally, the church exemplifies the Gothic Revival "Old English" style. Its architect, Gordon W. Lloyd, an Englishman, designed a number of Episcopal churches in the trans-Allegheny region, from Pittsburgh to Detroit, from Ann Arbor to Marshall

(Michigan). It is built in the form of a Latin cross, with Gothic arches, an apse chancel, and an imposing tower. The five windows in the apse symbolize the Holy Spirit in five different ways. Appropriately, the "McIlvaine window"—situated behind the bishop's chair at the rear of the apse—is the plainest of the windows. The glass shows one figure, that of a dove descending, the dove of the Holy Spirit. Its plainness testifies to the spiritual simplicity of the man it honors; to his straight-forward, Low Church style and to his opposition to what he considered to be the mystifications of Ritualism.

Built under the direction of McIlvaine's assistant and successor, Bishop Gregory T. Bedell, the church embodies in several ways the Evangelical tradition to which Bedell was equally dedicated. These features include the pews that line the nave and stand at right angles to the chancel. The arrangement allows worshippers to face one another across the central aisle—a position symbolic of their equality before God—as opposed to their gazing directly upon the chancel and sanctuary, as would "Romanists" intent on witnessing the ministrations of their priest. Worshippers seated in the additional pews in the two transepts are unable to see the communion table at all. By contrast, the pulpit and lectern, symbols of the Word of God, are clearly visible from all sides.

According to an 1871 article in the Evangelical periodical, Standard of the Cross, the building's chancel is arranged in the style "of the old Basilicas in the age preceding the novelties of worship and heresies of doctrine introduced by the Church of Rome." [1] That is, the chancel is arranged in the apse style, with the altar or communion table in the center and semicircular seating for the bishop and priests around and behind the altar. The feature was universal in early church architecture. By contrast, later developments in the Roman Catholic Church placed the altar against the back wall of the sanctuary, adding a note of mystery and making it remote from the laity.

In deference to the Evangelical tradition, the communion table in the Church of the Holy Spirit remained bare of hangings, flowers, or candles until 1908. Students from that period remembered that when Franklin Peirce, president of Kenyon College from 1896 to 1937, entered to conduct Evening Prayer in the wintertime, he was in the habit of tossing his hat and coat on the Table, to affirm that it was indeed a table and nothing more.[2] McIlvaine himself would have shied away from such common usage, but the symbolism of Peirce's gesture was indicative of the Evangelical movement's principles nonetheless.

Who was Charles Pettit McIlvaine? He was born January 18, 1799, in Burlington, New Jersey, the year George Washington died. He arrived with a silver spoon in his mouth and a golden tongue as well. These assets would serve him all his days in both worldly and otherworldly circles. The son of an influential family, surrounded from the start by men of means, he would in adulthood count as friends such notables as Abraham Lincoln, Salmon P. Chase, John C. Calhoun and Jefferson Davis. Among his notable clerical friends would be Phillip Schaff, Leonidas Polk, Charles Hodge, Henry Ward Beecher, Charles Simeon and the Earl of Shaftesbury. An Anglophile to his fingertips, he would move in the drawing rooms of high society both in America and abroad with the grace of good breeding and the mind of a man of learning.

In the tradition of his forebears, among whom were counted lawyers, politicians, and military officers, McIlvaine performed distinguished service on behalf of the young American republic. He did so as a Christian minister, a vocation chosen in the wake of a vivid conversion experience at Princeton College in his sixteenth year. First as chaplain, then as rector, then as bishop, he ministered to both highborn and low during a career that spanned fifty years. Though raised in the eastern United States, he answered a call to serve on the western frontier, as bishop of Ohio and president of Kenyon College and Theological Seminary. In

7

four strenuous decades as bishop, from 1832 to 1873, he saw the number of parishes in his diocese increase from forty to 116, the number of communicants from 900 to 15,000, and the number of clergy from seventeen to 108. In addition, during his years as president of Kenyon College and Seminary, he earned the title of "second founder" of those institutions (Bishop Philander Chase being the first), owing to his role in the construction of major college buildings, conscientious oversight of faculty and curriculum, and stabilization of the institution's financial situation.

Perhaps more importantly, McIlvaine came to be seen as the leader of the Evangelical party of the contemporary Episcopal Church, in which role he put to use his considerable talents as an organizer and a controversialist. As a born-again Evangelical, he emphasized the need of others to be born again as well. To be thus born again or "regenerated," he and other evangelicals believed, was to be subject to a spiritual change—generally of a striking nature—wrought in the heart by an act of God. By that direct and interior act, they held, rather than by baptism alone, God changed one's inherently sinful nature and enabled the penitent to respond for the first time to God in faith.

In addition, McIlvaine and other Evangelicals upheld the verbal inspiration and preeminent authority of Scripture; proclaimed the near return of Christ to redeem His elect; professed the supreme importance of preaching; stressed the urgent need for revival (both to convert the complacent and energize the faithful); rejected the doctrine of Eucharistic sacrifice in favor of a more symbolic understanding of the Lord's Supper; and nurtured a general suspicion of both the Roman Catholic Church and the Anglo-Catholic movement within the Anglican and Episcopal churches. Moreover, McIlvaine and his fellows celebrated their doctrinal roots in the English and Continental Reformations of the sixteenth century, whereby the Anglican, Lutheran and Reformed (Calvinist) churches had broken from the Roman Catholic Church and established themselves as independent entities. They celebrated as well their roots in the Evangelical Revival of the previous century, led by John Wesley and George Whitefield.

When, in the middle third of the nineteenth century, someone wanted to know something about Evangelical Episcopalians, they went to McIlvaine. There was no one more qualified than he to know what was on the minds of Evangelical churchmen, or to expound the doctrines that defined their beliefs, or to take the lead in pressing the Evangelical cause at the highest levels of the church. He believed the Episcopal Church in its Evangelical expression—owing to the central place it gave to Scripture, complemented by its three-fold order of bishops, priests and deacons, and enriched by its disciplined liturgy—was closer than any other Christian body to the primitive church.

Ever the man of action, and absorbed as he was by his Episcopal duties, McIlvaine found time to publish over seventy writings, many of them carefully researched and vigorously written treatises on the spiritual and doctrinal controversies of the day. In recognition of these accomplishments, he was honored by such leading educational institutions as Princeton and Brown in the United States and Oxford and Cambridge in England. His writings opposed both the Anglo-Catholic movement of the 1840s (and after) and the liberal or Rationalist trends of the 1860s.

The Anglo-Catholics whom he opposed, known as Tractarians because of the Tracts for the Times in which they initially espoused their cause, stressed the dogmatic and sacramental aspects of the Christian faith; the historical continuity of the contemporary Church of England—and, indirectly, of the Episcopal Church in America—with the church of the Middle Ages; and the agreement on essential principles between the Church of England and the unreformed Roman Catholic and Orthodox churches. Like High Churchmen in America, the Tractarians held that their principles alone expressed correctly the faith of historic Anglicanism. For their part, the liberals or

Rationalists (or "Broad Churchmen"), McIlvaine's other foes, objected to positive definition in theology and sought to interpret the Anglican formularies and rubrics in a broad and liberal sense. Whole-hearted adoption of the higher biblical criticism emanating from the German academy and a desire to reconstruct the Christian faith upon anti-dogmatic and humanitarian grounds were additional characteristics of the Rationalist trend within the Anglican and Episcopal churches of the time. McIlvaine sharply rebuked these diverse movements in both word and deed, while earning acclaim on both sides of the Atlantic for his Oxford Divinity Compared, a five-hundred page treatise targeting the doctrines of the Tractarians.

Recognition of McIlvaine's abilities reached beyond church circles. Early in the Civil War, President Lincoln chose him to serve as a special envoy at the critical time of the Trent Affair. McIlvaine thus interceded on behalf of the Union to help derail British recognition of the Confederacy and, owing to a surprising turn of events, defuse a potential war between the United States and Britain. According to his friend and memorialist, William Carus, McIlvaine's actions succeeded in large part because of the "entire confidence reposed in [his] wisdom and integrity" by all of the parties involved.[3] We will return to this dramatic incident in a later chapter.

Behind the public face of this imposing man—the commanding bishop, the trenchant critic, the judicious diplomat—was a complex figure, by turns humble and endearing, autocratic and intransigent. Although he had his adversaries in the public arenas of ecclesiastical debate and college politics, his friends and family, parishioners and students, colleagues and casual acquaintances testify overwhelmingly to McIlvaine's genuine goodness and authentic faith. In the eyes of those who knew him best, the manner and integrity of the man were consistent in private and public. His intervention on behalf of a student of color humiliated in the Kenyon College chapel; his courage during the cholera epidemic of 1832; his conciliatory words to Confederate prisoners; his tender care of a child shivering on the deck of an endangered river boat, all testify to the bishop's courage and kindness.

A lightness of spirit was evident as well. According to William Carus, McIlvaine displayed a "holiness of life and consequent spirituality of mind" that was "entirely free from all gloom or austerity; on the contrary, whilst always serious, he was eminently bright and cheerful—often, indeed, playful." Carus adds, in a phrase that borders admittedly on hagiography, "I never once saw him in any other temper but that which I wished to be in, in the last moments of my life."[4]

We might well ask, was this a man of flesh and blood or a plaster saint? Did McIlvaine's virtues place him on a pedestal above the common run of humanity? Clearly, he was "above average" in education, in leadership ability, in piety and purposeful living.

But his opponents, and even some of his admirers, were aware of certain faults. "He was capable of an anti-Catholic attitude, which approached religious bigotry," a generally sympathetic scholar says, adding that when McIlvaine "believed he was right, he was stubborn, often highly judgmental and cutting in controversy."[5] Not surprisingly, his opponents could be scathing, though they sometimes paid him his due. "Among all evangelical enthusiasts," wrote one, "especially ladies, Bishop McIlvaine was a hero, a sort of apostolic divinity....[Though] most violent and bitterly evangelical, with his high talents and fine elocution, [he] was something superhuman."[6] And McIlvaine was the first to admit his faults, at least when he saw them, which seems to have been often. He was, in the classic phrases of William James (The Varieties of Religious Experience), both a "sick soul" and a "divided self." As such, he spent a great deal of energy throughout his life in prayer and introspection, disciplines undertaken with the aim of healing his soul and unifying his self, all in accord with his evangelical faith. In these endeavors, however, he was only partly successful. In spite of his many attainments, he seems never to have found complete inner peace before the final days of his life, and even then not totally. He never achieved complete "unification" (another Jamesian term) either, the state wherein the formerly divided self enjoys the integration and equilibrium of a soul at rest. Then again, it could be argued, McIlvaine never sought complete unification. Surely, he would have believed that such harmony of soul was for the next world, not for this. But whatever his personal shortcomings and inner turbulence, he trusted completely that God had delivered him "unto salvation" through grace and faith, not by works. His "habitual walk" with God, Carus observed, while it "wrought in him increasing likeness to his Lord and devotion to His service, produced also an increasing sense of his own shortcomings. As he observed to me on his death-bed...'What I have left undone most troubles me;' adding, 'every enlightened conscience has, I suppose, an exceeding sense of shortcoming.'" [7]

The chapters that follow will present McIlvaine as at once a man of faith and a man of action, as a complex, divided personality excelling as an intellectual militant. They will reveal a Christian whose person and doctrine remain compelling more than 135 years after his death, for he was a man with a mission, an activist both practical and scholarly. Something of a religious prodigy, he proclaimed and ruminated on what he considered to be his spiritual poverty. Yet his unique assortment of qualities and gifts combined to produce a revivalist who was a loyal and steady churchman; a pastor and controversialist who was a commanding preacher; a reluctant but successful diplomat; a self-doubter but trusting believer; and an affectionate husband and father. He was, in short, a man of the highest order, and worthy of our continuing attention and respect.

INTRODUCTION

1. Quoted in Perry Lentz, The Anglican Digest, January, 1997.
2. Ibid.
3. William Carus, editor, Memorials of the Right Reverend Charles Pettit McIlvaine, D.D., D.C.L., Late Bishop of Ohio, in the Protestant Episcopal Church of the United States (Thomas Whittaker, New York, 1882), 5. Carus, who was canon of Winchester Cathedral, was a longtime friend of McIlvaine's. In the Memorials he gathered extracts from McIlvaine's correspondence, notebooks, journals and published writings and added commentary of his own. "They will," he wrote, "be useful materials for the future biographer."
4. Ibid., 3.
5. Loren Dale Pugh, Bishop Charles Pettit McIlvaine: The Faithful Evangel (dissertation, Department of Religion in the Graduate School of Duke University, 1985), 127.
6. Quoted in Diana Hochstedt Butler, Standing Against the Whirlwind: Evangelical Episcopalians in Nineteenth-century America (Oxford University Press, New York, 1995), ix. The remarks were made by Clarence F. Walworth, one of McIlvaine's severest critics, in his book, The Oxford Movement in America (New York, 1895), 165.
7. Quoted in Carus, 3.

CHAPTER ONE

Man and Mission

Charles Pettit McIlvaine was a descendant of the Makilvanes of Ayrshire in southwest Scotland. It was said that the Makilvanes, who were Presbyterian, wielded considerable influence in the early 1500s, thriving as landed proprietors before "high living and fines" impoverished them and led to emigration. Members of the transplanted family lived in or near Philadelphia in the early eighteenth century and later as country gentlemen on their estate of Fairview near Bristol, Pennsylvania. At the death of McIlvaine's grandfather, the estate passed out of the family.

Specifically, the future bishop was the son of Joseph McIlvaine of Burlington, New Jersey, and the grandson of Joseph McIlvaine of Bristol. The grandfather was brother to both William McIlvaine, "an eminent physician" of Burlington, and Mrs. Mary Bloomfield. She in turn was the wife of Joseph Bloomfield, governor of New Jersey for eleven years and a brigadier-general in the U. S. Army during the war of 1812. McIlvaine's father was a leading lawyer in New Jersey and a Democratic U. S. senator from 1823 until his death three years later. His mother, Maria McIlvaine, was a daughter of Bowes Reed of Burlington, who was in turn a brother of Joseph Reed of Philadelphia, who had served as confidential secretary to General Washington and was the first governor of Pennsylvania. She died in 1849. A man of intense family loyalty,

McIlvaine remained to the end of his life dedicated to the memory of his parents. "I was blessed," he wrote, "with the most affectionate, tender, devoted parents—wise and faithful—whose memory is treasured in my heart." [1]

McIlvaine was first educated at the Burlington Academy, of which his father was a trustee. The academy, which attained national renown, eschewed corporal punishment as much as practicable, preferring instead to dispense "tokens of disgrace...that the minds of offenders may be mortified." [2] One surmises that McIlvaine was duly mortified, either directly in response to his own wrongdoing or indirectly by observing the chastisement of others. Indeed, "tokens of disgrace," suffered directly or indirectly, may have wounded the sensitive child in ways that never quite healed, thereby explaining in part the sense of shortcoming that he felt throughout life in spite of his achievements. His father, too, though humane and affectionate, no doubt enhanced the exacting standards internalized by the son at the academy. Such influences may have sown the seeds of inner doubt and criticality that later shaded the personality of the otherwise confident and benevolent churchman.

McIlvaine attended St. Mary's Episcopal Church in Burlington from childhood until after his ordination as a priest. His parents and other members of the family belonged to the congregation as well but were not baptized and appear to have held no strong religious views. "My dear mother," McIlvaine later wrote, "having some scruples about presenting her children for baptism as long as she was not a communicant (which she afterwards became), I was not baptized until during my college course, when having been turned to the Lord, by His grace, I presented myself for baptism." It was during a revival at the College of New Jersey (now Princeton University) in 1815 that McIlvaine, a student, "was turned to the Lord" at the age of sixteen. More than half a century later, he recalled the impact of the revival: "It was powerful and prevailing, and fruitful in the conversion of young men to God; and it was quiet, unexcited, and entirely free from all devices or means, beyond the few and simple which God has appointed, namely, prayer and the ministry of the Word." How like McIlvaine, the cultivated Episcopalian, to remember the "quiet, unexcited" manner of the revival, thus contrasting it to the frenzied "camp meeting" style of the frontier or the innovative "anxious bench" that would be introduced by Charles Grandison Finney, the major evangelist of the 1820s and 1830s. "In that precious season of the power of God," McIlvaine further recalled, "my religious life began. I had *heard* before; I began then to *know*." [3] The young convert, who had intended to follow his father into law or politics, discerned another calling altogether.

He was graduated from Princeton in the spring of 1816, his mind duly trained in Greek and Latin, moral philosophy, natural and revealed religion, ancient history, mathematics, astronomy, chemistry, geography, and oratory. Two brothers, Reed and Bloomfield, had preceded him at Princeton; two others, Joseph and Henry, would follow. McIlvaine was imbued by Princeton with the certitudes of Scottish Common Sense philosophy and classic Protestant Christianity, certitudes that would furnish his mind and underpin his faith for the rest of his life.

Around the time of his graduation, McIlvaine heard of the Sunday school movement from a classmate, John Newbold, who had visited a Sunday school in Philadelphia. Sunday schools, originating in Britain in the 1780s, reached America before the turn of the century, coming first to Philadelphia and then spreading to communities in New England. They became a familiar institution in ante-bellum America, and in many Protestant congregations "Bible class" overshadowed regular Sunday worship. Designed not only to provide Scriptural and moral education, they became a vital means of reaching potential church members as well. Impressed by what he heard from Newbold, McIlvaine and several classmates raised $400 to form a Sunday School Society, with McIlvaine as treasurer. Four schools were set up in the Princeton area, with members of the Society teaching in them. "My first extempore address," McIlvaine recalled, "was...made to the School I was detailed to, in a barn of what was called Jug Town, a suburb of Princeton." Among participants in the Society were the young Charles Hodge, later a titan of Protestant orthodoxy at Princeton and McIlvaine's lifelong friend, and John Johns, later Episcopal bishop of Virginia. On returning to Burlington in the spring of 1816, after being graduated from Princeton College, McIlvaine determined to set up a Sunday school at his home parish of St. Mary's. "I first obtained Dr. Wharton's [his rector's] approbation," he said, "and then began to talk it up." He recruited teachers and arranged to have the school meet in the Burlington Academy. Forty children and six teachers were present when the school opened later that spring, with McIlvaine serving as both superintendent and as a teacher. According to the August parochial report, attendance at the Sunday school had more than tripled to 150 children by late summer.[4] Apparently pleased by this achievement of his early zeal, McIlvaine recalled with pleasure half a century later that the school was still in operation.

In September 1817, after a year of reading at home in Burlington—and with the prospect of a secular career abandoned—McIlvaine returned to Princeton to attend the theological seminary of the Presbyterian Church, the Episcopal Church having no seminary of its own at the time. At Princeton he received exhaustive training in the Bible, biblical languages, polemics and didactics, as well as the study of theological treatises (many of which, in deference to McIlvaine's denomination, had been assigned from a list prepared by Episcopal Bishop William White). In addition, he was taught apologetics, the defense of the Christian faith on intellectual grounds, a Princeton specialty. As a student of the discipline, he learned to parry objections to Scripture, objections based on apparent inconsistencies in the text or on challenges arising from history or reason. The apologetic arts he imbibed at Princeton equipped him formidably for later theological disputes.

Midway through his second year at seminary, McIlvaine returned home as the result of ill health, the first of several such collapses. At home, he engaged in private study for more than a year. But word of his abilities, nascent though they were, began to spread in the Episcopal Church, with interest surfacing here and there. Indeed, a call to serve as rector of a church in the nation's capital would soon be forthcoming. How this happened, even as he remained at home, we cannot be sure, but several suppositions are plausible. First, he had made influential friends among his classmates at Princeton, both at the college and the seminary, and no doubt had impressed his instructors as well, by his intelligence, character and piety. These friends and teachers presumably spoke well of the young man. Second, his family was well connected socially and politically. His father, as we have seen, was a prominent lawyer. In addition, two of his brothers were making names for themselves in business and law. Third, the rector of McIlvaine's home church, Charles H. Wharton, was clearly impressed by the young man's piety and initiative, having witnessed the founding and growth of the local Sunday school program. Fourth, McIlvaine's Evangelical inclinations, already evident in his college years, clearly piqued the interest of churchmen of a similar persuasion. In sum, it is clear that McIlvaine's name was being bruited about by people of influence, even as he remained in Burlington, closeted with his books. And no wonder: considering his abilities in general and his ambition for the religious life in particular. "Upon his graduating with endowments and advantages of no common order," wrote Alfred Lee, bishop of Delaware, many years later, "all the paths of worldly honour and advancement were invitingly open. Success at the bar or in the senate was all but certain. But he esteemed even the reproach of Christ greater riches than the world could give, and laid all his gifts, capacities, hopes and prospects a freewill offering at the feet of his crucified Lord." [5] He was called at the age of twenty-one to be rector of Christ Church Georgetown, in Washington, D. C.—an Evangelical parish in an Evangelical area—even though he had not yet been ordained. He accepted the offer nonetheless, and thereafter was ordained a deacon in July 1820. Yet owing to illness, he delayed going to Georgetown until late August.

Once in Georgetown, however, the ambitious McIlvaine—tall, slender, and of commanding appearance—displayed considerable power and charm as a preacher and parish leader. According to Alfred Lee (again, commenting many years after the fact), the young rector was characterized by "graceful manner, elocution, fervent and forcible style....The physical man corresponded well with the intellectual, and the lovers of oratory found his discourses a rich treat."[6] Word of such abilities spread throughout the larger Episcopal Church, a fact confirmed by a second call, this from the vestry of St. Paul's Church, Philadelphia. St. Paul's, a large, prestigious Evangelical parish (it had seven-hundred communicants prior to 1800), offered him the position of assistant rector. In that connection, and not without a bit of humor, McIlvaine's brother, Reed, wrote to him in words that testify not only to the skill but to the humility of the young preacher. "I have heard from various quarters," the elder brother wrote, "of the attention your sermons attracted in Philadelphia [;] however you may understate their merits, they appear to have been differently thought of by others mentioned in terms that must be wondrous gratifying....Ridgely [a friend] writes that he would rather be Charles McIlvaine than Emperor of Russia."[7] Brother Reed, tellingly, had opened with the salutation, "Dear Bishop." Other members of the family had used the sobriquet as well, indicating a teasing confidence in McIlvaine's future. In the event, the young clergyman declined the offer, apparently content for the moment to be in Georgetown.

McIlvaine experienced several pleasant changes in his status during the following two years. The first was his marriage to a childhood friend, Emily Coxe, on October 8, 1822. It was a marriage that would endure for more than half a century and by all accounts was a most happy match. In addition, on March 20 of the following year, at the age of twenty-four, he was ordained priest at St. Paul's Church, Baltimore, by Bishop James Kemp. Moreover, in December 1822, the young preacher had been elected chaplain to the Senate of the United States in the second session of the seventeenth Congress, the youngest clergyman to hold the post. The election occurred shortly after his appointment to Christ Church. Elected by members of the Senate, chaplains were charged with the preparation and delivery of convening prayers for the opening of legislative sessions. The position paid several hundred dollars a year, a welcome supplement to a young clergyman's salary. In addition, the position gave McIlvaine a stage in front of the leading political figures of the day. He was re-elected in 1824.

Britain's minister to the United States, Stratford Canning, was among the worthies who attended the church. A regular communicant, he took an interest in the young clergyman, especially in his attempts to preach extempore. To learn the technique, McIlvaine had begun to commit his sermons to memory. Finding the method onerous, however, he switched to studying his subject in careful detail, then preparing passages in the words he planned to use. Canning called upon the rector to offer some blunt advice: "Young man," he said, "you never will succeed if you go on in this way. Prepare your thoughts—have a distinct idea of what you mean to convey to your hearers; and then leave the words to come of themselves."[8] McIlvaine took the advice to heart and applied it, turning himself from a good preacher into a great one, much praised by laity and clergy alike.

While at Georgetown, McIlvaine became involved with the *Washington Theological Repertory*, a journal founded and edited by the staunch Evangelical educator, William Wilmer, rector of St. Paul's Church, Alexandria, Virginia. The journal gave voice in the 1820s to the Evangelical party of the Episcopal Church and to clergy, such as McIlvaine, who promoted its form of churchmanship. In its inaugural issue it defined itself according to six doctrinal principles: the perfection of God; the sinfulness of humankind; salvation from sin through the atonement of Jesus Christ; the power of God's grace to convert the human heart; the necessity of a personal religious experience, and the responsibility to conform one's life to the Christian gospel. These principles, it said, were "indispensable prerequisites for admission into Heaven."[9] McIlvaine's association with the *Repertory* and its principles placed him at the center of the Evangelical movement, earning him friends and foes alike and setting the stage for later achievements.

Among other men of influence who attended Christ Church was the future vice-president, John C. Calhoun, then secretary of war. The "cast-iron" but gracious Calhoun, busy reshaping the curriculum and staff of the United States Military Academy at West Point,[10] found the young clergyman an arresting preacher and an impressive figure. While the two men took tea one afternoon, he offered McIlvaine the appointment as chaplain of the West Point cadet corps and professor of ethics, history and geography. This was not totally unexpected. Though well received—and indeed, lauded—at Christ Church, McIlvaine had become restive, in part because of the difficulty of collecting pew rents, the source of his salary, in part, because of the effect on his health of the hot, damp Washington climate. A more elevated motive for seeking the position—the prompting of the Holy Spirit—was suggested in retrospect by his friend, William Carus. Regardless of motive, McIlvaine had been clearly angling for the post. He had written to a friend, the Rev. Mr. Ethan Allen, "suggesting that he would use his influence to get the chaplaincy for Allen, but proposing to try himself to 'stand' if Allen were 'not interested.'"[11] Political machinations followed and McIlvaine landed the appointment, departing Christ Church in January 1825.

True to type, the energetic McIlvaine brought to West Point—despite a lackluster beginning—a zeal that would revolutionize religious life at the academy. In his role as chaplain, he demonstrated a rare ability to stir the spirit of hardheaded military men and officers in the making. During his tenure, this bastion of rationalism and irreligion—for such it was at the time—was turned into a hotbed of religious revival. Before he left West Point, he had made for himself new friends and—yet again—new enemies. He also further established his reputation as a gifted preacher and man of God and, as we shall see later, for the first time entered the bracing waters of controversy in regard to revivalism. In addition, he became known as a bright and vigorous member of the faculty, even as he assisted the superintendent, Sylvanus Thayer, in planning and implementing curriculum reforms.[12]

After nearly three years at the academy and under growing pressure to resign—mostly from persons outside the academy unhappy with the growing religiosity of the place—the rising star decided in November 1827 to leave his chaplaincy and accept a call to become rector of St. Anne's Church in Brooklyn, New York, a parish which included many socially prominent business and professional people. Not surprisingly, McIlvaine ascribed the decision to God's will for his life. If in fact it was God's will, secondary causes were at work as well. According to one investigator, the decision may have stemmed in part from "a desire to move back into a place where he would not have to labor in such isolation and where there would be opportunity for upward mobility within the church."[13] In accepting the call to St. Anne's, McIlvaine declined two other attractive offers, one to become rector of St. Paul's Church, Rochester, New York, and the other to fill the dual position of president of William and Mary College and rector of historic Bruton Parish in Williamsburg, Virginia.

The decision to accept the call from St. Anne's was in part influenced by ecclesiastical and doctrinal controversy, attacks upon McIlvaine's churchmanship, and behind-the-scenes maneuverings by members of the High Church party, all of which conspired to rouse the fighting blood of the twenty-eight-year-old clergyman. The attack on McIlvaine was led by a partisan busybody, Henry U. Onderdonk, departing rector of St. Anne's and soon-to-be assistant bishop of Pennsylvania. Onderdonk, and his brother, Benjamin, would figure in subsequent controversies with McIlvaine. In this instance, the attack was aimed at his Evangelical churchmanship, reputed opposition to Bishop John Henry Hobart (the High Church leader and bishop of New York), alleged promotion of schemes to blend Episcopalians with Presbyterians, purported failures at West Point, and a claim "that his preaching was all show with no theological substance." In response, McIlvaine proved himself a resourceful opponent, going so far as to publish a pamphlet in his own defense. In the pamphlet he attacked Onderdonk for hypocrisy and defended himself on several counts, justifying his positions on Episcopal polity, liturgy and doctrine. Denying the High Church principle of exclusivity, he argued from an ecumenical or trans-denominational position, basing himself on the precedent of Anglican participation in the synod of Dort in the seventeenth century (at which the Dutch Reformed Church reestablished itself on firm Calvinist principles), and Episcopal participation in Bible societies. He also defended prayer meetings outside of church. Despite harsh opposition, McIlvaine was elected rector by the vestry of St. Anne's by a six-to-four margin, with the margin of victory influenced by a supportive letter from the vestry of his former parish of Christ Church. During his subsequent tenure at St. Anne's, parish membership nearly doubled and the amount of charitable giving increased twenty-fold. He also revitalized the parish's moribund Sunday school program.[14]

Yet despite these early successes, McIlvaine continued to suffer from puzzling illnesses. When he was in Georgetown, vestry minutes "reflect occasions where he was 'too weak to consider or continue' his duties and [therefore] had to be given extended periods of absence to recover his health."[15] Even so, as we have seen, he was much acclaimed for his ministry there. In the midst of attaining a like success at St. Anne's, illness struck again in March 1830. This time it was an attack of "neuralgia," prompting him to sail for England in search of respite. The ailment was probably the "tic douloureaux" he would complain of two years later, while contemplating a move to the western frontier to serve as bishop of Ohio. (Tic douloureaux is a nerve disorder—"neuralgia"—characterized by darting pain and muscular twitching in the face.) Today's diagnostician, however, might find in McIlvaine's physical problems something other than neuralgia or tic douloureaux by themselves. As will be seen in the chapters ahead, especially in chapter two, his habitual complaints would fit the profile of what today would be called "neurosis" and, on at least one or two discreet occasions, such as the "attack by Satan" discussed in the next chapter, "psychosis." But though today's doctor might use such terms from the psychotherapeutic handbook, there is no reason that believing Christians are obliged to do so. Indeed, the "attack by Satan" may have been just that, for McIlvaine was not one to apply such dramatic language without cause. Regardless of how one wishes to label his chronic health problems, his partial triumph over them stands as a tribute to his character. Be that as it may, his illness in 1830 led to a five-month visit to the mother country, during which time he formed friendships with leaders of church and state, spent time in prayer and meditation, and learned to love the life of the English upper classes. In addition to meeting the renowned Anglican Evangelical, Charles Simeon, an event that would influence him for the rest of his life, McIlvaine was introduced to a number of other evangelical leaders. Among them were Daniel Wilson, later bishop of Calcutta; Wriothesley Noel, named in 1840 as one of Queen Victoria's chaplains; Thomas Chalmers, professor of theology at Edinburgh University, and Charles R. Sumner, John B. Sumner and Henry Ryder, bishops respectively of Winchester, Chester and Lichfield. He also met several prominent church leaders and eminent scholars at Cambridge University, among them regius professor of Hebrew, Samuel Lee, the foremost linguist and oriental scholar of the day;

William Farrish, Jacksonian professor of natural and experimental philosophy, and James Scholefield, regius professor of Greek, all of whom were evangelicals.[16]

After returning from Britain to St. Anne's, he took on added duties as an adjunct professor at the newly founded University of the City of New York, where he lectured on the evidences of Christianity. He had been chosen to present the series owing to his growing fame as a leader of the Evangelical party. The lectures, similar to a series he had presented at West Point, were a resounding success. Indeed, they were published by the university, the first book ever by a member of the faculty of that institution. The work, *Evidences of Christianity in their External Division*, was much acclaimed and went through several editions, including an immediate reprinting in England. He owed the latter printing to several of the aforementioned scholars, men who had been impressed by the theological resourcefulness of his work. (Even late in the century, his *Evidences* remained an approved text for seminarians of the Reformed Episcopal Church.) His reputation was growing at home and abroad. He was ready for the next step.

That came when the Convention of the Diocese of Ohio voted unanimously to make him bishop on September 10, 1831, to fill the vacated bishopric of the stormy Philander Chase. Chase, a Low Churchman, had grown up in a prominent Congregationalist farming family in New Hampshire. His father, enamored of a poem entitled *Young's Night Thoughts*, had named his thirteenth child after a character in that work. Years later, while attending Dartmouth College, the singularly named young man came under the influence of the Book of Common Prayer and by a tract trumpeting the merits of Anglicanism, leading him to renounce the church of his forebears and to join the Episcopal Church. After becoming a bishop in 1819, he consolidated Ohio's frontier parishes into a diocese and founded Kenyon College and Seminary, becoming the first president of each. The goal of these institutions was to train young men raised in the West to serve as frontier clergy, prior experience having shown the difficulty of recruiting clergy from the East. Chase's accomplishments came at the price of much personal sacrifice. Owing to the meager resources of the diocese, the sturdy bishop supplemented his income by operating a sawmill, running the local post office, and farming. He found it necessary to travel extensively as well, not only to visit the parishes of his diocese but to appeal for funds to support the college and seminary. Fundraising missions took him to both the eastern United States and to Britain.

Despite his tireless efforts during a twelve-year episcopate, not all was well in the diocese. Chase was as autocratic as he was industrious, thereby fomenting conflict and making enemies. In 1831, following the mandate of his diocesan convention that he could not be both bishop and college president, he resigned both offices. For a time he returned to farming, first in Ohio and then in Michigan. Yet the irrepressible churchman was not one to keep his candle burning under a bushel basket. In 1835, he accepted election as the first bishop of Illinois, where he subsequently labored to plant churches in towns and rural areas and to found Jubilee College.

McIlvaine, just thirty-two-years-old in 1831, was considered for the Ohio vacancy for at least two reasons. First, he had attained a position of prominence in the church, especially among Evangelicals, and second, he was well known in England by Lords Kenyon and Gambier, whose financial support was vital to the survival of Kenyon College. Yet during the deliberations of General Convention, McIlvaine found himself ambivalent about the contemplated move west. He considered himself a contented and happy pastor in Brooklyn, where the people of his parish were "so harmonious, affectionate, attentive."[17] Good things had been done and were being done, he felt, and the separation would be painful. In addition, he must have ruminated on his fitness to withstand the rigor of frontier living. A genteel hypochondriac, he was something quite unlike his predecessor, Chase, a rough-hewn original toughened by farm and frontier from an early age. Intimidated by the prospect of the move, he spoke of "tic douloureaux," commenting, "I cannot stand exposure, fatigue, or anxiety."[18] In addition, there was technical doubt about whether an Episcopal vacancy truly existed, even as bishops Hobart and Onderdonk—yet again—threw their weight against McIlvaine's election. Yet he felt the tug of duty. "Great as was the rebellion of my heart when the election first came, it is now passed. I can say, 'Here am I, Lord; send me, if I am such as Thou seekest.' Duty seems as plain as if I heard a voice from heaven. But it [acceptance of the position] will call for great self-denial."[19] On October 19, 1832, General Convention voted that the Episcopal office of Ohio was indeed vacant and on October 31 McIlvaine was consecrated bishop in St. Paul's Church, New York City.

Thus began the lengthiest and most productive chapter of McIlvaine's life. For more than forty years he would serve as bishop of Ohio, ruling his diocese even as he engaged in the rough-and-tumble of national Episcopal Church politics and in drawn-out debates on doctrine and practice. In going to Ohio, he would enact in his own person the archetypal American journey. The young man would indeed "go west," to exercise his aristocratic mien and abilities within the rambunctious environment of Jacksonian democracy and frontier expansion. He would live and lead among a people optimistic in temper and egalitarian in spirit. Equipped by Princeton with the angular doctrines of evangelical orthodoxy and the tenets of Scottish Common Sense philosophy, and by his church with the Book of Common Prayer and its liturgical safeguards, he was prepared— whatever shortcomings he might have had in regard to physical stamina—to pastor a people in the ways of Gospel rigor.

Frontier folk—the present and potential members of McIlvaine's flock—lived in that era an ethic of personal ability, both spiritually and materially. For many of them, Protestant orthodoxy—the complex of doctrines based on the Bible as the only source of revealed truth; of justification by faith alone; of emphasis on the Fall and original sin; of the impotence of the unaided human mind to obtain any knowledge of God, and of high if not austere standards of personal morality—had been weakened if not everywhere displaced. Because nature abhors a vacuum, souls emptied of orthodox certitudes were ripe to be filled with other views altogether. They were—in the eyes of traditional churchmen like McIlvaine—in danger of succumbing to the heterodoxies of the day. These dangers included Arminian inconsistency, the lure of Unitarianism and the residues of Deism. Arminianism, with its stress on free-will in regard to salvation; Unitarianism, with its rejection of "tangled trinities" in favor of God's unipersonality; and Deism, with its system of natural religion bereft of divine revelation and a supernatural realm—each of these views found an audience among the frontier populace. Challenged by such a milieu, McIlvaine would rise to the occasion, overcoming obstacles of man and nature, trusting God in all things and putting his matchless ethic of hard work to what he saw as the noblest of ends.

He demonstrated his mettle from the start. Arriving in Ohio late in 1832, at the age of thirty-three, he defied the approach of winter by embarking on a journey through the diocese, which at that time encompassed the entire state. The itinerary was daunting, especially as daylight shortened and the weather changed for the worse. He preached day and night, lectured, held prayer meetings, and ordained a priest. He traveled on horseback from Zanesville to Newark, Berkshire to Delaware, Mount Vernon to Gambier. He traveled also to Columbus to meet the trustees of Kenyon College.

In addition to his episcopal duties, McIlvaine assumed the presidency of both college and seminary. During the year-and-a-half interregnum that had passed between the resignation of Philander Chase and the new bishop's arrival, the financial situation of the school had worsened. To address a $15,000 debt as well as a general malaise, vigorous leadership was needed. Once on the scene, McIlvaine provided it. His ample energies were enlisted in behalf of an institution that, if it could be saved and strengthened, would be, he said, "of immense importance."[20] In a visit to the East, he succeeded in raising $28,520 to be spent mainly on buildings, while a loan of $15,000 was secured to pay off pressing debts. The building program was aimed at completing the college's physical plant and providing houses for the faculty. Although McIlvaine had intended to reside in Cleveland or Cincinnati instead of Gambier, while leaving the faculty to manage affairs on its own, he was smitten by "the charms of that alluring village" and arranged that a house be built for his residence.[21] Convinced of the potential of the theological department, he decided to be its head while naming a vice-president to preside over the college. Even before coming to Ohio, he had raised subscriptions in New York City and Brooklyn—where Evangelical friends and former parishioners remembered his earlier services with affection and admiration—to pay the salary of an additional professor of theology.

McIlvaine can be credited with a number of achievements at Kenyon. It was he, building upon the rudiments established by Chase, who organized the seminary and provided a full course of theological studies. It was he, also, who sailed to England in November 1834 to raise money for a separate building for the theological department. The mission was a success. He returned to Gambier the following June to begin work on Bexley Hall, named after its principal benefactor, Baron Bexley (Nicholas Vansittart), the pious financier, promoter of the Church Missionary Society, and longest serving Chancellor of the Exchequer ever. Owing to delays, however, work on the building did not begin until 1839, and another two decades would pass before it was finished, although it was used extensively during the interim. In the meantime, Rosse Chapel, begun under Chase in 1829, occupied McIlvaine's attention as well. Five years after the cornerstone was laid, the plan for the church was altered (to Chase's displeasure) and the building was not completed until 1845. Owing to its redesign, the original tower at the front and a forty-foot-deep chancel were eliminated, as was the intended Gothic style of the overall structure. Moreover, the features originally planned for the exterior front of the church were replaced by twin pillars bearing Ionic capitals. Other building projects during McIlvaine's tenure included erection of six brick houses for the faculty, a "beautiful mansion" for the bishop and his family,[22] and a substantial brick building for younger students who attended a grammar school. Like his predecessor, McIlvaine quarreled with faculty and trustees and nearly removed himself to Cleveland in 1838 owing to a sense of isolation and opposition. But for a time he triumphed. By 1839—owing to favorable action at the diocesan convention—he attained a virtual supremacy of leadership at the college, something Chase had sought but never achieved. He was elated at his sweeping victory. Writing to his mother, he said that certain "jealous professors" had caused him problems for three years but when he brought the matter before the convention, it was "well settled by the diocese, who have no idea of letting two or three men disturb the peace of their Bishop."[23] But the victory was short-lived; relations with faculty and trustees soon returned to their former state of tension and conflict. Saddled as he was by the worries and burdens of diocesan matters and national church politics as well, McIlvaine moved the seat of his episcopate to Clifton, a suburb of Cincinnati, in 1846.

In addition to handling the day-to-day affairs of his diocese as well as college and seminary affairs, McIlvaine had established himself in the 1830s and 1840s as the leader of the Evangelical party in the Episcopal Church. Yet this did not prevent him from joining forces with High Churchmen when necessary. For example, early in his episcopate, he had joined with others in attempting to curb the revival excesses that he witnessed in Ohio. He discovered that the enthusiasm and sectarianism of the West's freewheeling revivals, along with their frequent doctrinal aberrations, were quite unlike the ordered and liturgically-based revivals that he had both conducted and witnessed in the East. Owing to these discoveries, he became more appreciative of the Episcopal office and liturgy of his own church in contrast to the overwrought doings of the revivals of Charles Grandison Finney and other traveling evangelists. As a result, he and fellow Evangelicals made common cause with the High Church party, inasmuch as the two parties shared the vision of an ordered church polity and thereby stood as bulwarks against the more popular evangelical bodies and their relatively unchecked activities. He went so far as to stress the distinctive merits of the Episcopal Church—a High Church view of long standing—as over against other denominations, putting behind him for a season his earlier stress on cooperation with churchmen of other denominations.

Yet in time, the revival frenzy that swept the country declined in importance in the overall scheme of national religious activity. With its abeyance, McIlvaine turned again to intra-church issues, especially those involving the Tractarian (or Oxford) Movement, which by the late 1830s was emanating from Britain and capturing the attention of a growing number of Episcopalians. Principled Protestant that he was, he became—as noted in the introduction—an unbending foe of Tractarianism and the first American to challenge in a sustained manner the movement's beliefs, practices and alleged strategies. That attack, expounded in the five-hundred-page *Oxford Divinity Compared* published in 1841, brought him praise from evangelicals on both sides of the Atlantic and won the sympathies of a handful of High Church traditionalists. He accused the "thoroughly Popish" Tractarians of undercutting the Protestant foundations of the Anglican and Episcopal churches—most directly by subverting the Protestant teaching of "justification by faith alone"—even as they lured unwary Protestants in the direction of Rome itself. McIlvaine's dispute with Tractarianism overlapped with his opposition to the High Church party of his own denomination, which he had engaged on issues of belief and practice over many years. In fact, the growing influence of the Oxford Movement on High Churchmen helped bring to an end the relatively peaceful relations that the two parties had enjoyed in the 1830s, thereby reigniting

McIlvaine's opposition to his erstwhile allies. In later years, he would continue to oppose High Church and Anglo-Catholic tendencies within his own denomination while taking up his pen against a new theological enemy, the Broad Churchmen, whose Rationalism and McIlvaine's response to it will be discussed in a later chapter.

Although McIlvaine, like most clergy of the ante-bellum period, prudently observed the distinction between church and state, he was unable to avoid a measure of involvement in the vexing issues touching on the growing rift between the states of the North and the South, principally over slavery and states' rights. Early on, he spoke in favor of purchasing slaves from their owners in order to repatriate them to colonies established in Africa. When that movement faltered, he sided cautiously with other Evangelicals in favor of eventual emancipation of slaves on American soil. Though opposed to slavery, he remained aloof in regard to supporting whole-heartedly the abolitionist movement then agitating the nation. Yet as civil war loomed, he became increasingly aligned with the policies of the new Republican Party and outspokenly opposed to the secession of the southern states. Owing to his friendship with high officials in Washington, President Lincoln among them, he was asked to serve as a special envoy to Great Britain during the first year of the war, at the time of the notorious Trent Affair. His success in that vital endeavor, which will be discussed in chapter eight, demonstrated to the full his gifts of wisdom and tact.

In the years following the war, McIlvaine remained active in church politics and theological disputes. Though approaching the age of seventy, he remained a force to be reckoned with, especially in opposition to the Broad Church influence of the period. He successfully presented his views at the first Lambeth Conference in London in 1867, a gathering convened in large part to counter the new movement's theological novelties. As we have seen, the journey to London was not unique. Despite ill health—and in part because of it—he remained to the end of his days an inveterate traveler. The last months of his life found him moving about Italy, in the domain of the popes, in a "Romish" land par excellence. His eventual death in Florence, far from the scenes of his pastoral and polemical triumphs, was an irony no one could have predicted for the Ur-Protestant himself. "From Genoa," he wrote to his wife, "we took steamer to Leghorn; then to Pisa and here [Florence]. I feel a sort of famine for letters, but we shall get some at Rome." Characteristically, he provided details of the area—the warmth by day and the chill by night, the snow on the Apennines—plus censure of the social backwardness of "the Continent" and especially of the country he was visiting. His last illness commenced the day after he had written to his wife. According to William Carus, who recorded McIlvaine's lingering confrontation with the final enemy, the bishop died as piously as he had lived, and in greater peace of mind. At the time, the event attracted much attention. In the words of Archibald Tait, Archbishop of Canterbury, "Much will the Bishop's loss be felt in England and America. He was a true bond of union, not only between the two Churches, but also between the two countries; and this union was cemented by his genuine Christian character."[24]

We will examine in the chapters that follow McIlvaine's impressive achievements in church politics, doctrinal controversy, and Civil War diplomacy, as well as his travels abroad and life-threatening incidents at home. These were the acts and experiences of the public man. The private McIlvaine, as revealed in letters to family and friends as well as in his journal, is every bit as compelling. His highly developed interiority was a marked aspect of his nature from his earliest years, and it begs to be investigated at length. His loves, his loyalties, his regrets, his nostalgia, his playfulness—above all his abiding concern over the state of his spiritual and physical health and his frequent meditations on death—all of these were no less a part of him than the forceful and competent self he presented to the world. As already noted, McIlvaine endured bouts of ill health, both physical and emotional, throughout his long life. These afflictions were an intractable and telling aspect of his character. They appear in part to have been psychosomatic. Given his strenuous and stressful labors, coupled with his less than robust constitution, it may be that periodic collapses were the necessary means of telling himself it was time for rest and a change of scene. One could cite numerous letters and other documents to confirm this pattern, as well as his related hypochondria and obsession with death. In a letter of April 1857, for example, he related to Francis Wharton, professor at Kenyon College, the means by which he was attempting to keep his delicate health from further decline, and averred to the pressures that weighed upon him. He was concerned especially about his ability to conduct parish visitations. "I do not see that I can…escape a sudden and entire break down, except I can restrict my preaching to about once a Sunday, and perhaps once in the week (on visitation), and be exceeding quiet in the intervals." In such times of ill health, he dreaded facing the burden of "incessant talking," the worries and needs of small parishes, and the press of expectations he could not gratify. "I think my prospect of much more work, except in a very quiet way, is not good."[25]

Despite his apparent fragility, McIlvaine survived another sixteen years. Indeed, in a letter to his daughter on his seventy-third birthday, he noted that he was the longest lived of any member of his family, parents included, and that such longevity had not been expected. It would seem that the elixir of an arduous course of life and the constancy of his sturdy faith had been the keys. For his life had been one of "constant, exacting labour, and great tension of mind, having had much mental trial and bodily exposure, and having suffered many dangerous accidents…. '[But] by the care of my Heavenly Father I am…standing here so near Eternity.'"[26]

We find in the private McIlvaine—despite his stresses and illnesses—a love of family that was unalloyed and reciprocated. "It is a sad thing for the head of a family to be so much away from it," he opined in a letter to the Rev. Noah H. Schenck in May 1856.[27] In lauding his parents, praising his wife, and teasing his daughters, he showed himself to be a dutiful and affectionate son, a loving husband and a doting father. His mother's death in Burlington, far from his home in Clifton, brought forth a characteristic effusion of emotional and pious hope, expressed in the ornate style of the ante-bellum period. "She lived a long time before her death as if always ready," he wrote. "I feel…sure that she was in Christ, and that He had taught her, that she…is safe, blood-washed, white-robed, full of blessedness before the throne and the Lamb." Convinced of the reality of heaven, he was not reluctant to speculate upon its inhabitants. "Dear, sweet mother," he asked, "will you come and welcome me when I go likewise? Do you know my sweet children there?"[28] The second of the questions most likely referred to two of his literal children, a son and a daughter having died in childhood a dozen years before. McIlvaine had written to his mother a decade earlier, apprising her of his episcopal duties and praising her person and station. He observed at that time also his sadness to be away from family as well as the trying nature of visitations in the diocese. But memories of his family, especially of his mother, solaced him. "Often the sweetest thoughts I have amongst strangers…are upon my precious mother," he wrote. "No name comes with precisely the same savour. None away from wife and children brings such music as that of mother." He told her that he elicited tears among parishioners in the churches he visited by introducing a "good mother" and venerating her. "I speak of mothers in general, but the fire of my thoughts comes from recollections of one dear mother, whom I do indeed love to honor."[29]

McIlvaine could be playful as well, as in an early letter to his mother-in-law, Mrs. William Coxe Jr. The letter mixed pious praise of his new bride—of his "dear little wife"—with less serious remarks. "[Emily] is not only a good wife," he wrote, "but a most excellent Christian….She is an example as well as a companion; preaching in her private ways, as I do in my public services." Seized by an impish spirit, he added that he "would not exchange her for most folks wives." Warming to the task, he concluded: "I pretend to scold now and then and sometimes *beat* my wife but never do *anything worse.*"[30] Thus the droll clergyman, at twenty-three.

Fifty years later we find the aging bishop in a reflective, nostalgic mood, as evident in a letter to his daughter, Maria (Mrs. George Washington DuBois), regarding the marriage of her eldest daughter, Emily McIlvaine DuBois, to the Rev. William R. Mackay. In this missive, he waxed eloquent about his granddaughter and her "precious" mother on their joyous occasion but warned of the feeling of loss that would accompany the separation of mother and daughter. He recalled to "Mamy" his own distress in the same situation. "Dear Emmy will have left you for her new life and work and you my Mamy will have passed through a time of keen pain of heart...you will have realized what your dear Father felt when you went away—and I walked about the house and knew I could not find there my sweet Mamy and that she was never again to be mine."[31]

McIlvaine was in turn remembered fondly by his daughter. In reminiscing of the bishop's life in Gambier to a sister, she recalled "helping him here and there, and everywhere, with his favourite trees, transplanting flowers with him," and on his spending the occasional evening on the long portico after the heat of a summer's day. She recalled how impressively he would converse, especially in regard "to the second advent [the second coming of Christ as judge at the last day], and the signs of prophecy being near its fulfillment." She remembered his voice in Rosse Chapel at missionary meetings and the "beautiful sermon" he preached at her confirmation. "But all the rest seems like a lovely dream as regards him: his delight in having us with him, taking all three of us with him sometimes, on his short visitations in our large buggy, stopping at noon to water old Mike while we ate our dinner, walking up all the steep hills while we drove." On these occasions, he talked in "a sweet, winning, simple way—very playfully too...full of fun...bringing home roses, clematis, etc. to plant in our garden." She concluded with a bittersweet reflection on how "Providence" had fixed her home far from his, and how she had for many years nothing to remember him by but his "beautiful letters; but they are indeed a treasure."[32]

Despite his regret of family partings, McIlvaine relished new places and the company of new and old companions far from home. Much of his time away can be accounted for by his episcopal duties, which caused him to travel throughout the diocese for two months of every year. Additional absences were the result of his trips to England, generally to recuperate from the physical and emotional collapses that plagued him. His sometimes ambivalent attitude toward these latter travels was confided to his daughter, Mrs. DuBois, from the English cathedral town of Winchester, five months before his death. "So here I am till April next at least—perhaps May. The only drawback is your Mother being left so much alone—and that is not a little serious." Still, he was satisfied with the results of the trip. "I *know* it is very important for me—I have so much improved in health that I have good reason to hope that by spring I shall be able to go home and *stay* at home—and be of some use." [33]

Clearly he loved England and made the most of his visits, at ease in church and society. Despite his ailments, he appeared on these visits to be something of an ecclesiastical whirlwind. The following account, filled with color and detail, is typical of the epistolary bishop. It touches on the requirements of his spiritual life (praising as it does the nutritional value of a sermon); it notes in passing his scholarly achievement, recalling his honorary doctorates from England's premier universities; it mentions the "several good homes" that welcomed his visits, and it sounds the note of a solitary aesthete, a man among men who needed time alone with himself.

I spent last Sunday at Cambridge with my friend Dr. Guest, head of Caius (pronounced Keys) College. I went in the morning to Trinity Church…and heard a *feeding* sermon. At two, went to St. Mary's to the University sermon—and heard Dr. Vaughan, Master of the Temple (London)—preaching the last of four sermons. I went in with the Heads of Houses—and sat with the Vice Chancellor in what the young men call the…place of sculls [sic]—because there sit the *Heads* of Colleges….In the Evening at 7 I went to the service at Trinity College….*All* the length of the chapel was occupied by undergraduates in surplices….There were probably 500—besides Fellows. The whole Evening service was gone through *chorally* and in regular cathedral style….I know of no spectacle more striking than that chapel thus filled. As I am a Doctor of both Universities, I do not know which to prefer in all respects. There is nothing at Oxford equal to the Chapel of King's Cambridge—and the grounds behind. I always go into them for a solitary walk and with a feeling that Oxford has not their equal….I have several good homes in England and am very much blessed in that way. Dear, dear—how I should like to take my Mamy about in this green land. [34]

In April 1853, nearly two decades earlier, McIlvaine had sailed to England as an American delegate to the jubilee meeting of the British and Foreign Bible Society in London. In a journal entry he remarked the kindness shown him by the Archbishop of Canterbury "and many others of the English Episcopate," as well as the role granted him in the meetings "of many noble benevolent institutions," several of which he addressed. In addition, he assisted the archbishop in consecrating the new bishop of Lincoln, "which I had great pleasure in doing." [35] The day of the consecration, he was introduced at Lambeth Palace (the archbishop's London residence) to no less than twenty-eight bishops of the Church of England and Ireland. On another occasion, he assisted the Bishop of Winchester in ordaining twenty-eight candidates for holy orders, at which event he preached the sermon. It was on that trip, on June 7, that he received an honorary degree from Oxford along with such prominent members of the English establishment as future prime minister Benjamin Disraeli and statesman and historian Thomas Babbington Macauley. In 1858, five years later, he would receive a similar degree from Cambridge. There were times when McIlvaine returned the favor, playing host to eminent men. In 1860, he welcomed to Clifton the charming and fashionable Prince of Wales (later Edward VII) and his top-hatted retinue, consisting of the Duke of Newcastle (Henry Pelham), Sir Henry Holland, the Earl of St. Germans (Edward Granville Eliot), and Lord Richard B. P. Lyons, the British ambassador at Washington, none of whom he knew at the time. The following year, several of these men would assist him when he served President Abraham Lincoln as emissary to Britain at the start of the American Civil War.[36] In such circles did McIlvaine move, yet even he expressed a measure of awe at having the prince and the duke under his roof. McIlvaine could wax nostalgic in recollecting England. In writing to William Carus during Christmas 1862, from his house in Clifton, he recalled happier days. Noting that he had been lying on the sofa in his study, that he was "not well," and that a dark and rainy day was ending in snow, the bishop confessed to closing his eyes and imagining that he was back in Winchester Cathedral as he had been the year before. "It was too sweet not to be painful," he confided, "But I had not thought long of *you in my room,* looking out of *my window* on St. Cross—of the Hallelujah Chorus in the Cathedral on the 24th—and on all the precious visits between…when I got up and said, 'I must write.'" Energized by reverie, he proceeded to pen a letter of some length, devoted to the "Rationalistic flood" and other matters of mutual concern, before reverting to pleasanter memories of England. In those final remarks he recalled a room in which he had stayed, a room since converted by Carus into a study. "It is so cheerful," he said of it, "with the light of that sweet green prospect, and the train rushing through flirting its plume of steam. How I can see it all."[37]

England was a part of McIlvaine's mental furniture for more than half-a-century, a source of sweet longing when he was away from it and a cause of joy and pleasure when he was there. It lightened his burdened soul like a glimpse of paradise or a hint of heaven, a ready reminder that good things awaited the diligent clergyman at the end of his days. But in these thoughts we are getting ahead of our story. In the next chapter, we will look at the beginning of that sojourn, at the time of his conversion and the early fruit it bore.

We will consider the soul of a "divided self," and how that self attempted to find both inner peace and outer achievement.

1. Quoted in Carus, *Memorials*, 8-9.
2. Quoted in Pugh, *Bishop Charles Pettit McIlvaine*, x.
3. Quoted in Carus, 9, 11.
4. George M. Hills, *History of the Church in Burlington, New Jersey* (Trenton: William S. Sharp, Printer, 1876), 383.
5. Quoted in Carus, 15-16.
6. Ibid., 15.
7. Reed McIlvaine to Charles P. McIlvaine, Lexington, Ky., June 14, 1822 (Kenyon College Library Archives, Gambier, Ohio), no. 21-06-14.
8. Quoted in Carus, 17.
9. David Hein and Gardiner H. Shattuck Jr., *The Episcopalians* (Praeger, Westport, Connecticut, 2004), 67.
10. James B. Bell, "Charles P. McIlvaine," *For the Union: Ohio Leaders in the Civil War*, edited by Kenneth W. Wheeler (Ohio State University Press, 1968), 236.
11. Pugh, 49.
12. Bell, 237-238.
13. Pugh, 61.
14. Ibid., 64, 65-66, 68.
15. Ibid., 48.
16. Bell, 239-240.
17. Quoted in Carus, 67.
18. Quoted in Pugh, 74.
19. Quoted in Carus, 67.
20. Quoted in William B. Bodice, *The Kenyon Book* (Theological Seminary of the

Protestant Episcopal Church, Diocese of Ohio, 1890), 119-120.

21. Ibid., 120.

22. George Franklin Smythe, *Kenyon College: Its First Century* (Yale University Press, New Haven, Connecticut, 1924), 121.

23. Quoted in Bodice, 130.

24. Quoted in Carus, 342, 284.

25. Charles P. McIlvaine to Francis Wharton, April 29, 1857, Cincinnati, Ohio (Kenyon Archives, no. 58-09.

26. Quoted in Carus, 318-319.

27. Charles P. McIlvaine to the Rev. Noah Hunt Schenck, May 26, 1856 (Kenyon Archives, no. 56-05-26.

28. Quoted in Carus, 137.

29. Ibid., 121, 122.

30. Charles P. McIlvaine to Mrs. William Coxe Jr., Dec. 3, 1822, Georgetown, District of Columbia (Kenyon Archives), no. 22-12-03.

31. Charles P. McIlvaine to Mrs. George Washington DuBois, Nov. 15, 1872, Winchester, England (Kenyon Archives), no. 72-11-15.

32. Quoted in Carus, 135, 135-136.

33. McIlvaine to Mrs. DuBois.

34. Ibid.

35. Quoted in Carus, 154.

36. Bell, 241.

37. Carus, 237, 239.

CHAPTER TWO

The Divided Self

For all of his fine social and intellectual qualities, Charles Pettit McIlvaine was a "divided self," to use the now classic phrase coined by William James. The divided self, described by James in his famous work, *The Varieties of Religious Experience,* is marked by an interior separation, with first one tendency and then another getting the upper hand. Moreover, in the type, discrepant feelings and impulses come and go in response to a deep-seated wish to possess incompatibles. As we shall see, McIlvaine's soul reflected such patterns.

Expanding on his insight, James observes that some persons are born with an inner constitution that is harmonious and well balanced. Others—like McIlvaine—are quite the opposite, and are so in degrees that vary from the merely odd or whimsical to a discord of which the consequences may be severe. In the latter instance, two selves, one actual and one ideal, vie for control. In religious terms, two elements, spirit and flesh, battle one another. In this, one thinks of St. Paul's spiritual travails, described in Romans 7, in which he says he delights "in the law of God" in his inmost self, but sees in his members "another law at war" with the law of his mind, making him "captive to the law of sin."

In the case of persons thus "divided," James writes, life is "one long drama of repentance and of effort to repair misdemeanors and mistakes." [1] Thus it was for McIlvaine. Moreover, his dividedness made of him a "sick soul," to borrow another Jamesean phrase. He suffered from severe feelings of anxiety, obsessive thoughts, and physical complaints (often without objective evidence of disease). Such symptoms, expressed in hypochondria and an obsession with death, dogged him throughout his adult life. Divided and "sick," he was thus prone to physical pain and psychological distress. He possessed also a keen awareness of the brevity of life. He was quick to note the passing of others and to contemplate his own demise. He saw no purpose in life—life reduced to the natural or horizontal plane—that would not be undone by death.

McIlvaine's dividedness presents something of a mystery in the case of a man so accomplished and so affectionately raised as he was. As suggested in chapter one, likely causes appear to be his early schooling and the influence of his father, combined with a temperament predisposed to such behaviors. He was thought to have, in his own words, the "least vigorous constitution" [2] of his family, a phrase hinting of uncommon sensitivity and a disposition to sickliness as a child. The rigor and discipline of the preparatory school he attended, with its "tokens of disgrace," as well as the humane but exacting example set by his father, surely sowed seeds of self-doubt and self-repudiation in the sensitive youth even as they imparted high standards of conduct and scholarship. His less-than-vigorous physical and emotional constitution, seemingly so sensitive to the demands placed upon it, would have made him a classic melancholic type, complete with excess of sentiment, deep and reflective thought, preoccupation with painful impressions, and a predisposition to judge and evaluate himself and others strictly.

Joseph McIlvaine's manner of addressing his son, exemplified in a letter of August 1820, indicates several traits of character likely imparted by him to the younger man. The letter, which offered advice on a variety of subjects, made it clear that mother and father were "extremely anxious" about the health of their son, who had recently left home while suffering an unspecified ailment after graduation from Princeton and its seminary. The young man would thenceforth, his father wrote, be the arbiter of his own actions and of his "final destiny;" the "prerogatives of man hood and self government" having become his. The elder McIlvaine expressed "deep regret" at the son's departure, mingled with hope for the young man's future. He wrote of the "dearly cherished" affection between the son and his parents, and said it was "an awful period in the lives of...parents strongly attached to their children" to see a much-loved son depart, especially as they were "sensible of the dangers and difficulties" that must of necessity be encountered in life. "But we must hold to the course of nature," he wrote, and dutifully fulfill our destiny. "Take good care of your health—our happiness now depends on that." [3] One detects in these remarks the anxiety and gravity, mixed with affection, which marked the son as they had the father. One also detects hints of the religion that would belong to the son throughout his life. For in the "father figure" of Joseph McIlvaine, many of the traits that would shape the child's views on love, virtue and God were present. That is to say, in the flesh-and-blood father the child had perceived no doubt the outlines of a "heavenly father" who was kind, honest, trustworthy, and acutely concerned for the welfare of his progeny. In one way or another, McIlvaine would serve this personal deity—superimposed in part on the Bible's deity—to one degree or another throughout his life, even after theological sophistication had rendered his immature sense of God a thing of the past.

The young Charles McIlvaine, talented yet anxious like his father, found the shifting sands of quotidian existence unable to afford the needed foundation for his life. He sought perforce a rock on which to build his house. He would find his rock at the Princeton revival, at the age of sixteen, in the *euaggellion*, or "good news," of Christian faith. It was a message that would sustain him in bouts of depression and delight him in periods of joy. Owing, it seems, to what traditional Protestants call regeneration ("rebirth") and sanctification (the process of becoming holy), he would be empowered—despite his dividedness—to live the life of a humane and accomplished churchman, one notable for good cheer and equitable temper and for love of God, the church, and his family.

McIlvaine's inner divide may have derived from other, secondary causes as well. In addition to his temperamental disposition, the rigor of his academic training, and a strong paternal influence, already mentioned, there may have been a youthful but serious indiscretion that caused him spiritual discord. Also, he may have been torn by a sense of duty to serve the church, on the one hand, and a desire to escape an unhappy episcopate on the other. Then again, he might have been tormented by the tenets of a tyrannical theology. That he was simply the victim of the "ontological predicament" as experienced by a sensitive soul might seem insufficient, all things considered, to explain his complex condition.

That McIlvaine's dividedness might have stemmed from a serious or embarrassing sexual sin committed in his youth and thereafter kept secret is a possibility that readily comes to mind today. The pervasive influence of psychotherapeutic categories in our time— especially the fading shadow of Freud—makes the suggestion all but inevitable, and thus necessary to be addressed. But that such a sin was committed has nothing to document it. To be sure, a concern to curb "sins of the flesh" did play a role in the Princeton revival, as indicated by an eleven-page pamphlet published at the time and addressed to students. The pamphlet, "Questions and Counsel for the Students of Nassau Hall...Who hope that a Work of Saving Grace Has Been Wrought Upon Their Hearts," begins by asking each student to consider if he is "by nature and by practice, a lost and helpless sinner." It then implores students to "flee youthful lusts" and to "shun every excitement of them." To this end, dozens of questions are provided for an examination of one's moral and spiritual life. Urging students to ponder these questions weekly over a period of several months, the pamphlet concludes with the following sober advice: "Mirth and laughter are not always sinful; but let your indulgence in them be clearly innocent, not very frequent, and never of long continuance." [4]

Like most adolescents, McIlvaine presumably experienced erupting drives of sex and aggression to some degree, drives that tend to confuse and conflict young people. One suspects, however, that whatever sins he may have committed of a sexual nature were of the most harmless sort, the faults of a model child with a tender conscience. Had he committed serious sexual sins, they would likely have been alluded to in a later journal entry. Perhaps, in the manner of the age, they would have been cloaked in figurative language; but they would have been there nonetheless. McIlvaine was ever a person of candor.

He did in fact write of early sinfulness in his journal but it was mostly sinfulness of a general kind, sinfulness of condition rather than of specific transgression. A particular and disturbing sin, a severe moral lapse or indulgence of the flesh, was implicitly denied. "When first called and persuaded in my sixteenth year in College," McIlvaine wrote in his journal in 1860, "I had been kept comparatively exemplary in point of morals—a profane expression had never crossed my lips. But how ignorant I was of all Thy truth and way and word!" [5] One sees in this testimony an awareness of the classic "conviction of sin," of having involuntarily offended against God. McIlvaine saw himself as a sinner by nature but not as particularly sinful in deed. His friend, William Carus, reinforced this view: "The strong terms which he [McIlvaine] uses, when…describing his natural alienation of heart from God previous to his conversion, are not…any painful remembrance of a sinful course in youth: for [his] early life was exemplary for its morality." [6]

In looking elsewhere to explain McIlvaine's dividedness, the scholar Mark Heathcote Hall focuses on the adult and not the youth. He suggests that McIlvaine's illnesses were caused by subconscious urges to escape from the burdens of an uncongenial episcopate aggravated by pessimistic theological views. He argues that the burdens of the Episcopal office in a frontier setting, complicated by a strong sense of duty, played a major role in McIlvaine's discontents. "There is...evidence," Hall writes, "that the good bishop just did not fit in socially in some of the areas and among some of the company of his diocese." Nor, perhaps, did he adjust well to the rough and frequent travel demanded of him. When one considers his often expressed love of home, family, quiet and order, Hall suggests, one might suspect he would have been happier "in an urban, socially respectable parish or area, [and] would not find happiness and fulfillment in the rough, rapidly growing semi-frontier of Ohio." Moreover, he argues, McIlvaine's theological convictions played a role in his discontent. Emphasis on "the utter sinfulness and unworthiness of the individual," Hall writes, "does concern the Bishop's life. As a preacher and practitioner of evangelical principles, [he] seemed to have entirely adopted these ideas regarding the nature of man and applied them to himself, in a way which burdened him with a heavy sense of responsibility and a vivid concept of self-guilt." [7]

Hall's argument bears some plausibility. Unable to admit that his bishopric, to which he believed he had been called by God, was basically untenable, McIlvaine may have become, as Hall says, an "exile from himself."[8] Moreover, he suggests, he may have attempted to "escape" by employing a four-fold strategy. Two of the four stratagems derived from his theological position: his role as a leader and theologian of the Evangelical movement, which exercised his talents as a man of consequence and a writer of clarity and power, and his hope of heaven, which set before him the ultimate escape through death. The other two were his "head troubles" and other ailments, which seem to have been partly of a psychosomatic nature, and his enchantment with England, which drew him from home many times. That McIlvaine employed these stratagems to escape may have been the case, though one might just as well be inclined—if less captive to modern psychologizing—to see them (with the exception of the psychosomatic symptoms) as healthy means of fulfillment rather than as "escapes" from occupational distress and emotional imbalance. Clearly, he needed to absent himself from time to time from the burdens and troubles of his office, which by his own account placed a heavy strain upon his high-strung nature, but this is to say no more than that he was like other men in his need for rest and recreation. In addition, one might question whether his evangelical principles burdened him with self-guilt, as Hall suggests, or whether in fact he turned to evangelical principles to make sense of the guilt he already felt. Rather than burdening him, his evangelical principles may have provided him with a mirror in which to see and better understand his inner discomforts, and a framework in which to find meaning and purpose in spiritual and temporal endeavors.

That McIlvaine's divided nature could have been caused by his attachment to evangelical theology has also been addressed by another scholar, Diana Hochstedt Butler, who disagrees with Hall's view. As she sees it, McIlvaine's "anxious depression" was typical of the times, regardless of theological persuasion. Furthermore, many men and women, if means were available, traveled to Europe for rest cures, just as McIlvaine did. In addition, she notes, obsession with death—a pronounced trait in McIlvaine—was prevalent in the ante-bellum United States. In other words, in these respects, the bishop was a man of his times. [9]

Neither Hall nor Butler asks whether McIlvaine's afflictions might have been aggravated by an organic infirmity. It seems possible that, in light of today's medical knowledge, he might have suffered a chemical imbalance, thereby intensifying if not causing his periodic anxiety and depression. Chemical imbalances leading to depression, stemming from low serotonin levels in the brain, are regularly diagnosed in patients today. Perhaps McIlvaine was thus afflicted.

Moreover, the possibility that McIlvaine's theological scruples helped cause his emotional troubles depends in part—as suggested above—on whether he was neurotic before or after adopting such scruples. If his disorder preceded his adoption of evangelical principles, then evangelicalism did not cause it. Indeed, his "divided self" and "sick soul" appears to have taken shape, at least in embryo, before any formal commitment to a theological system. It is quite possible that the discomfort of divided selfhood was already in place at the time of his spiritual rebirth and that the discomfort, prompting him to search for relief, thus led him to a new way of life and its concomitant belief system.

The notion that evangelicalism was McIlvaine's bogey may also depend, at least in part, on a mistaken view of this theological system. In this view, evangelicalism is linked to simplistic, hell-fire preaching, total depravity, repressive morality, a world-denying narrowness, judgmentalism, and a strong dose of Calvinist gloom. Would not anyone, it is insinuated, be anxious and depressed by internalizing such views? Yet evangelicalism—which comes in more than one form—is both more complex and more subtle than this caricature allows, and arguably more liberating than oppressive to its adherents. It appears that McIlvaine's evangelicalism was of a moderate strain and fully congruent with Episcopal distinctives and prayer book formularies. It is less likely, in short, that it oppressed him than that it freed him, at least partially.

In analyzing McIlvaine's dividedness, we should take into account the "ontological predicament" that transcends the contingencies of individual lives. The predicament, alluded to above, can be sketched in a few simple statements: everyone is susceptible to ill health; everyone faces unexpected circumstances; everyone faces the threat of meaninglessness, and everyone faces the certainty of death. Thus the predicament that McIlvaine faced, and which drew his sustained attention, was no different from the one faced by other sensitive human beings. Among the classic personality types—the buoyant sanguine, the languid phlegmatic, the fiery choleric—each in his own way must face the same uncertainties. That McIlvaine the melancholic was concerned to the point of obsession with such matters is not surprising. There is nothing unusual about a man of sensitive nature and keen intellect reflecting on the data of his earthly sojourn, his frequent illnesses, his rising or falling fortunes, the meaning and purpose of his life, and the certainty of his death. To be sure, his brooding seems to have been excessive. Though his predicament was universal, his expression of it bore a decidedly personal stamp.

Regardless of the exact cause of his dividedness, McIlvaine was prepared by the age of sixteen to embrace the evangelical paradigm. He was ready to submit to rescue and to embrace rebirth. "I had *heard* before; I began then to *know*." His conversion, one could say, was a means of getting into right relationship with the transcendent realm over against the shifting sands of the natural realm. Writing on his sixty-first birthday, he recalled the condition of his alienated heart at the time of his conversion: "While I was spending nearly sixteen years in entire rebellion against Thee, while sin rioted in my heart, and the world was all…for which I cared…Thou didst then visit my dark, blind, corrupt, wretched heart with Thy free and sovereign grace, mercifully calling me to know and serve thee." [10] The healthy-minded man or woman, William James says, needs to be born but once to be eligible for happiness (happiness as the world understands it, that is). Not so the sick soul. Not so Charles Pettit McIlvaine. "Peace cannot be reached by the simple addition of pluses and elimination of minuses from life," James says. The sick soul, in other words, must be born twice. [11]

What was it to be born again as McIlvaine understood it? In the Gospel of John we learn that one "must be born again [or 'from above'] by water and the spirit" in order "to see the kingdom of God." But Scripture by itself does not present fully the richness of the doctrine in its developed forms. Regeneration (the technical term for spiritual rebirth) is, in some churches, incorporated into baptism, especially in the Roman Catholic, Orthodox and (if the Book of Common Prayer is read literally) Episcopal churches. In others, it is part of a conscious experience detached from sacramental rites. In the view of McIlvaine and the Evangelicals, the latter opinion was upheld. To support their view, they interpreted the prayer book—despite its clear statement of spiritual regeneration in the baptismal rite—against the backdrop of the Thirty-nine Articles, especially articles twenty-five and twenty-seven, which call baptism a "sign" of regeneration and allude to those who "receive Baptism rightly," statements that mitigate against baptismal regeneration. There was no *opus operatum*, as in Roman and Anglo-Catholicism. Only faith in God, exercised by the baptized person through grace, could save. Baptism of an infant, therefore, placed the individual in covenant with God but did not change his moral or spiritual nature.

This understanding of rebirth was rooted in both Anglo-American Puritan and Continental Pietist movements of the sixteenth and seventeenth centuries. The Great Awakening in New England as well as the Wesleyan and Whitefield revivals in Britain and America kept the doctrine alive throughout the eighteenth century. At its core was the Puritan focus on new birth, with the example of St. Paul on the road to Damascus as its emblem. The Puritans, many of whom were Anglicans opposed to what they deemed an over-emphasis on formalism and traditionalism in the Church of England, called their people to a "spiritual awakening." They expected from penitent sinners an identifiable experience of rebirth. The experience need not be as dramatic as St. Paul's;

indeed, only the most unusual was. But such an experience there had to be.

So vital was this experience to Puritan identity that, over time, rebirth became standardized in Congregationalist New England life, with specific features regarded as signs of election. The process involved at least four essential beliefs: that sinners were in need of being converted and saved; that God had sent his Son to the cross on behalf of sinners; that the risen Christ called burdened souls to himself for their release and salvation, and that the road to rebirth would not be an easy one. As a modern exponent of this tradition writes, there would be "ups, downs, blockages and pitfalls that face us as we travel the road from ignorant complacency about our spiritual state to informed, self-despairing, clear-headed and whole-hearted faith in Christ."[12] This journey could be an arduous, agonizing one for the conscientious penitent, complete with psychological strain, insecurity, intermittent self-abhorrence and a redundant search for signs of regeneration. Even then, assurance of rebirth could be problematical. Assurance that the transition had been made was often the result of prolonged self-analysis. In the words of a prominent authority, the Puritans "liberated men from the treadmill of indulgences and penances, but cast them on the iron couch of introspection." [13]

The born-again experience, in its classic Puritan form, generally occurred at the end of a period of restlessness, anxiety and confusion. It might have appeared to the onlooker and perhaps to the subject himself as a sudden and unprecedented occurrence, but subconscious preparation (the working of prevenient grace, theologically speaking) had been under way for some time. In the *Varieties*, William James describes the process in a typically horizontal and psychological manner, but accurately nonetheless despite its limited scope. "In all of us, however constituted," he writes, "but to a deeper and greater in proportion as we are intense and sensitive…does the normal evolution of character chiefly consist in the straightening out and unifying of the inner self." Feelings and impulses, at first a comparative chaos, must in the end form a "stable system of functions in right subordination." The period of order-making and struggle is an unpleasant one. If the individual has a sensitive conscience and a religious turn of mind, the unhappiness will take the form of feeling inwardly vile and wrong in relation "to the author of one's being and appointer of one's spiritual fate." (Such, James believed, was the religious tension and "conviction of sin" that played so large a part in Protestant Christianity.) But once unification or partial unification of the soul had occurred, it brought with it "a firmness, stability, and equilibrium succeeding [the] period of storm and stress and inconsistency." Stated otherwise, one could say the process involved the unification of fragmented thoughts, ends and "selves." Thus, the subject's previous ideas, aims and objects were understood to have formed diverse internal groups and systems within the soul, relatively independent of one another. There may have been a pleasure-loving self, an intellectual self, a moral self, a melancholy self, a hopeful self, an ambitious self, an altruistic self. But in the wake of conversion, one idea or closely related group of ideas attained supremacy and expelled or subjugated its previous rivals. Residues of the once-born self remained in the form of "indwelling sin," but with no power to dominate and distort the personality as they formerly had done. [14]

This understanding of regeneration was based on an evangelical interpretation of Scripture. The idea of sin in the Bible, according to this view, involved first and foremost an offence against God, an offense that disrupted the proper relationship between the human and the divine. Sin was not primarily a social concept but a theological one. It was measured against the yardstick of God's total demand for righteousness. Against that measure, human beings were "convicted of sin." Humanly speaking, McIlvaine was a righteous man. He had committed no grave sin against his fellows or against society at large. Nonetheless, he saw himself as a transgressor meriting retribution. He saw himself in the perspective of God as understood by evangelical theology. "Sin rioted in my heart, and the world was all the object for which I cared." His heart was "dark, blind, corrupt." Yet in the moment of need, the penitent was rescued. "Thou didst then visit…with Thy free and sovereign grace, mercifully calling me to know and serve Thee, and graciously constraining my heart to love thee and choose thy ways." [15]

In sum, salvation—free, sovereign, merciful—came to McIlvaine in classic evangelical form. He felt himself *justified*—redeemed from guilt by the work of Christ crucified; *converted*—his prior state of sinfulness replaced by a state of righteousness, by grace through faith, the curse of Adam lifted; *regenerated*—"born again," become a babe in Christ, a new creation, ready to take baby steps on the road of sanctification. According to the evidence, this is how McIlvaine understood what he had experienced.

Several types of evangelicalism had found a congenial climate in the America of the seventeenth and eighteenth centuries. There they contributed to the shaping of a distinctive form of revival-based, conversionist religion. By 1811, this form of piety had achieved self-identity in the Episcopal Church, where it began to contest for influence with the more traditional High Church party. Thus the evangelical nature of McIlvaine's conversion may be less puzzling than it might at first appear.

Such notable divines as Devereux Jarratt, John Wesley and George Whitefield were among the first to preach evangelical principles to Episcopalians. Jarratt, rector of Bath Parish, Dinwiddie County, Virginia, helped revive the spiritual life of southern Anglicanism during the eighteenth century. He was a tireless propagator of the Gospel, especially at a time when the Episcopal Church was in dire straits, during and just after the War of Independence. The dynamic Wesley, for his part, brought pietism (the Continental version of Puritanism) to both England and America in modified form. The Anglican founder of Methodism was influenced by both the Moravian Pietists and their leader, Count Nicholas Zinzendorf, as well as by the piety and courage of a band of Moravian emigrants who sailed with him to Georgia. Following his conversion at Aldersgate, where he felt his heart "strangely warmed," he too propagated the evangelical faith tirelessly, bringing the message of personal religion and born-again experience to many thousands of hearers. The melodramatic Whitefield, an Englishman like Wesley, spread the evangelical message in the American colonies as well, and is thought by some scholars to be the defining figure in the history of American evangelicalism itself. According to historian Mark Noll, "Whitefield's style—popular preaching aimed at emotional response—has continued to shape American evangelicalism long after [his] specific theology (he was a Calvinist), his denominational origins (he was an Anglican), and his rank (he was a clergyman) are long since forgotten....Almost every one of Whitefield's sermons is marked by a fundamentally democratic determination to simplify the essentials of religion in a way that gives them the widest possible mass appeal." [16]

Owing to Wesley and Whitefield, the separation of regeneration from baptism, begun a century earlier by Calvinists and Puritans, was completed. Hence, by McIlvaine's time, evangelicals took it for granted. Yet near the end of McIlvaine's life, issues raised by the separation would sow tension within Evangelical ranks, and calls on the part of some clergy to revise the prayer book to remove all signs of ambiguity on the matter. McIlvaine's attempts to mediate this crisis will be discussed in chapter nine.

In addition to the evangelical features that had found their way into the Episcopal Church, McIlvaine had witnessed evangelical worship in other churches at an impressionable age. These experiences may have played a role in his later evangelical sympathies. He recalled in old age that as a child his nurse had taken him on occasion to the local Baptist church, and that from time to time as a boy he had looked in "out of curiosity" at the Methodist church near his home. "Until I went to college," he said of these experiences, "I had never seen the worship of any other denomination." [17] Perhaps these early incidents, still vivid at the age of seventy-three, impressed the boy favorably. Perhaps the sight of Baptists and Methodists at worship—evangelicals of the purest strain—rendered McIlvaine amenable to evangelical religion in ways that he would not otherwise have been. Regardless of the precise reasons, McIlvaine found at Princeton an evangelical solution to his needs. Previously religious in a nominal way, he became religious in a profound way. Through conversion he became a "new man." Half a century later, in the notes of his personal history, he praised the Princeton revival for its affect on him and others.

It was powerful and prevailing, and fruitful in the conversion of young men to God; and it was quiet, unexcited, and entirely free from all devices or means, beyond the few and simple which God has appointed, namely, prayer and the ministry of the word. [This was a vital point to McIlvaine the Episcopalian: that "devices" and "means"—by which he referred to the "engineered" revivals of Charles G. Finney and others—were in no way necessary.] In that precious season of the power of God, my religious life began. I had *heard* before; I began then to *know*. I must doubt the deepest convictions of my soul, when I doubt whether that revival was the work of the Spirit of God. Many that laboured faithfully in the ministry, and are now at rest with the Lord; some that are still in the work; many whose mark has been strongly made on their generation on the side of the Gospel, were the subjects of that work. [18]

The Presbyterian Charles Hodge was among the "many" who went on "to labor faithfully in the ministry." Hodge, who became a professor at Princeton Seminary and a famous theologian, remained McIlvaine's friend from Princeton days onwards. In his recollection of the revival, he recalled "there was only a gradual change in the spirit of the College, and state of mind of the students....Personal religion—the salvation of the soul became the absorbing subject of attention." He listed McIlvaine among the dozen or so students "most seriously impressed" by the revival. For his part, McIlvaine recalled the effects in a letter written nearly six decades after the event. "By the grace of God making us new creatures in Christ Jesus, we became brethren one of another, in every near and affectionate association. We were then, as now, of different churches in the one ever-living Church of Christ; but I am thankful to be able to say, that no dividing lines have every touched our oneness of heart." [19]

"New creatures in Christ Jesus." Such is, in evangelical eyes (and in the words of St. Paul), the sum and substance of the true believer. The "evangelical soul," so to speak, thirsts for deliverance like that experienced by McIlvaine and Hodge. No halfway measures are sought or accepted. According to the *Varieties* of William James, "The deliverance must come in as strong a form as the complaint, if it is to take effect; and that seems a reason why the coarser religions, revivalistic, orgiastic, with blood and miracles and supernatural operations, may possibly never be displaced. Some constitutions need them too much." [20] There was nothing coarse about Charles Pettit McIlvaine—let alone "orgiastic"—but the needs of the sensitive youth appear to have required, all the same, a strong measure of revival religion, of a religion of the heart. Such a religion, present at the Princeton revival, was tailored in every particular to the shape of his soul. He was, as he saw it, reborn not by moral effort or religious ritual but by the gift of God, given in grace and known experientially. "I began then to *know.*"

According to the Rev. Ashbel Green, president of the college at the time of the revival, "Every religious service, both on secular days and on the Sabbath, was attended with a solemnity that was very impressive....There were very few individuals in the college who were not deeply impressed with a sense of importance of spiritual and eternal things....For a time it seemed as if the whole of our charge was pressing into the kingdom of God." [21]

Indeed, the students were ripe for repentance, as indicated by contemporary records. Moreover, the offenses of some had gone far beyond breaches of piety. In January 1814, for instance, a year before the revival, students had both burned the college privy and exploded the "big cracker"—a hollow log filled with two pounds of gunpowder—against a doorway at Nassau Hall. The blast blew away the door, cracked masonry and shattered glass. And in January 1817, on the other side of the revival, a riot erupted when students angry over the length of their reading assignments sealed the entrances to Nassau Hall and the rooms of tutors and theology students. Attempts to punish the rioters sparked additional violence in which pistols, clubs and knives were wielded. The president was struck by a chunk of ice and the pulpit from which he preached was partially destroyed. [22] The revival of 1815 appears to have been an island of peace in a sea of discontent. Other riots had occurred as well, among them the "Great Rebellion" of 1807. After each disturbance, troublemakers were expelled from the school, sometimes by the dozens.

In the wake of the revival of 1815, the pious McIlvaine returned to his home parish, St. Mary's Episcopal Church, in Burlington, where he presented himself for baptism and received the Lord's Supper for the first time. [23] Although considering himself but a "worm and miserable sinner," [24] he was convinced of a call to the ministry. Thus convinced, he returned to Princeton to enroll in the seminary. He also began to preach and conduct Bible classes. With his friends Charles Hodge and John Johns, later

59

Episcopal bishop of Virginia, he started—as we saw in chapter one—an interdenominational Sunday school, becoming a pioneer in that movement. [25]

In retrospect, McIlvaine considered himself a slow learner in the school of Christian life and doctrine. "How cloudy was my understanding of divine things!" he wrote in his journal in 1860, of his early life in the faith. "And as the morning light advanced, how long was it a misty morning!" Though it was ever so slow, he was grateful for the spiritual progress he made, and gave all the credit to God. "Thou didst lead me, and hold me, and bear with me, and was so compassionate and long-suffering." Like a kindly father—not perhaps totally unlike the flesh-and-blood father in Burlington—the Father of Spirits was believed to be close at all times. "All has been Thy leading, Thy sustaining, Thy feeding—all Thine, the grace of God in me, with me—else had I been nothing but a poor, blind, useless, lost sinner!" [26] It was all "sola gratia"— by grace alone.

Within a year or two of McIlvaine's conversion, a singular and dramatic incident occurred. Demonstrating his remarkable memory for detail, he recounted the incident from a distance of more than fifty years, when describing it in his journal entry for February 7, 1869. [27] He was reminded of the event, he said, while reading 2 Corinthians 12:7, where St. Paul speaks of a "messenger of Satan." McIlvaine, noting that he had seldom mentioned the event to anyone, said he would never think of it "but with a solemn awe, and a sort of consciousness of having once known that buffeting from such a messenger, in a manner too impressive to be forgotten."

The incident, he remembered, occurred at his father's house in Burlington at about the time he graduated from college, when he was between seventeen and eighteen years of age, a year to eighteen months after being "turned to the Lord." Conscious of his lack of maturity in the faith, and feeling a need for times of prayer (and "there being at that time in the town scarcely any intelligent, earnest, Christian society" to aid him), he had vowed to retire each evening at sunset to his bedroom to pray. While sitting in the parlor with company late one afternoon, he said to himself: "The sun is down, go to your room. But I answered to myself, They will go directly, and I will wait." Aware, however, that his disposition to pray was flagging, he rose and left the company. He had no sooner entered the hall than an "indescribable dread" fell upon him. It was, he said, "as if some mysterious agency of terror" were resisting him. Clutching the banister, "by force" he began to ascend the stairway. "As I went up," he recalled, "the dread increased to such a degree that I trembled in every limb, and perspiration broke out at every pore." By the time he had reached the first landing, he was "so overpowered with dread" that he was unsure whether to proceed. "I knew...that something, some power, some darkness, some unutterable *dread* was upon me and before me." He continued to the head of the stairway, trembling more than before. Again, he paused, uncertain of whether to proceed. Again, he "pushed forward," reaching his room at the end of the passage. He took hold of the door handle. "The dread increased," he said. "It seemed a *horror* of darkness." After yet another pause, he opened the door and rushed to the chair by which he was accustomed to kneel, at the opposite end of the room. There, kneeling, he prayed in broken sentences, while "two or three times looking behind me, as if I expected to see some being there." Finishing his prayer, he rose up, and "instantly" the dread began to lift. In a few moments, all had passed. "I was drenched with perspiration," he said, "my limbs shook, my nerves were thoroughly shaken." Thirty-six hours would elapse before his "nerves" recovered. Never again would he undergo such an experience. "What it was precisely I say not," he reflected. "I believe it was a messenger of Satan. It was an awful encounter. I mentioned it to nobody for years." Yet he found a silver lining in the event. "It has helped me," he said, "to believe solemnly in the

Bible teaching of that adversary [Satan], who goeth about as a roaring lion to devour; and whom we must resist, by praying with all prayer and supplication in the spirit."

McIlvaine's memory of the encounter points up several telling features of our subject. For in it we see a young man conscious of his own religious immaturity; an earnest convert dutifully at prayer; a deviser and follower of rules; a gifted student disdainful of the humdrum piety of his home town; a conscientious host, and a sensitive soul aware of spiritual promptings. Each of these elements proved to be characteristic of the man throughout his life. Moreover, there is in the story a vivid sense of *opposition*, of a spiritual counterforce at work in him, of an entity (the "adversary") eager to prey on his soul's dividedness. Thus the incident foretold a lifetime of "spiritual warfare."

That McIlvaine was a complex and divided soul prior to his conversion is certain. That he remained one following conversion is no less certain. He had, in the evangelical view, been saved but not sanctified. His divided selves were only partly bridged; the sick soul only partly healed. The process of sanctification—of growth in holiness—had been started but not finished. At the Princeton revival, his center of gravity had been repositioned, stabilizing him in a new life. Yet he would remain imperfectly stable. The revival had moderated his habitual tendencies, not erased them. Faith would henceforth equip him to make sense of his dividedness and to transcend its greatest liabilities but not to abolish them.

Later in life, McIlvaine would adopt as his own a "precious hymn" entitled "Just as I Am," written by an English invalid named Charlotte Elliott in 1836. He applied it to his entire life as a believer. "That hymn contains my religion, my theology, my hope," he said. "It has been my ministry to preach just what it contains. In health it expresses all my refuge; in death I desire that I may know nothing else, for support and consolation, but what it contains. When I am gone, I wish to be remembered in association with that hymn." [28] This hymn, which remains in the hymnal of the Episcopal Church (1982 version), has been used by the evangelist Billy Graham for many decades to accompany the altar call at his crusades.

Two of the hymn's seven stanzas capture the essence of McIlvaine's spirituality:

Just as I am—though tossed about
With many a conflict, many a doubt,
Fightings and fears within, without –
O Lamb of God, I come.

Just as I am—poor, wretched, blind:
Sight, riches, healing of the mind,
Yea, all I need, in Thee to find –
O Lamb of God, I come.

McIlvaine sought a framework for his life that would provide peace, joy and meaning. He sought a unification that would bind together, whether in whole or in part, the divides and disparities of his youthful self, thus equipping him for a life that would be at once faithful, ethical and useful. The foundation for that life, laid at Princeton in the revival of 1815, would serve him all his days.

1. William James, The Varieties of Religious Experience (Penguin Books, New York, 1986), 168-169.
2. Quoted in Carus, Memorials, 319.
3. Joseph McIlvaine to Charles P. McIlvaine, Aug. 13, 1820 (Kenyon Archives) no. 20-08-13.
4. "Questions and Counsel for the Students of Nassau-Hall (At Princeton in New-Jersey) Who Hope that a Work of Saving Grace Has Been Wrought Upon Their Hearts" (Concord, 1815), Princeton Weekly Bulletin, May 22, 2000, Vol. 89, No. 28.
5. Quoted in Carus, 35.

6. Ibid.

7. Mark H. Hall, "Bishop McIlvaine: the Reluctant Frontiersman," Historical Magazine of the Protestant Episcopal Church 44 (1975): 85, 86, 82.

8. Ibid., 86.

9. Butler, Standing Against the Whirlwind, XI-XII.

10. Quoted in Carus, 36.

11. James, 166.

12. J. I. Packer, A Quest for Godliness: The Puritan Vision of the Christian Life (Crossway Books, Wheaton, Ill., 1990), 299.

13. Perry Miller, quoted in Sydney E. Ahlstrom, A Religious History of the American People (Yale University, 1972), 128.

14. James, 170-171, 176.

15. Quoted in Carus, 36.

16. Mark Noll, The Scandal of the Evangelical Mind (Inter-Varsity Press, Downers Grove, Ill., 1994), 61.

17. George M. Hills, History of the Church in Burlington, New Jersey (Trenton: William S. Sharp, Printer, 1876), 391.

18. Quoted in Carus, 11.

19. Quoted in A. A. Hodge, The Life of Charles Hodge (Charles Scribner's Sons, New York, 1880), 30, 32, 527.

20. James, 162.

21. Quoted in Butler, 24.

22. Questions and Counsel.

23. Butler, 24.

24. Quoted in Carus, 36.

25. Butler, 24.

26. Quoted in Carus, 36.

27. Ibid., 13-14.

28. Ibid., 199-200.

CHAPTER THREE

Birth of a Controversialist

As observed earlier, Charles Pettit McIlvaine was not one to hide his light under a bushel basket. Whatever personal dilemmas might have afflicted him as a youth, his conversion experience put them into perspective, providing the spiritual energy and emotional harmony that would propel him through life. In his first years as a priest, he would competently lead two parishes, stir a religious revival at the U. S. Military Academy at West Point, cross swords with powerful High Churchmen, join the work of both Episcopal and non-Episcopal voluntary societies, and hone his skills as a preacher. These experiences laid a foundation upon which the mature clergyman would build, as he pastored the diocese of Ohio, administered a college and seminary, and led the Evangelical party of the Episcopal Church. His years as bishop, educator, and partisan would bring him equal shares of conflict and accomplishment.

McIlvaine's aptitude for controversy was fortified by his studies at two Presbyterian institutions: Princeton College, from which he graduated in 1816, and Princeton Theological Seminary, where he was resident from 1817-19. (Although the Episcopal Church had no seminary at the time, General Theological Seminary was in the process of being organized in New York City.) The curriculum at Princeton College was demanding, as it included ancient languages and history, moral philosophy, mathematics and natural science, natural and revealed religion, detailed study of Scripture, and more, as noted in chapter one. For its part, seminary instruction was rooted in Reformed theology and its bulwarks, including the Westminster Confession of Faith and the scholastic theology of Francois Turretin.

The Westminster Confession, to which McIlvaine was exposed, had been completed in 1646, during the period of the English Civil Wars. Arguably the ripest fruit of Reformation creed-making, it was the product of twenty-seven months of labor by a commission appointed by Parliament. It quickly established itself as the definitive statement of Presbyterian doctrine in the English-speaking world and has ever since had significant influence on Reformed doctrine (the doctrine of Calvinist-based churches in contrast to Lutheran-based churches). Both the confession and Turretin's theology were in turn undergirded by the philosophy of Scottish Common Sense Realism (or "Scottish realism"), which was America's common intellectual property in the nineteenth century, and to which we will return. [1]

Despite its Presbyterian roots, instruction at Princeton College was in fact broad –based, transcending denominational boundaries. Remarkably, McIlvaine attested that his studies "involved nothing distinctive of the Presbyterian Church." [2] A later student, Edward Mansfield, who matriculated at the college in 1820, also affirmed that he "never heard Presbyterianism as such preached at Princeton College." [3]

Another commentator asserts that the seminary itself avoided a narrowly confessional viewpoint. "Princeton Seminary," Loren Pugh writes, "during the period when McIlvaine was a student, was broadly evangelical rather than narrowly Presbyterian or Calvinistic....It is possible that the seminary wished to broaden its appeal, and it also is possible that it was merely perpetuating the tradition of Princeton College." [4]

McIlvaine's required reading for Episcopal orders included a number of works selected by William White, presiding bishop of the Episcopal Church at the time. Taught to both Evangelicals and High Churchmen, it consisted of readings in Post-Restoration Anglicanism, the Caroline Divines, and assorted latitudinarians, rationalists, moralists and Nonjurors. In the words of one scholar, "Except for Richard Hooker, White included no figure from the English Reformation, and in line with his almost fanatical dislike of Calvinism, he included only anti-Calvinistic works." [5] We have every reason to believe that McIlvaine, converted at the Princeton revival of 1815, found White's course of study, with its targeted hostility towards Reformation theology, at odds with his growing conviction of the rightness and usefulness of the evangelical paradigm.

Although broad in scope, instruction that was specific to Princeton Seminary had an edge to it nonetheless. Ashbel Green (who was also president of the college), Samuel Miller and Archibald Alexander, the first three professors at the seminary, were ardent defenders of traditional Protestant distinctives. Hence, they served as anodynes to McIlvaine's exposure to Anglican rationalism in its various forms. Buttressed by Scottish realism, Turretin, and other foundational sources, they expounded orthodox doctrine and philosophy as understood through the eyes of the Reformation. Consequently, their institution was noted for a "siege mentality;" not only for its opposition to the rising philosophies of the day—which it deemed dangerous to religious and ethical life—but to the perceived emotionalism and subjectivism of much American religion. Not surprisingly, in light of its self-identification as a defender of orthodoxy, the seminary was noted for its apologetic stance, thus emphasizing the branch of theology that seeks to defend or prove the truth of the Christian faith.

It was by way of Ashbel Green that Scottish realism made its way to the seminary. Green had learned it from the Scotsman and patriot, John Witherspoon, first president of Princeton College and signer of the Declaration of Independence, who in turn had imbibed the tenets of Thomas Reid, the philosophy's most eminent spokesman. Archibald Alexander was a devotee of it as well, having been exposed to it by his mentor and tutor, the Rev. William Graham. Graham had also studied the teaching under Witherspoon at Princeton. Alexander, who wielded the weapons of Scottish realism with skill and verve, maintained they provided "the basis for an irrefutable apologetic concerning the existence of God and the reality of biblical revelation." [6] This tough-minded philosophy, in conjunction with Reformed principles and the carefully worded structures of Reformed confessions, equipped McIlvaine to become an intellectual militant with few equals.

Scottish realism's principal aim was to create "a position free from absurdity or unreasonable subtlety," a fault attributed to the thinking of such as David Hume and George Berkeley. In keeping with their age, Scottish realists "rang the changes on the greatness of Bacon and Newton," seminal figures in the birth of modern science, and thus insisted on being empirical. [7] They argued that human beings experienced the world objectively, without mediation of "ideas," and held to the ancient dualisms of mind and matter, subject and object, creator and creation. By these means, they escaped a whole string of potent "isms," among them materialism, idealism, subjectivism, pantheism and skepticism. An Enlightenment philosophy itself, Scottish realism challenged other Enlightenment philosophies on their own grounds, thus recommending itself as a weapon in Christian apologetics. Throughout much of the nineteenth century, it dominated the thought of Episcopalians, Congregationalists, Unitarians and Lutherans, as well as Presbyterians.

The spirited Archibald Alexander, who was vital in shaping McIlvaine's theology, was grounded not only in Scottish realism but in the seventeenth-century scholasticism of Francois Turretin, the doughty defender of orthodoxy at Geneva who attacked efforts to modify a strict understanding of predestination and a literalistic view of scriptural inspiration. Having imparted vital intellectual and doctrinal guidance to Alexander, Turretin's four volume *Institutio Theologiae Elencticae* became an established text at the seminary, and remained one until 1873, when it was replaced by the *Systematic Theology* of Alexander's protégé—and McIlvaine's friend—Charles Hodge. During its many decades of use, observes historian Sydney Ahlstrom, Turretin's theology provided "both structure and content for the message which hundreds of the seminary's graduates carried across the land and into many foreign mission fields." [8] McIlvaine was among its carriers.

"Princeton Theology," built on the intellectualism of Turretin, Alexander, Hodge, and others, became a bastion of Reformed orthodoxy in America. Hodge later boasted that during the years of his dominance at Princeton the institution never brought forward "a single original thought." [9] He judged this a badge of honor. Indeed, owing to its breadth and rigor, Princeton theology was, in Ahlstrom's view, "A great positive force, affording theological substance wherever revivalism threatened to vaunt experience only, fostering education and the learned tradition, and striving desperately to provide a Christian message that was not simply an amalgam of folk religion and Americanism."[10] According to Ashbel Green, primary drafter of the plan of Princeton Seminary, students were required to know and explain "the principal difficulties which arise in the perusal of the Scriptures...translations...apparent inconsistencies...and real obscurities." In addition, each "must have read and digested the principal arguments and writings relative to what has been called the Deistical controversy. Thus will he be qualified to become a defender of the Christian faith." [11] Upon this foundation, McIlvaine would stand immoveable. For in Scottish realism and Protestant orthodoxy he found truth, not novelty, guidance, not questions. They marked out for him a path both clear and consistent. They equipped him to fight a battle royal in defense of the faith.

Such considerations bring up the remark of a scholar who has studied McIlvaine closely, to wit, that he was a man of "careful, if unimaginative, theological formulations." [12] McIlvaine, one suspects, would not have been in the least discomfited by the remark, although he might have resented its implication that his writing lacked in any way the verve and color that it does in fact possess. That reservation aside, he was indeed beholden to the notion that theology should be more of bedrock than of blowing sand. Progressive understandings were not for him; the Bible, once given, and filled as it was with what he considered to be inspired, propositional testimony, could be formulated theologically in unwavering terms—and should be.

In addition to its carefully formulated dogmatics, the Princeton Theology that McIlvaine imbibed had a strong experiential component. Archibald Alexander himself had been a revivalist— as well as an educator, a pastor and a theologian—prior to coming to Princeton Seminary in 1812. During the 1780s and '90s, he had witnessed or led revivals in his native Virginia, initiatives that grounded him in the importance of experiential religion. Nor was Charles Hodge, subsequent leading light at the seminary, confined to a narrow intellectualism but rather, according to one scholar, "succeeded in bringing together more elements from the Reformed heritage, American culture, and pastoral concern than anyone in the [Princeton] tradition." The "quickening power" of the Holy Spirit, as understood in classic Reformed teaching, played a vital role as well. Princetonians stressed the importance of religious experience as understood through Scripture, Christian nurture, preaching and the sacraments. "None of them neglected the importance of religious experience, even if they insisted that such experience not be opposed to the propositional testimony of Scripture and the intellectual structure of the confessions." [13]

Under Alexander's inspired tutelage, McIlvaine and several of his fellows became increasingly serious about their Christian faith. This does not surprise us. Alexander was a compelling teacher and preacher. As professor of didactics and polemic theology, he shaped minds that were lively, logical, consistent, and committed to the spread of the Gospel. He preached regularly each Sunday evening, initially in the junior recitation room in the Old Library building. "That room is to this day sacred in the eyes of the old students of the College," Hodge recalled later in the century. "It was...the birth-place of many souls. We were thus brought under the influence of a man, who, as an 'experimental' preacher was unequalled and unapproached." Alexander taught that religious and moral elements were universal and indestructible, and sought to demonstrate how vain it was to struggle against them. Conscience, he taught, was the master of all men, a faculty, as Hodge put it, that "could neither be silenced nor sophisticated....All [men's] efforts to make themselves infidels were abortive....However calm may be the surface, there is always the rumbling of an earthquake underneath." [14] Owing to the testimony of conscience, in sum, those who committed sin without repentance were without excuse and doomed to the "second death."

Alexander demonstrated a marked talent for leading students step by step along the road of repentance and to a solid belief in Christian teachings. With uncanny ability to peer into the soul, "he would detail the experience of those under the conviction of sin; show how such convictions often came to nothing; [then explain] what was essential, and what incidental and variable in such experiences." He would, as Hodge further recalled, take a student "by the hand, and tell him all about himself, leading him along from point to point, until the inquirer was left behind, and could do nothing but sit and weep." It was this ability to intuit the motives and mainsprings of action that riveted and inspired both new and advanced Christians. "Whether doubting, desponding or rejoicing...all [were] edified and strengthened." [15] To this influence, young McIlvaine and his companions were subject.

An instance of advice from this great teacher is illustrated by the counsel he gave to McIlvaine, when asked by the latter whether he should remain an Episcopalian or become a Presbyterian. Alexander advised him to remain an Episcopalian because his church had great need of men of ability. In the view of one scholar, this "was at once arrogant and generous." Regardless, it was advice the young man followed. Interestingly, the incident casts light on McIlvaine's commitment, or rather lack of commitment, to a particular denomination at the time, making "clear that [his] ecclesiology was rather fluid and his church identification rather tenuous." [16] It was a sign of immaturity but a mark also of an evangelical viewpoint, given the evangelical predilection to place private and experiential religion ahead of formal church structures.

This irenic spirit among Episcopalians and Presbyterians at Princeton was not limited to McIlvaine and Alexander but instead characterized relationships throughout the seminary. As noted above, McIlvaine and Hodge remained lifelong friends and admirers of one another's work. Hodge was an admirer too of the Thirty-nine Articles of the Church of England, formularies adopted by the Protestant Episcopal Church of the United States in only slightly altered form. By its centennial in 1912, Princeton Seminary could count among its alumni no less than five bishops of the Episcopal Church. [17]

Hodge and McIlvaine took from Princeton Seminary not only a similar theology but a similar rigor of mind. The irenic and cooperative spirit they enjoyed between themselves was not extended to the assorted Arminians, Pelagians, rationalists and others whom they deemed enemies of orthodox belief. In the words of one historian, "It was the stout consistency of Hodge's theology and the rigorous defense he gave of it" that singled him out as the great and formidable scholar and leader that he was. [18] One could say the same of McIlvaine. He too was equipped by training and temperament—by an angular theology and a rigorous mind—to fight the battles of his own church.

The battles were not long in coming. Newly married and filled with evangelical zeal, McIlvaine was called in 1820 to be rector of Christ Church, Georgetown, in Washington, D. C. There, as we have seen, he took little time in making a name for himself. His subsequent election as chaplain of the U. S. Senate in late 1822 gave a further boost to his career. Though largely ceremonial, the position—along with the pulpit he occupied at Christ Church— gave him visibility before people of high rank. In addition, the nation's capital, as the center of activity for the Evangelical party of the Episcopal Church, provided a friendly environment in general for his ambitions and views.

Evangelical Episcopalians in and around Washington were led by the scholarly activist William Holland Wilmer, four times president of the House of Clerical and Lay Deputies of the General Convention and the first professor of systematic divinity at the Virginia Theological Seminary. He was author in 1815 of *The Episcopal Manual,* a devotional work that expressed Evangelical doctrines, and in 1819 the founder and editor of the journal, *Washington Theological Repertory.* He and his colleagues were founders also of the Evangelical Education Society, which led to the creation of Virginia Seminary. For his part, McIlvaine served as director of the education society and as an editor of the *Repertory,* which was founded a year before his arrival. By such means, Evangelicals taught classic Reformation doctrines, insisting on God's perfection, the sinfulness of humanity, the need for Christ's atonement and mediation, the necessity of new birth, and the need to live a holy life. The principles of the *Repertory,* stated by the editors in the first issue, were based on Scripture "as illustrated in the Articles, Liturgy, and Homilies of the Protestant Episcopal Church," and their chief object was "to inculcate sound theological knowledge and to delineate and recommend pure and vital religion." [19]

This summary of principles did not recommend itself to members of the High Church party, who stressed instead ecclesiastical authority, the claims of the episcopate, the centrality of the sacraments, and continuity with Catholic Christianity, not the Reformation. They accused the Evangelicals of being Calvinists and therefore outside the mainstream of Anglican tradition. Furthermore, they were incensed at the Evangelical Education Society's plans for a seminary, an institution that would, they charged, compete with the High church-centered General Theological Seminary, founded in 1817. The project was viewed as an assault on the unity of the church. James Kemp, bishop of Maryland (and McIlvaine's bishop), denounced plans for the seminary and Evangelical initiatives generally in a pastoral letter. Despite such protests, Virginia Theological Seminary opened its doors in 1823.

Along with other High Churchmen, Kemp accused Evangelicals of departing from correct doctrine, mangling the liturgy, and attempting to give the doctrines of the church "a Calvinist cast." "I have thought that time and consideration would cure these things," he opined patronizingly in regard to Evangelical initiatives, "and while they continued to be viewed as the peculiarities of individuals, or the aberrations of young men, I viewed them as of little consequence, believing that more enlarged views...would correct all these." He said he looked upon the "present business...as an attempt to systematize and to perpetuate those peculiarities and aberrations." [20]

McIlvaine and two associates, Stephen Tyng and William Hawley, did not take the scolding lightly. They denied charges of liturgical innovation and defended themselves against the accusation of Calvinism. In fact, they specifically denied that they held such Calvinist doctrines as particular redemption and unconditional reprobation, thereby agreeing that such notions—and their outworking in double predestination (which holds that God predestines some persons to Heaven and some to Hell)—were un-Anglican. But on other points, they admitted to Calvinist sympathies, and observed that Anglican notables of the past had done the same, among them the sixteenth-century reformers Thomas Cranmer and Nicholas Ridley. "What is the theology of the Lambeth articles?" they asked. "Calvinistic of the very highest description." Therefore, they claimed High Churchmen had not "the least warrant, from the history of the Church, or the opinions of its best divines, to insinuate that our sentiments are at variance with the doctrines of our Church." [21] They charged that

> The fashion is at present to denounce, as the disciples of Calvin, those followers of Christ who shun not to declare the whole counsel of God, and preach to sinners as men that must render to the Judge an account....But these men have the comfort of knowing that it is not so much their holding some of the opinions of Calvin, as because they hold the doctrines of the Gospel; and the persons who are so fond of denouncing them should be extremely careful that they mistake not the Bible for the Institutes of Calvin, and the spirit of Christ for the spirit of heresy, lest haply they should be found fighting against God. [22]

McIlvaine's convictions were evident also in regard to the Education Society and its goals. He regarded the society as independent and therefore not answerable to either Bishop Kemp or the convention of Maryland. "None of the proceedings of the Society have had any connections with the deeds of the Convention," he wrote to Benjamin Allen, a fellow clergyman. "They are doubtless associated with the Convention in some way or other in the minds of the members from Maryland...but as acts of the Society, they have not the smallest reference to the Convention...and are properly to be considered as the acts of an independent society." [23] Such a view was at variance with High Church principles but very much in agreement with evangelical notions of independent action.

McIlvaine thus demonstrated, at a young age, his eagerness to join in the factional struggles that would absorb a great deal of his energies in the years to come. It is no wonder that fellow clergy of opposing views complained to Bishop Kemp of McIlvaine's popularity. The Rev. William Rafferty, for instance, in a complaint to the bishop, referred to McIlvaine as an "ignorant youth." [24] There is a grain of truth to the charge. Historian Diana Hochstedt Butler agrees that neither McIlvaine nor Hawley nor Tyng knew "very much about Anglican theology at this early point of their careers" [25] and were not beyond confusing theologians and centuries. The afore-mentioned Lambeth Articles, for example, though most definitely Calvinistic, were never authorized for use by the Church of England. Even so, McIlvaine and friends were correct in asserting that many early Anglican divines had been Calvinists in the same sense that they were.

The High Church party, led by the energetic and impetuous John Henry Hobart, bishop of New York, vigorously espoused its principles while opposing Evangelicals on any number of points. Stressing episcopacy and sacraments, High Churchmen held that Christ had established a particular form of church polity and ritual that should not be altered. Owing to this exclusivist principle, they considered other churches something less than real churches and, as a result, opposed Evangelical cooperation with interdenominational bodies. In addition, they stressed liturgical uniformity and communal spirituality, thereby opposing the more personal, experiential worship promoted by Evangelicals. Further, they rejected Evangelical emphasis on seminal or original sin, holding instead that human guilt was due to specific transgressions, not natal influences; that Christ's atonement was made for all people, and that good works were necessary for salvation.

In addition to his specific episcopal duties, Bishop Hobart wrote devotional manuals as well as other works. His *The Companion for the Festivals and Fasts* and *The Companion to the Altar* exemplify the emphasis on liturgy and ritual that characterized the High Church party. But he was not untouched by evangelical influences. Despite his later opposition to the Evangelical party, he too was a graduate of Princeton College where, says Sidney Ahlstrom, "he imbibed an evangelical outlook that he never lost, while at the same time [sharpening] his arguments for episcopacy." [26] One of the great leaders in the history of the Episcopal Church, he reconstituted and reinvigorated his struggling diocese, demanded fellow Episcopalians claim their exclusive heritage, vigorously advocated the founding of a seminary, and later became a mainstay of General Theological Seminary, which opened in New York City in 1819. He served the seminary as professor of pastoral theology and pulpit eloquence and thus greatly influenced a generation of students. In addition, between the years 1809 and 1817, he helped establish the New York Bible and Common Prayer Book Society, the Protestant Episcopal Tract Society, the New York Sunday School Society and the Protestant Episcopal Press, as well as the *Churchman's Journal,* which became a semiofficial voice of the High Church party. Also, he founded a college at Geneva, New York, in 1821. Ironically, his preaching "was accounted by many as unduly enthusiastic, even Methodistic." [27]

The year 1811 was a watershed for the Episcopal Church, marking as it did the emergence of distinct intra church parties with the consecration of Hobart as bishop of New York and Alexander Viets Griswold as bishop of the Eastern Diocese (comprised of Rhode Island, Massachusetts, Vermont and New Hampshire). The late-blooming Griswold became the first of the Evangelical leaders, although Evangelical seeds had been planted among Episcopalians in the previous century by Devereaux Jarratt, John Wesley and George Whitefield, as noted in the last chapter. At the time of the consecrations of Hobart and Griswold, neither the High Church party nor the Evangelicals had more than a few parish ministers to provide leadership, so low had sunk the fortunes of the church in the decades following the War of Independence. Indeed, Griswold's sprawling diocese counted only sixteen priests and twenty-two struggling parishes. By the time of his death in 1843, however, he had ordained well over a hundred priests and watched his original jurisdiction develop into five dioceses with a total of one hundred parishes. This achievement was something of a surprise, in light of his early career. It was only after he experienced a religious crisis at the time of his consecration that he became a vigorous preacher of experiential Christianity and subsequently a tireless visitor in his diocese. Known for his humility and pleasing personality, he was vigilant against High Church encroachments, fearing that too great a stress on sacraments, episcopacy and exclusivity would obscure more vital doctrines of the faith.

In opposition to Hobart and the High Churchmen, Griswold and the Evangelicals placed their stress on the person of Christ, especially his death on the cross; on identification of the Bible as the ultimate authority in matters of faith; on the necessity of conversion as a life-changing experience, and on a concern for sharing their faith, especially through evangelistic preaching. Since conversion was at the center of their theology, they placed less stress on the sacraments—Holy Communion was administered but once a quarter—and episcopacy. They also opposed the doctrine of baptismal regeneration, of which McIlvaine would write extensively in his volume *Oxford Divinity Compared*. Church buildings, as mirrors of public worship, displayed a near-puritanical austerity, with the pulpit dominating the "Lord's Table" (it was never an "altar"), crosses and candles a rarity, and even Gothic architecture suspect because of its Roman Catholic associations until the Romantic revival made it popular. There was, however, an affirmation of the traditional threefold ministry of deacons, priests, and bishops, which Evangelicals held to be in agreement with primitive church practice. In addition, they expressed concern for the lower classes by interdenominational promotion of Sunday schools, as seen in the case of McIlvaine; prison reform, temperance, and frontier evangelism. They also advocated extemporaneous prayer and special night meetings for devotional exercise while opposing dancing, theatre-going, gaming and dueling.

McIlvaine's involvement with the Evangelical Education Society and the *Washington Theological Repertory* gave him his first taste of theological as well as church controversy. He would soon see more of it but in a different venue. As mentioned in chapter one, he was offered the position of chaplain at the U. S. Military Academy at West Point. Also, as indicated earlier, certain political machinations assured that President James Monroe would choose McIlvaine over other contenders for the position. McIlvaine's friend, the Rev. William Carus, would later intimate that the success of the nomination was the work of the Holy Spirit. There is evidence that secondary causes were at work also, by way of human hands in high places, among them McIlvaine's own. In the event, he received the appointment and arrived at West Point on March 1, 1825.

At the time, the academy was not propitious for a man of the cloth, for it was a bastion of rationalism, of hardheaded men more interested in military science than the gospel of peace. The previous chaplain, the Rev. Thomas Picton, a Presbyterian, had been dismissed by the academic board for perceived shortcomings in classroom instruction (he taught in the department of history, moral science and geography), as well as for his long and dull sermons. The academy decided that he should be succeeded by an Episcopalian, in the belief that the liturgy of the Episcopal Church was more suitable to discipline and order. Despite his dismissal, Picton had his supporters and there was residual bad feeling to greet the new appointee.

McIlvaine suffered an entire year at West Point with little result to show for his efforts. Like his predecessor, he was required to teach as well as to fulfill the duties of chaplain. And like his predecessor, he too ran afoul of the academic board, which judged his classes "imperfectly and superficially taught." [28] The superintendent, Sylvanus Thayer, a man of competence and character, defended McIlvaine against the charges and suggested that any shortcomings in his work owed not to lack of pedagogic ability but to lack of available time. Colonel Thayer and McIlvaine would maintain a warm relationship throughout their lives. The cadets, some of whom resented the dismissal of Picton, and others—by far the greater number—who were hardened in religious indifference if not hostility, refused to accept the new chaplain. Undeterred, McIlvaine pressed ahead, preaching and teaching against all odds. He was determined to treat his military and scientific congregation as differing in no respect from any other congregation. "I would remember what they were," he recalled, "only to give a certain...direction sometimes to what I said; but they were sinners, lost sinners, with hearts and consciences and wants like all others; they needed the same Saviour, the same Gospel." He preached "the Cross" to them, in "simplicity and directness and boldness and confidence," but could not break the wall of opposition. A year passed "before anything of the least encouragement appeared, except as evidences of offense, taken at what I preached." Yet even these "indicated something better than perfect indifference." As he left church one Sunday, several junior officers walked behind him, speaking indiscreetly. He heard them say his preaching was "getting hotter and hotter." Such indications of "character," McIlvaine recalled, surfaced "from time to time, giving me *bearings* to shape my course by." Soon thereafter, while dining in company at the home of a junior officer, a lieutenant said something interpreted as insulting to the chaplain. In response, McIlvaine left the table. The next day the lieutenant—"an infidel of the most scoffing and sneering kind"—came to apologize. McIlvaine learned later that the other officers who had formed the dinner party had insisted that the lieutenant was bound as a gentleman to make amends, and so he had. "Now and then such incidents showed that something was at least stirring," the chaplain remarked. [29]

According to the Rev. G. T. Fox, a member of McIlvaine's subsequent parish in Brooklyn, the thaw came when "one of the eldest and most high-spirited of the cadets came to him," one whom McIlvaine did not know by name, and unburdened himself on spiritual matters. According to Fox's account, which must have been supplied by McIlvaine himself, the cadet had talked with no one beforehand about the meeting. Yet in a day or two, another "case of conviction," as solitary as the first, presented itself. Then "another and another," seemingly unconnected, found their way to the chaplain. These were followed by three officers "in the same mind," of whom two were professors and one an instructor of artillery. Within a few days, prayer meetings had commenced in the chaplain's study. They were "crowded with cadets and officers; but silent, quiet, calm. [They] were confined to prayer by the Chaplain, and the simplest exposition of truth." [30] Soon they were being held two and three times a week. Revival was underway.

In the weeks that followed, cases of conversion multiplied. "Some who had not been baptized," McIlvaine said, "came forward before all the corps, and...confessed Jesus." [31] Among them was Leonidas Polk, later to serve as Episcopal bishop of Louisiana. The episode of Polk's conversion had begun earlier with another cadet's visit to the chaplain. The cadet had promised his father that he would seek spiritual counsel, and was doing so following his father's death. In response to the visit, McIlvaine gave the young man a tract entitled *Evidences of Christianity* by Olynthus Gregory. He requested that once he had read it, the cadet leave it somewhere in his barracks. The tract was found by Polk, who was in a troubled mind owing to a reduction in rank because of a poor grade in drawing. As he picked up the tract, he noticed it was by the author of his textbook on mechanics. In reading it, he was moved to visit the chaplain to discuss the condition of his soul. Owing to the exchange that followed, Polk was converted to Christian faith and counseled to make a public profession. At worship the following day, McIlvaine recalled, "I could hear his movement to get space to kneel, and then his deep tone of response....It was a new sight, that single kneeling cadet. Such a thing had not been supposed to be possible." [32] Throughout the revival, Polk displayed a sterling character that served to draw additional cadets to prayer meetings. So popular did these become that a room in the prison was refitted to accommodate the cadets and officers who were attending.

Though some of the conversions were transitory, others endured, as McIlvaine learned in later years when he received word from former students or their friends. Polk was among those whose conversion endured. Following graduation from the academy in 1827, he resigned his military commission and entered Virginia Theological Seminary. Ordained a priest in 1830, he spent most of the decade serving parishes in Virginia and Tennessee, as well as owning and managing a plantation. In 1838, he was appointed missionary bishop of the Southwest and, in 1841, was elected bishop of the diocese of Louisiana. Yet the military skills he had learned at West Point found a use in his later life. Nearly four decades after attending the academy, while serving as a general in the Confederate army during the Civil War, the "fighting bishop" was killed at Pine Mountain, Georgia.

Other notables attending West Point during McIlvaine's chaplaincy included Robert E. Lee and Jeb Magruder, Confederate military heroes; Robert Anderson, commander of Fort Sumpter at the start of the Civil War, and Jefferson Davis, president of the Confederate States of America. Of these, only Davis appears to have left a tangible memory of the chaplain. The recollection appears in his autobiography, which he wrote in 1889, sixty-one years after leaving the academy. In it, he recalled that McIlvaine seemed

> to belong to the pulpit, and...had a peculiar power of voice, rarely found elsewhere than on the stage. From its highest tones it would sink to a whisper and yet be audible throughout the whole chapel. His sermons, according to the usage of the

church—the Episcopal—were written before-hand; but, occasionally, he would burst forth in a grand tide of oratory, clearly unpremeditated, and more irresistible than it probably would have been had it been carefully written. [33]

Though "done decently and in order," the West Point revival—and by extension its leader—stirred controversy beyond the academy. McIlvaine was informed in a letter from his friend and fellow Evangelical, James Milnor, that "enemies of truth" were accusing him of turning West Point "into a theological seminary, and aiming to make young men soldiers in the Church militant." [34] The New England Galaxy, for instance, lamented the presence of "revival in the very sanctuary of algebraic symbols and curves, redoubts, and bastions, gunpowder and projectiles!..who has dared to introduce the demon of fanaticism among the flower of a free country's chivalry?" Mrs. Anne Royall, of Newport, registered dismay following a visit. "[A] better lesson on the danger of priests (to say nothing of sects) was never exhibited than this of West Point. It shows them in their true colours." [35] Rumblings were heard also from the diocese of New York, the locus of High Church agitation. High Churchmen considered revivals disorderly, irrational and unbiblical by definition, and the one at West Point to be no exception. They were especially unwilling to remain quiet about a revival under the auspices of a fellow churchman. Even McIlvaine expressed concern. Some aberrations had occurred, he conceded, and some of the charges leveled in New York were based in fact. Further, a visiting committee from the government had been unfavorably impressed with the happenings and made its displeasure known. "They did not report this dissatisfaction in their formal report," notes historian Diana Hockstedt Butler, "but pressured McIlvaine through informal channels to find a new position." [36] Owing to the revival and its purported excesses, the chaplain eventually lost his position at the academy.

But controversy can help as well as hurt. In 1827, during his time at West Point, McIlvaine received a call from St. Paul's Episcopal

Church in Rochester, New York, which was eager to avail itself of the chaplain's reputed skills. When the call was made public, it was questioned by the Rev. Henry Ustick Onderdonk, soon-to-be bishop of Pennsylvania. The meddling Onderdonk wrote to the vestry of St. Paul's and accused McIlvaine of being a "half-churchman, a great opponent of Bishop Hobart, and a zealous promoter of the schemes that would blend us with Presbyterians."[37] He published the letter in a Philadelphia newspaper, where it caught the eye of a member of McIlvaine's previous parish in Georgetown. The Christ Church vestry bristled at the attack on their former rector, who remained very much in their affections. The vestrymen responded by lauding McIlvaine's zeal, piety, ability, and general popularity. The following year, by which time Onderdonk had entered the episcopate, they retaliated by refusing a proposed visit from Pennsylvania's new bishop.

Episcopalians intent on revival continued to seek out McIlvaine. In the end, he accepted a call from St. Ann's Church in Brooklyn, New York, in the middle of the denomination's most thoroughly High Church diocese and under the bespectacled eyes of none other than John Henry Hobart. Bishop Onderdonk—ironically, the previous rector—characteristically pledged his resolve to do everything in his power to prevent McIlvaine's election at Brooklyn. Despite his efforts, seventy-five of the 105 pew-holders voted in favor of the Evangelical candidate, knowing full well that he was clearly disliked by their former rector. McIlvaine arrived in November 1827, and thus began a successful pastorate, marked by steady growth in membership, sound instruction in Christian basics, and participation in ecumenical charitable activities. In the years ahead, however, Onderdonk, a leader in the Anglo-Catholic movement, and his younger brother, Benjamin Tredwell Onderdonk, bishop of New York, would continue to oppose McIlvaine on matters of theology, church politics and personal pique.

Ushered into St. Ann's on a wave of acclaim and controversy, the new rector continued to make waves. Throughout his five years at the parish, he would not only serve its members but also join interdenominational Christian societies that were designed to reform the nation. New York was a strategic center for such initiatives, among them the American Bible Society, the American Tract Society (of which McIlvaine was elected president), seamen's societies and temperance societies. Predictably, McIlvaine's participation in these societies displeased his critics. Although High Churchmen promoted voluntary societies also, they did not cooperate with other Christian bodies in doing so. By contrast, McIlvaine and the Evangelicals joined with other churches to promote the general Christian good. High Churchmen believed that such participation would undercut the exclusive claims of the Episcopal Church, always a key notion for them, while Evangelicals believed that ecumenical participation would increase godliness in the nation.

McIlvaine was keen to increase godliness in his parish as well. He did so based on the tenets of Evangelical belief, with a stress on the conversion experience and justification by faith as the keys to salvation. In doing so, he did not neglect the standard Episcopal requirements to teach the Apostle's Creed, the Lord's Prayer, the Ten Commandments and the catechism. He added, however, spiritual qualifications that stressed the need of experiential rebirth. He did so in particular in the rite of confirmation, which Evangelicals saw as the appropriate vehicle for the baptized to publicly profess a personal faith in Christ and to experience salvation through new birth. To this end, McIlvaine prepared a series of questions for the confirmands at St. Ann's. Although his questions followed the sense of the confirmation rite in the Book of Common Prayer, they reflected also the distinctive Evangelical concerns regarding sin and total reliance on grace—and not the church as such—for salvation and subsequent holy living. This emphasis on conscious rebirth led McIlvaine and other Evangelicals to reject baptismal regeneration, which doctrine (shared by High Churchmen and Roman Catholics alike) held that anyone who was baptized was the recipient not merely of a sign of grace but of saving grace itself, provided the recipient placed no obstacles in the way of God's action. But as Evangelicals saw it, regeneration was impossible without repentance towards God, saving faith in Jesus Christ, and the visible fruit of the Spirit. Consequently, they denied that divine life "implanted in infancy at baptism could take ten, fifteen or twenty years to manifest itself in a conversion experience. For them regeneration had to be a visible change of character and attitude." They understood infant baptism in the context of covenant theology, wherein the promises of salvation were declared and a sign and seal of them given in the belief that God would honor his covenant promise. "Thus baptism involved no immediate, inward change but the confirmation of God's covenant promise that he would, when the child reached an age of discretion, work salvation in the life." [38] This vexed question will be addressed in chapter six, in the discussion of McIlvaine's opposition to Tractarianism, and in chapter nine, as a divisive factor in the Episcopal Church of the 1860s and '70s.

McIlvaine was comfortable at St. Ann's. The parish provided a new parsonage, modest challenges and a cultivated environment. He was happy with his parishioners and they were happy with him. During his tenure, the church grew dramatically, from 180 members to 327 in five years. Financial support to charitable causes rose dramatically as well, from a negligible $89 in 1827 to a robust $1,845 in 1832, with donations to eight charitable causes. In addition, the rector, always a strong proponent of Sunday schools, worked to reestablish the school at St. Ann's. So successful was this initiative that by January 1829, just eight months after the school's founding, it became necessary to construct a new building to accommodate it. By May 1831 there were thirty-eight teachers and 453 children participating in the program. [39]

CHAPTER THREE – *Birth of a Controversialist*

Following a hiatus in Britain in 1830, where McIlvaine had retreated to recover from a bout of illness ("neuralgia" in this instance), he returned to his parish and took on the additional responsibility of adjunct professor at the recently founded University of the City of New York. There he delivered a series of lectures on "the evidences of Christianity." These lectures, which received fulsome praise, were subsequently published as a book of the same title. The apologetic nature of the volume was in keeping with McIlvaine's strengths, for he was logical, consistent and masterful. In exercising these attributes through the written word, he added to his achievements that of a scholar of marked ability.

Though barely thirty years of age, McIlvaine had established himself as a growing force in contemporary American church life. Eloquent preacher, successful revivalist, affectionate pastor, obdurate controversialist: the pattern was set. He would employ his talents and opportunities to advance "the kingdom" and to teach the truth as he saw it, without wavering. He would do so first in the east and then in the west, "meaning it" from first to last.

1. Mark A. Noll, "The Princeton Theology" in *Reformed Theology in America: A History of Its Modern Development*, edited by David F. Wells (Baker Books, Grand Rapids, Mich., 2000), 27.
2. Carus, *Memorials*, 10.
3. Quoted in Loren Dale Pugh, *Bishop Charles Pettit McIlvaine*, 45.
4. Ibid., 45.
5. Diana Hochstedt Butler, *Standing Against the Whirlwind*, 25.
6. Noll, 16, 21.
7. Sidney Ahlstrom, *A Religious History of the American People*, 355.
8. Ibid., 463.
9. Quoted in Noll, 17.
10. Ahlstrom, 463.
11. Quoted in Pugh, 44.
12. Ibid., vi.
13. Noll, 16, 23.
14. Quoted in A. A. Hodge, *The Life of Charles Hodge*, 26.

15. Ibid., 27, 28.
16. Pugh, xi.
17. Noll, 24-25.
18. David F. Wells, "Charles Hodge" in *Reformed Theology in America*, 39.
19. Quoted in Butler, 29.
20. Quoted in E. Clowes Chorley, *Men and Movements in the American Episcopal Church* (Charles Scribner's Sons, New York, 1950), 76-77.
21. Quoted in Butler, 30.
22. Quoted in Chorley, 78.
23. Quoted in Pugh, 47.
24. Quoted in Butler, 52, n. 20.
25. Ibid., 53, n. 32.
26. Ahlstrom, 626.
27. Ibid.
28. Quoted in Pugh, 54.
29. Quoted in Carus, 26-27.
30. Ibid., 27-28.
31. Ibid., 28.
32. Quoted in Butler, 39.
33. Quoted in Pugh, 56.
34. Quoted in Butler, 40.
35. Quoted in Pugh, 58-59.
36. Butler, 40, 57.
37. Ibid., 45-46.
38. Peter Toon, *Evangelical Theology, 1833-1856: A Response to Tractarianism* (John Knox Press, Atlanta, Georgia, 1979), 191.
39. Pugh, 68-69.

CHAPTER FOUR

Meaning It

Evangelical Episcopalians had a special integrity in McIlvaine's day, both spiritually and intellectually. They had a logical and consistent mindset that lent itself to the search for, and the acquisition of, truth, truth as understood within the context of orthodox Protestant theology of the Reformed tradition. This is not to say that churchmen of other stripes lacked integrity. It is to say that Evangelicals had a special *kind* of integrity, a particular *form* of intellectual honesty, a singular *manner* of "meaning it." Their dedication to moral principles and emphasis on moral character informed both their doctrinal orthodoxy and their everyday piety.

The Evangelical commitment to "meaning it," to trying in all things to integrate faith and doctrine into everyday life, led to the articulation of a consistent pastoral theology. In this theology, they attempted to guide the faithful along the bumpy road to holiness. The present chapter will examine how this pastoral theology was used to shape the lives of believers; it will show how it was integrated into both McIlvaine's life and the lives of Evangelicals as a whole.

McIlvaine's integrity—his integrated and Evangelical Episcopalian view of things both physical and metaphysical—was true to type personally, theologically, and practically. *Personally,* like other Evangelicals, he modeled himself on a significant figure of reputed holiness and integrity. That figure was the eminent Anglican Evangelical, Charles Simeon (1759-1836), a fellow of King's College, Cambridge, and minister of the nearby Trinity Church. Simeon was to McIlvaine an example of all that was good, holy, gracious, and learned in the Evangelical tradition. *Theologically,* like other Evangelicals, McIlvaine's views were informed, detailed, and committed. There was no vagueness, no latitudinarian blur, no mystical obscurity. His theology—Anglican and moderately Calvinist—was clear, distinct, and propositional. It was bibliocentric—tied to Scripture first to last—yet grounded in the common sense of Scottish realism. *Practically,* like other Evangelicals, McIlvaine put his theology into practice. He lived through it and it lived through him, so as to embody the Evangelical creed both experientially and intellectually. He expected others to do no less. He taught this doctrine to his family, to his parishioners, and to his readers. He insisted they must be converted to Christ and sanctified thereafter.

To McIlvaine's mind, no one represented the Christian life better than the Rev. Charles Simeon, whom he had met on two of his visits to England. So smitten was he with the person and doctrine of the aged churchman that he remained under his spell for the rest of his life. According to historian Diana Hochstedt Butler, "He read and admired no one more."[1] Simeon's British colleagues took note: upon Simeon's death, they gave his cassock to McIlvaine. Later, McIlvaine would edit the American edition of Simeon's *Memoirs.*

By the time McIlvaine met him in 1830, Simeon had enjoyed decades of respect and devotion for his work as both a teacher and a spiritual leader. His piety was notable. He rose at four o'clock each morning, even in winter, and devoted the first four hours of the day to private prayer and study of the Scriptures. An Evangelical to the core, he expended great energy on the British and Foreign Bible Society, the Church Missionary Society, and the London Society for promoting Christianity among the Jews. He also founded the Simeon Trust with a family inheritance. That entity had, by the end of the nineteenth century, appointed clergy to leadership in more than a hundred parishes. Lord McCauley, the famous historian, who was at Cambridge during Simeon's later years, wrote to his sister, "If you knew what his authority and influence were and how they extended from Cambridge to the remote corners of England, you would know that his real sway in the church was far greater than that of any Primate." [2]

In a letter of 1860 to his friend the Rev. William Carus, general editor of the British edition of Simeon's *Memoirs*, McIlvaine praised the book and confided his abiding interest in its subject. "I am at Mr. Simeon again," he wrote. "Yes, I am again reading your Memoir of that dear and very remarkable character and minister. I admire him more than ever." Though he read the *Memoirs* regularly, he did so "only in short portions, as a sort of morning stimulant." He discovered in the *Memoirs* a parallel between himself and his hero: "I found that [Simeon] encountered just what I do, in similar circumstances, when he was called to abstain from work on account of health." Simeon's ill health, to which McIlvaine referred, began unexpectedly at the age of forty-seven and lasted for thirteen years. It was marked by bodily weakness, low spirits and difficulty in speaking. Yet Simeon persevered in ministry and, at the age of sixty, unexpectedly found himself restored to health, a turnabout that allowed him to preach another seventeen years. The discovery of Simeon's health problems was no doubt of capital importance to McIlvaine, as his own periodic bouts of ill health were a marked characteristic of his otherwise dutiful and active life. How reassuring to find a similar trait in Simeon!

McIlvaine also expressed admiration for Simeon's patience in facing opposition during his early years at Cambridge. To be sure, much of the opposition was provoked by Simeon himself, owing to his affected manner, sense of self-importance, excess of zeal over knowledge, uneven preaching (a mix of striking remarks and incorrect statements), and, to his credit, willingness to speak the truth to hostile listeners. Despite opposition, the young curate persisted, all the while allowing his character to be molded by "his Master" (Christ). Instead of breaking his spirit, the sustained opposition he faced softened his harsh and self-assertive air and rendered him a better man and a better priest. "I think," McIlvaine said, "that part of his history [the period of opposition] was one of the strongest exhibitions of his Master's spirit, because it was so contrary to the peculiar impulsiveness, and *uppishness* of his natural temperament."[3]

In 1835, following his second and last visit to Simeon, McIlvaine wrote in his journal that "The old man was...as vigorous, and sprightly in spirit, as when I saw him five years since. He seemed as young and fresh in mind, as if the joys of religion were new every day, and every step towards the grave were revealing to his eyes some new beauty of the heavenly inheritance." In recalling the visit in his introduction to Simeon's *Memoirs* seventeen years later, McIlvaine remembered the "peculiar feelings" he experienced moments after Simeon left the room.

> I was sensible of an impression on my mind of a very unusual kind. It was one which I had never been conscious of before....I asked myself what it was and whence it came. It partook of the solemnity which one would feel in the presence of a spirit come down from heaven; though I know that such a description will, to many, seem extravagant. But so it was, and I could then explain it only as arising out of the sense I had, when conversing with that holy man, that in a very unusual degree, he *walked with God,* and was very near God, and belonged a great deal more to the heavenly world, than to this.[4]

The passage reads like a counterpoint to McIlvaine's unhappy experience of nearly twenty years before, when he was "attacked" in his parents' home in Burlington by a "messenger of Satan." It appears that his sensitivity to "presences" had not abandoned him in maturity. In Simeon's room in Cambridge, however, the "spirit" was perceived as a heavenly one, precisely the opposite of the malevolent spirit of the earlier event. Perhaps McIlvaine's mild euphoria was prompted by the harmonizing factors of friendship, freedom from stress—he was after all far from the obligations of his diocese and the cares and concerns of his family—and immediate circumstances much to his liking. Perhaps it was something of a mystical experience. McIlvaine himself, as we can see, believed that the moment was inspired by the aura of a singularly holy man, and there is no reason to conclude he was mistaken. At the least, it was emblematic of his relationship to a figure that would inspire him throughout his days.

McIlvaine's theology exemplified the Evangelical stress on both biblically-centered doctrine and commitment to truth-seeking, truth-telling, and truth-living in the light of Scottish realism and Reformed teaching. He and his colleagues were no different in this respect than are Evangelical Episcopalians or Evangelical Anglicans today, who, in the words of Evangelical scholar J. I. Packer, maintain a sense "of being entrusted with revealed truth, and of having a steward's responsibility to keep the deposit intact." [5] In guarding this deposit, and in using it as the standard by which to measure other theologies, McIlvaine and his allies were sensitive to deviations of every kind. Specifically, in putting the Bible first, they rejected both the reason-centered approach of liberal or Broad Church theology and the tradition-centered approach of Roman and Anglo-Catholic theology.

This sense of responsibility to preserve revealed truth was at the core of the biblically informed conscience of nineteenth century Evangelical Episcopalians even as it was at the core of conservative Protestantism more generally. Owing to this sense of responsibility, Evangelicals of that day were careful to use their freedom of conscience in such a manner as would be consistent with their overall view of biblical inspiration and infallibility. In

Packer's view, "Private judgment, as evangelicals inculcate it, has to do not with the layman's luxury of disagreeing with the organized church, but with the universal necessity of agreeing with the Bible, and therefore with the universal duty of...searching the Scriptures to see whether what men say in God's name is really so." [6] McIlvaine did just this, purposing to ground his doctrine principally in what he considered to be the revealed words of Scripture rather than in the ideas of human speculation.

In sum, McIlvaine took seriously the view that the Bible was a once-for-all revelation designed to teach specific truths about God, man and nature. The Bible was, he held, neither myth nor fable nor allegory. It was primarily factual and historical, while not denying it contained such non-historical (though spiritually true) forms as psalms, proverbs and parables. Again, Packer: "The tolerant indifferentism which reflects belief that there are no revealed truths and no given certainties, so that no finality can attach to any biblical or post-biblical formulations and therefore Christianity must be viewed as essentially a life rather than a doctrine, is as far as possible from the evangelical outlook." [7] So it was for McIlvaine. Nothing was less congenial to him than what he saw as "tolerant indifferentism" in regard to the revelation of Scripture. He believed Scripture meant what it said, just as he meant what he said.

In addition to their theological acumen in regard to biblical doctrine, Evangelicals were experiential as well. They attempted to combine elements of theological rigor with pious emotion to produce a practical faith that was incorporated, ideally, into every aspect of life. McIlvaine embodied in full this dual focus of the Evangelical. He taught that Christian life began with conversion or "new birth," as discussed at length in chapter two, but he taught also that conversion was only the beginning. In the wake of rebirth, he, like other Evangelicals, urged believers to aspire after the sanctified life, to increase in holiness as they experienced victories and joys, losses and crosses. In the work of sanctification, he urged believers to focus on Christ and the conviction that Christ offered a direct, unmediated relationship between God and them.

Inasmuch as Christian faith was to be incorporated into every aspect of life, McIlvaine and other Evangelical clergy provided a pastoral theology of considerable range. Pastoral theology, which provided practical advice on the conduct of Christian living, was intended to keep the faithful on the biblical "straight and narrow." McIlvaine was diligent in offering such advice to members of his diocese. "Whoever has become a true Christian," he wrote in a pastoral letter to his diocese in 1848, "has been 'born again' of the Holy Ghost, and 'is a new creature in Christ Jesus.'" As a new creature, he said, the new Christian is expected to live differently than he has in the past. McIlvaine's letter, prompted by perceived threats from "worldly conformity" and "worldly amusements," enlarged on the notions of rebirth and its outworking in the life of holiness or sanctification. In it, he described the true Christian as one who had not only undergone a "radical and wonderful change, which only the power of God could effect," but as one who should henceforth seek "to grow in grace, and thus to make it continually more certain that he is *in* grace, and 'alive unto God.'" To guard and preserve the new life, he said, the Christian must understand the link between the high calling and character of his religion, on the one hand, and the Scriptural portrait of the world, on the other.[8]

Warning of the "world" in his pastoral letter, McIlvaine cited passages from the first letter of John—"the whole world lieth in wickedness"—and the letter of James: "Whosoever will be a friend of the world is the enemy of God." To keep "unspotted from the world," he said, was essential to "pure and undefiled religion." Therefore it was imperative that everyone "born of God" should "overcometh the world." He observed that Christ, in chapter seventeen of the Gospel of John, spoke of the faithful as "in the world" but "not of the world." Twice in the same chapter, he noted, Christ used "that strong expression concerning the unworldly character of his people." St. Paul too, he observed, wrote that believers "have received not the spirit of this world, but the Spirit which is of God," and that they should "be not conformed to this world, but…transformed by the renewing" of their minds. He drew on specifically Episcopal liturgy as well. "The vain pomp and glory of the world," from the baptismal rite, and the "pomps and vanity of this wicked world," from the catechism, should be enough, he said, to make Christians wary of worldly amusements. Such things, he said, were in principle formally renounced in baptism. Therefore, the spirit of the world and the Spirit from God "are considered as essentially antagonistic." [9]

In opposing such amusements, he clearly revealed—again in the letter of 1848—his pietist and puritan strain. Among his targets were "fashionable balls, expensive, crowded, fashionable assemblies, with all 'the pride of life,' and all the vanity of person, and dress, and demeanor which they promote." [10] He had, no doubt, witnessed such events in his childhood, as his socially prominent parents entertained their friends and acquaintances in Burlington. He had, no doubt, witnessed them also in Georgetown and Brooklyn. Now, it appears, he had detected them in the diocese of Ohio, as frontier austerity gave way to civilized abundance. Thus, it seems, he felt compelled to preach to the faithful of the dangers of worldly vanities.

Thus, he chided people for listening to "the most earnest claims of God" on the Sabbath while giving themselves to "dances and theatres" during the week. Such Christians, he asserted, harmed the image and reputation of the church. Their partaking of such amusements, he charged, went beyond the intrinsic tendency for good or bad of the activities themselves. For the "world," he said, is dependent for its estimate of religion on the example of those who profess it. Hence the importance of holy living was vital not only to the believer but to the observer as well. No "epistle written with ink" could so easily be read as the visible conduct of the Christian. Therefore, the "living epistle," written by the Spirit of God in the hearts of Christians, was that on which the world depended. *"Some epistle, or other,"* he observed, "honorable or dishonorable to the Gospel, [practicing Christians] are continually giving out in their daily examples, and the world cannot help reading and being influenced by it." Consequently, believers must "avoid being hinderers of God's word, by an unholy example and influence, [and be] positively 'workers together' with their ministers in promoting among men the highest attainments in piety." [11]

McIlvaine's view—echoing the Reformation ideal of the "priesthood of all believers"—held that "The godly minister has no more part in [God's work] than every other believer." That all Christians were not licensed preachers, he said, is no excuse for their not being zealous promoters of the Gospel and careful of their conduct in the world. One might think him naïve in this view. After all, "clericalism" in one form or another had been a feature of most Christian churches from their beginning, and rank-and-file believers had always looked to spiritual leaders—be they elder, priest or pastor—to make important decisions in the life of faith. Though aware of this well-nigh universal tradition, McIlvaine nonetheless promoted vigorous lay participation. Everyone who professed the name of "Christian" was expected to mean it, just as he did. There were to be no exceptions to the rule. Yet he knew he was fighting an uphill battle. The view of many believers, he noted, seemed to be that while "it is the duty of the minister to promote as much as possible an unworldly spirit in his people, it is a duty in which they are not expected to feel and to work with him." Many believers, he said, were like schoolboys in relation to their teacher. They were "ever contriving how they may escape his requirements and get opportunity for play." How far they may go, he said, in disregarding their pastor's instruction in Christian duty was their main interest. [12]

Also, in the letter of 1848, McIlvaine insisted that the "worldly" themselves were adept at catching out the hypocrisy of worldly believers. The worldly, he said, were alert to Christians not "in their most proper and consistent place when attending on [worldly amusements]." Hence, believers who abstained from such amusements gained the most respect. Believers who did otherwise, he charged, did a disservice to the faith. "When one hears a communicant praised," he said, "by those who make no pretensions to religion, for his liberality and freedom from bigotry and from narrowness of mind, because he has no objection to engaging in these [amusements], I know not a more questionable compliment." [13]

McIlvaine's admonitions regarding "worldliness" were in harmony with the views of other Evangelical clergy. Warnings against the dangers of worldly pursuits were sounded from Episcopal pulpits and at general and diocesan conventions both prior to and during McIlvaine's years of ministry. As early as 1815, the convention of the diocese of Virginia had adopted a canon describing the offenses for which laymen could be tried by the church. These included drunkenness, incontinence, "profane" swearing, general neglect of public worship, Sabbath-breaking, irreverent behavior during public worship, and gaming. To these strictures, the laity rebelled and the canon was suspended for a time. Yet at the convention of 1818, clergy voted unanimously, and laity by a margin of seventeen to nine, to pass a resolution urging church members to foreswear gaming, attendance at theatres or public halls, and horse-racing. In a similar vein, the poetic patriot Francis Scott Key, lay Episcopalian and author of *The Star-Spangled Banner*, introduced a resolution to the House of Deputies of the General Convention of 1817 declaring that "conforming to the vain amusements of the world, frequenting horse races, theatres, and public balls, playing cards, or being engaged in any other kind of gaming, are inconsistent with Christian sobriety [and] dangerous to the morals of the members of the Church." The deputies were reluctant to legislate on such matters but the House of Bishops, in its convention journal, expressed sympathy with the resolution and urged clergy to advise their parishioners to refrain from gaming, theatrical representations, and amusements "involving cruelty to the brute creation." William Meade, an ally of McIlvaine's, sounded a similar note while bishop of Virginia in 1841, as he criticized young communicants who "were going from place to place, from ball to ball, even as the veriest devotees of pleasure." Also, he drew up an elaborate memorandum condemning card playing. Stephen H. Tyng, rector of St. George's, New York, another ally of McIlvaine's, kept the flame alive by warning parishioners in 1845 of the "gay and giddy amusements of fashionable society" and urged them "to keep themselves unspotted from the world." On such matters, he said, "we cannot...yield a single point of duty...to the hostility or caprice of men." [14]

Today's reader is likely to find such strictures narrow and harsh. In their defense, however, McIlvaine and others could point to Scripture and the Prayer Book. They had much of Christian history on their side as well. Theologians and church councils in the early centuries frequently targeted both dance and theatre as openings to sin, and medieval churchmen did much the same. The dancing and theatrical presentations that did occur in the Middle Ages took place mostly outside church walls, despite the fact that Holy Day dramas, labyrinth dances, and mystery and morality plays had religious themes. Calvinist and Puritan condemnation of dance and theatre, though neither so vehement nor encompassing as many think, more directly affected the early American scene. From the eighteenth to the twentieth centuries, condemnations of "mixed" or couple-dancing were frequent, alongside criticisms of theatre-going, horse-racing and card-playing. In the minds of conservative Protestants, dance and theatre were invitations to degradation, especially of women. Horse-racing and card-playing, for their part—as well as "gaming" generally—drew criticism because, it was charged, they encouraged participants to put their trust in fortune or luck rather than in God.

The character of the "world," McIlvaine said in a sermon published in 1855, was the "natural or unregenerate state of man." Consequently, it was not in its essence marked off by external boundaries. Its identification was not a question ultimately of "less or more in worldly vanities, or worldly devotedness." Therefore, despite his opposition to "fashionable balls" and the vanity of dress, McIlvaine went beyond them in analyzing the worldly spirit. He located the divide at deeper levels, deeper even than the lines that separated the visible church from the world beyond its walls. "The true line of the world," he said, "runs within the visible sanctuary and separates to right and left the partakers of the sacraments. It is simply the question, who are they that have been born again, and have the spirit of Christ?" Thus, to his mind, the "sheep" and the "goats" sat side by side in the pews of the churches themselves. [15]

Appearances, then, can be misleading. According to the 1855 sermon (aptly titled "The Christian Not of the World"), many whom the world would judge to be among the redeemed are not among the redeemed at all. The worldly in their variety populate a wide spectrum of types, ranging "from the most profligate sensualist, to the person of pure morals and delicate refinement; from the men of most brutal inclinations and habits, to the elevated tastes of those who find their pleasures in intellectual culture; from the most selfish of mankind, to those whose benevolence is the blessing of their neighborhood." What was it that put this variety of human types within the kingdom of this world while excluding them from the kingdom of heaven? The answer, McIlvaine said, was found in the affections. Their affections were set on things on the earth and not on things above, on things of the flesh and not on things of the Spirit. Yet, he allowed, the worldly were sometimes the benefactors of others. "Many of the most worldly in their affections," he said, "are among the most laborious in endeavors, by outward works, which require no change in the current of the affections." But alas for the humanitarian or the philanthropist, if he or she was but once-born. Like other evangelicals, McIlvaine did not preach salvation by works. He held good works to be the "fruit" of salvation, not its cause. [16]

Consequently, that which was "habitual"—that which governed or controlled the heart—determined the kingdom to which one belonged. It was the heart—focus of one's strongest motivations—that accepted or rejected the sacred deposit; that chose blessing or curse. Stated otherwise, it was the disposition of the heart, the spiritual organ, rather than the disposition of the brain, the rational organ, that determined one's posthumous destination. Yet in thought and behavior, neither the spiritually nor the worldly-minded were totally consistent. In admitting to incongruities on the part of the genuine Christian, McIlvaine allowed that worldly affections were never entirely cast out, that the believer's "weak and wayward heart" would never be totally purified this side of the grave, and that the grace that had brought rebirth would be needed throughout the process of sanctification. But, he said, the temptations of the world that continue to beset the spiritually minded are not entertained by them willingly. Rather, they endure them unwillingly, "as clay on the garments, and mire on the feet of the traveler through a marshy way." [17]

The idea that a Christian was *in* the world but not *of* the world, he continued, was typified in the Old Testament by the nation of Israel. The ceremonial law, he said, from its inception before the Israelites left Egypt to its completion at Mount Sinai, "was the wall of separation between them [and all other nations] as a visible Church of God's peculiar people." The outward separation, he said, was a "type" of the inward or spiritual separation that divided the true Israel—the church—from all other peoples. God chose, he said, to shine his light on a particular people, both spiritually and physically. That light, present in the dwellings of the Israelites, shown during the plague of darkness, singling them out for blessing and illumination. Though they were *in* Egypt, they were not *of* Egypt. Though surrounded by spiritual darkness, they did not experience that darkness, for light shown upon them. [18] So too, McIlvaine intimated, was the condition of the true Christian of the current age. The true Christian was *in* the world but not *of* the world. The true Christian—chosen, reborn, sanctified—was set apart by grace, rescued from darkness, and illuminated by light.

The true Christian, McIlvaine continued, was clearly identifiable in times of trouble. When God sends afflictions on the people of darkness and the people of light, he said, the people of darkness are "disquieted" within themselves; they perforce lose hope when the world on which they have centered their affections ceases to meet their needs. By contrast, those who fear the Lord and "think upon his name" are able to "glory in tribulations," finding consolation even as trials increase. To the faithful, God gives "songs in the night," surprising joys and comforts amidst trouble. These "songs" confound the worldly minded, who by nature sing in joy but not in sadness. "Songs in the day time are easily given," McIlvaine said. "Such is the rejoicing of the world." But in the night, when the candles by which the worldly light their life have gone out, especially in the night of death, then the worldly have no songs. Quite different it is for those who believe. For them, the Gospel shines brightest at the darkest hour. "It will be with them in all their journey," even as they enter the "valley and shadow of death." [19]

Such considerations, present not only in the sermon of 1855 but in much of McIlvaine's preaching, posed a moment of decision to those who were listening, a moment dramatized by the preacher lest anyone's attention wander. "Let each of us ask himself," he urged, "to which class do I belong? *Of the world or not?* There is no neutral position. To those who know where they belong, and that the world is their all—allow me a few kind, earnest words." Here, he would sharpen the crisis and ask the listener to make a decision without qualification, to render a decision on life or death, light or darkness, blessing or curse. Thus he continued: "Do I hear you say, 'Suppose we would become more serious and thoughtful, as regards religion; less interested with the idols of the world?...And suppose we should be unfailing in attendance on all religious services, private and public, would this translate us into the condition of those who are *not of the world?*" In McIlvaine's view, the answer was a simple "no." Such a turnabout would be insufficient. Such a change would affect the "outer man" only. "You might shut yourselves up in a monastery," he declared, "and by a process of self destruction, become, in a sense, dead to the world; but it does not follow that you would be alive unto God...there is but one answer. *'Ye must be born again.'* Nothing will do but a *new heart.*"[20] In such unequivocal terms did McIlvaine present the Gospel. He posed the question of life or death in terms of black or white. The choice was "either-or," never perhaps or maybe. There was no "neutral position." One must be born again; one must become a new creation in Christ. No half measures would do. McIlvaine meant what he said; he expected his listeners to respond in kind.

McIlvaine did not direct his criticism only at others. He knew that worldly tempers were active in him as well. Thus on January 13, 1829, five days before his thirtieth birthday, while serving as rector of St. Ann's Church in Brooklyn, he expressed in his journal a clear understanding of what he was pursuing while admitting that he had fallen short in reaching it. "What to me is all the world, what all the universe of worlds, in comparison with my never-dying soul? I have a battle to fight, a race to run. The prize is not in my hands." Despite his singular dedication, he had found arrayed against him both interior and exterior enemies. "I have," he said in the same entry, "a wicked and deceitful heart to contend with, a powerful adversary from hell to fight, an ungodly world to overcome. I have much holiness to gain; deeper repentance to feel; stronger faith to put on." Yet he did not despair. Like a good soldier, he found safety in attack not retreat. "To be continually advancing, I must *redeem the time.* Time advances rapidly. It waits for none. Before I have realized that it comes, it passeth away." He regretted that "scattering moments" were so often lost, that time, devoted to self-examination, was so inadequately spent. "How many more precious visits might I make to the invisible world?" he asked. "How much more would all my engagements be intermingled with spiritual thoughts and exercises?"[21]

McIlvaine's journal was an exercise in self-interrogation. While at St. Ann's, he made the following entry on January 18, 1830, a little more than a year after the one cited above. The entry reflects his preoccupation with the possibility of an early demise, the fleeting nature of time, and his perceived failure to attain holiness. It reflects also an antinomy of Reformed thought, in which the sinner was expected to strive obediently after holiness while realizing his utter dependence on grace to attain that holiness. (The antinomy is implicit throughout Scripture, and explicit in Philippians 2:12, where St. Paul urges believers *to work out their salvation* with fear and trembling, knowing *it is God* who works in them, to will and to work for his good pleasure.) McIlvaine sought to pray more, to feel more, to believe more and to seek more, even as he expressed total reliance on Christ alone for all that he might attain. "I have lived *thirty-one years*," he wrote. "How they have fled!" Having completed nine-and-one-half years in the ministry, he found himself plagued with "pictures of unfaithfulness." With Christ his only hope, he pondered his future course, or "as much of this my thirty-second year as God shall give me!" He resolved to live under the "believing impression that I am soon to die—that I know not how soon, or suddenly; and to view death so frequently and closely, that when it comes I may be acquainted with it, and know how, in the strength of God, to meet it." Thus fortified, he believed death would hold no terrors for him, if he could "feel a near, tender, strong attachment to Jesus." He resolved to do more "in and by prayer" and to agonize longer in secret prayer. He would pray, he said, for his own soul, for his wife and children, and for his "precious mother" and his "dear brothers and sisters." "My birthday is just now fading away," he said as night approached. "But it is a sweet evening, cool but clear—a bright unclouded sky, affording hope of a sweet and beautiful morning." He wished the evening of his dying day to be so beautiful. "While cold with the chill of death," he said, "may my soul be peaceful, my heart comforted—the sky of hope all brightness and glory—not a cloud—affording…a bright and glorious eternity."[22]

A journal entry of 1834, after becoming bishop of Ohio, found him in no less a pensive mood. He was more deeply discontented with himself than previously, yet equally ready to throw himself on the mercies of God. He confessed to being "overwhelmed with shame and confusion…by my sinfulness—my spiritual declension." In contemplating his many duties, he bemoaned his "cares innumerable…too heavy for me to bear." Plagued by "sloth, coldness of heart, selfishness, pride, worldly mindedness," he feared his inner turmoil would make of him "a mere lifeless formalist, a barren husk." Between the cares of the college, the diocese and his home, "all spirituality of mind" was being lost. But the impulse to pray remained. "Lord, lift Thou up the light of Thy countenance upon me!" He felt the need for a new beginning and a "new heart." He prayed God would awaken "all the motives and calls to diligence and zeal, and holiness and prayer." He prayed the Holy Spirit would receive him back, raise him "higher." *"I need a single steady aim,"* he declared, even as he confessed to "so much sloth and vanity within….Oh, for faith—habitual faith –working by the continual exercise of love!"[23]

McIlvaine's self-recriminations may strike non-Christians and perhaps most Christians of today as excessive. They may appear as yet another sign of his neurotic nature. Perhaps in part they were. But they also reflected an age of obsessive journaling, as educated people of all walks of life dutifully kept diaries of their every sentiment. Moreover, readers of his epistles might have remembered St. Paul calling himself "the chief of sinners." If St. Paul could refer to himself thus, could not McIlvaine do likewise? Arguably, the more self-aware a person is, the more aware of his shortcomings. The bishop's friend, William Carus, spoke to the matter. "Confessions of demerit and sin," he recalled of McIlvaine's self-appraisals, "which to the world are unintelligible, and appear perhaps morbid or exaggerated, are in truth the irrepressible expressions of the deep humiliation of the saint." [24] The saint sets the bar high and thus falls short.

McIlvaine's ruminations on the state of his soul did not end in despair. Rather, they appear to have spurred him to greater effort on behalf of himself and others. He worried in particular about those whom he was called to serve. Their souls were in jeopardy, he believed, therefore he must be vigilant for their welfare. "Besides my own soul, a whole congregation of immortal souls is committed to my charge," he wrote in his journal in January 1829. "I am occupying the awful station of a steward of souls—a shepherd of a flock which looks to me for guidance unto eternal salvation." Lapses in responsible teaching or behavior on his part, he believed, could doom members of his flock. "If unfaithful to my work, souls will perish on my hands, and I must answer for their death....What responsibility is this!" Predictably, he regretted deeply his failures to better serve his "fellow-worms" and lacerated himself for "my worldly-mindedness, and my indolence." [25]

To reach sinners both inside and outside the church, to fulfill his obligation to save souls, McIlvaine preached as simply and sincerely as he could. His insistence on simplicity in preaching was stated clearly in *The Work of Preaching Christ*, a charge delivered to his clergy in 1863. In it, he urged his clergy to preach after the manner of the Apostles, spiritually and simply, using little of the "devices and mixtures and dilutions and subterfuges of man's wisdom." Such counsel came naturally. For though eloquence and presence were a part of him, pulpit theatrics were not. According to Bishop Alfred Lee, McIlvaine's aim "was not to delight the ear and gratify the tastes, but to arouse the conscience and convert the heart...his speech and his preaching were not with enticing words of man's wisdom, but in demonstration of the Spirit and of power." [26] By such means, McIlvaine believed, God's blessing would be forthcoming.

In seeking the "lost," McIlvaine preached only what he held to be—in the Pauline phrase—"sound doctrine." Classic Reformation orthodoxy—"justification by righteousness of Christ imputed" and "sanctification by the Spirit of God imparted to the believer"—was the sum and substance of his teaching. Anything else he held to be a half-Gospel at best. But though appealing to some, his teaching repelled others. To some, the battle cries of the Reformation had grown stale in the course of three centuries, and for others the tenets of orthodoxy had been eroded by Enlightenment theologies and philosophies. Yet McIlvaine held to the old orthodoxy, to those doctrines that men "will not endure." [27] That so many *did* "endure"—and profit by—his teaching, is clear by the spread of Evangelical belief among Episcopalians in Ohio and elsewhere in the 1830s and '40s. He did indeed acquit himself well in reaching the "whole congregation of immortal souls" committed to his charge.

As we have seen, McIlvaine believed his vocation the most solemn of all callings. Far from seeing the ministry as an adjunct to civil religion, as a sub-specialty devoted to baptizing, marrying and burying, he saw it as "prophetic," as the calling to preach salvation and live out God's word. He therefore preached and taught and wrote with special fervor. Neither guile nor irony marked his teaching. He said what he meant and meant what he said. Even as old age encroached, a fire burned in him to reach those with ears to hear. "I have recently, in preaching," he mused at sixty-seven, "had peculiar pleasure and trust, from thinking, when I go into the pulpit, of the Lord's petition. *'Sanctify them through thy truth.'* I say to myself...[the Lord] is praying that same prayer!...and I get strength—I believe that the word will not be void." [28]

Although he never lost his passion for communicating the truth as he understood it, McIlvaine admitted to weariness with the interminable doctrinal and ecclesiastical debates of the age. At sixty-eight, as he pondered the growing influence of Rationalism and Anglo-Catholicism on the Church of England, he confided to his journal that "The truth is more precious to me than ever, but the trials...I feel bound to maintain in its behalf, affect my spirits more than they once did. I get no comfort in looking to the future, except as that future is found in the promises of God." In the same entry, he asked for patience "to wait and pray, and work, and contend, and watch." He prayed for continued usefulness: "In my declining years make use of me, to maintain Thy precious Gospel in the hearts of sinners, and to lead souls to Thee." [29]

McIlvaine's contemporaries applauded his integrity, learning and zeal. Though he made enemies, though he was not without fault, his virtues and accomplishments patently outweighed his liabilities. "Of all whom it has been my privilege to know," said Edwin Guest, master of Caius College, Cambridge, "he came nearest to my ideal of the Christian man. There was in him a balance of qualities not often met with, a clearness of intellect and decision of character united to a singular humility, and a kindliness of nature....I shall always look upon it as one of my greatest privileges to have known Bishop McIlvaine." The archbishop of Canterbury put it succinctly, on receiving word of the last days of McIlvaine's life. "It was," he said, "impossible to know our dear friend without loving him." [30]

---

1. Butler, *Standing Against the Whirlwind*, 31.
2. Quoted in Roger Steer, *Guarding the Holy Fire: The Evangelicalism of John R. W. Stott, J. I. Packer, and Alister McGrath* (Baker Books, Grand Rapids, Mich., 1999), 133.
3. Carus, *Memorials*, 198.
4. Charles P. McIlvaine, editor, *Memoirs of the Life of the Rev. Charles Simeon* (Robert Carter & Brothers, New York, 1852), xviii.

5. J. I. Packer, *The Evangelical Anglican Identity Problem: An Analysis* (Latimer House, Oxford, 1980), 8.

6. Ibid.

7. Ibid.

8. McIlvaine, "Pastoral Letter, Addressed to the Members of the Protestant Episcopal Church in the Diocese of Ohio" (William B. Thrall, Columbus, Ohio, 1848), 3, 12.

9. Ibid., 12-13, 19.

10. Ibid., 19.

11. Ibid., 20, 14, 16.

12. Ibid., 16-17.

13. Ibid., 18-19.

14. Chorley, *Men and Movements*, 109, 107, 108.

15. McIlvaine, *The Truth and Life: Twenty-Two Sermons* (Robert Carter and Brothers, New York, 1855), Sermon IX, "The Christian Not of the World," 195.

16. Ibid., 195-196.

17. Ibid., 197-198, 200.

18. Ibid., 200-202.

19. Ibid., 202-203, 205.

20. Ibid., 209-210.

21. Quoted in Carus, *Memorials*, 38.

22. Ibid., 42-44.

23. Ibid., 85.

24. Carus, 3.

25. Quoted in Carus, 38, 39.

26. Ibid., 15.

27. McIlvaine, "The Work of Preaching Christ. A Charge: Delivered to the Clergy of the Diocese of Ohio" (Anson D. F. Randolph, New York, 1864), 62-63.

28. Quoted in Carus, 264.

29. Ibid., 265, 267.

30. Ibid., 6.

CHAPTER FIVE

The Revivalist

McIlvaine's call to convert the unconverted both within the church and beyond its walls was coterminous with revival movements of a far different sort than his own, both theologically and practically. Even as he labored to midwife the new birth in once-born souls—by applying the ordinary means of Scripture, prayer, preaching, a set liturgy, and sometimes fasting—the fabled Charles Grandison Finney labored to the same end. Yet few evangelists were as unalike in theology and method as these two. The contrast between them is instructive regarding both McIlvaine's approach to revival and the history of revivalism in ante-bellum America.

Most revivals in the decades before the Civil War were in fact simplifications, echoes, or amplifications of the eighteenth-century revivals of Jonathan Edwards, George Whitefield and John Wesley. These famous men, though learned themselves, preached to crowds that included members of the poor and uneducated classes who were, when aroused, given to bumptious and even bizarre behavior. Whitefield especially stirred his listeners' emotions by employing a pronounced talent for showmanship. Finney's revivals were an updated version—albeit an "engineered" and orchestrated version—of those of Whitefield and Wesley. They were orgies of emotion, with "protracted meetings" held every night for a week or more, with "almost saved" sinners sitting on the "anxious bench," the objects of special exhortation and prayer as they awaited the second birth, while the newly saved swooned in conversion on the floor. By contrast, McIlvaine's revivals were orderly and sober events, though never without an element of charged if restrained emotion.

Many early nineteenth-century revivals were extensions of an event that transpired in August 1801 at Cane Ridge, Kentucky, one that encapsulates in every major respect the American religious revival writ large, in legend and cliché. The Cane Ridge revival drew as many as twenty-five thousand persons, the bulk of them frontiersmen and their families, to a week of day-and-night-long singing, praying and exhorting under guidance of Methodist, Baptist and Presbyterian preachers. Many of the participants were profane, hard-drinking backwoodsmen, drawn by the prospect of a frolic as well as the hope of heaven. "We all," remembered Barton Stone, a Presbyterian clergyman, "engaged in singing the same songs of praise—all united in prayer—all preached the same things—free salvation urged upon all by faith and repentance." [1]

In the course of events, Stone threw off the yoke of his Calvinism, while others threw off their inhibitions in less theoretical ways. "Conversions and lovemaking intermingled" in what one investigator labels an "Orphic unison." Conversion phenomena were multiform. Bodily agitations included the falling exercise, the jerks, the dancing exercise, the barking exercise, and the laughing and singing exercise. "The falling exercise," Stone reported, "was very common among all classes, the saints and sinners of every age and grade, from the philosopher to the clown." Repentant sinners in the throes of the falling exercise, he said, would emit "a piercing scream" and then "fall like a log on the floor, earth, or mud, and appear as dead." The "fallen" would thus lie for moments or hours, eventually reviving and "exhibiting symptoms of life by a deep groan, or piercing shriek, or by a prayer for mercy most fervently uttered....The gloomy cloud, which had covered their faces, seemed gradually and visibly to disappear, and hope in smiles brightened into joy—they would rise shouting deliverance." [2]

In the words of one historian, ante-bellum America experienced "almost obsessive concern with exorcising spiritual deadness." [3] The pioneer multitudes of Cane Ridge shared that concern and addressed it in their extended camp meetings. Those who followed them sought the same end, though generally in a less uninhibited manner. In the words of historian Perry Miller, revivalism was the "dominant theme" in America from 1800 to 1860. "We can hardly understand Emerson, Thoreau, Whitman, Melville," he writes, "unless we comprehend that for them this [revivalism] was the one clearly given truth of their society. By its basic premise, revivalism required—indeed demanded—that between outbursts there come lulls, which would shortly thereafter be denounced as 'declensions.' This was the accepted assumption...for the mass of American democracy." [4]

Though late summer was the gathering time at Cane Ridge, the winter months became at other times and places the accepted season for revival. The choice of winter fit well with the seasonal demands of an agrarian society. Yet the cold and barren nature of the season served also as a metaphor of spiritual death. Whether it was endured in New England, Ohio or Minnesota, winter was by nature bleak and withdrawn. In a Concord December, Henry David Thoreau wrote, "You come near eating your heart now." The dormancy of the season prompted in turn a longing for rebirth. According to historian Lewis O. Saum, "The religious excitements of the [pre-Civil War] generation involved not so much a summery equation of camp meeting-revival as a wintry progression of protracted meeting-revival." The need for "spiritual showers" was felt deeply by Americans of all classes. Even as the showers of rain in the spring would thaw the frozen ground, so the showers of the Holy Spirit would thaw their frozen hearts. "To a later, naturalistic age," Saum observes, "the pre-Civil War period frequently appears a phantasmagoria of religious frenzy." [5] For to members of those generations, there was never enough revival activity. Be they lawyers, merchants or clerks; mechanics, farmers or students; men or women, young or old, they thirsted after new life in the cold and dark of the winter months. McIlvaine, Finney and a host of other preachers, aware of this thirst, showered the people with the "words of life." McIlvaine bid them come forth within the liturgical structures of the Episcopal Church, "decently and in order." Finney, by contrast, invented his own brand of revival based on the needs of a less cultivated clientele.

Born in 1792, seven years before McIlvaine, Charles Grandison Finney was raised in frontier circumstances in western Connecticut and New York, where he received virtually no exposure to Christianity. This deficiency would appear to be due more to his own lack of interest than to anything else, for churches were active in the environs of his childhood. He did, however, avail himself of such educational opportunities as were at hand, attending school until he was sixteen, after which he began the study of law at home. He later taught school as a way of supporting himself. At twenty-six he joined the law office of Benjamin Wright in Adams, New York, and was a success from the start. A natural advocate, the skills of the legal profession would serve him well all his days. He made his way as a lawyer for four years before undergoing an experience that would alter his destiny. Although a "godless scoffer," as he later called himself, the young lawyer was converted to Christianity at a revival in the autumn of 1821. "Finney emerged from his conversion a new man," writes an authority on the matter. The skeptic and scoffer "had become the believer and zealous propagandist. His devotion to the legal profession fell away at once with his old man; he assumed immediately the new profession of bringing men to Christ." [6]

From 1825 to 1832, Finney staged a series of revivals as remarkable as any ever seen on the North American continent, with the exception perhaps of Cane Ridge. After launching himself as a fulltime revivalist, he transferred his church membership from the Presbytery of St. Lawrence to that of Oneida, thus turning his back on frontier work and turning his face towards the towns and cities of a richer and more populous region. There he began the "Western Revivals" that established his enduring reputation, revivals that added his particular brand of fire to the "Burnt-Over District" of upstate New York, so famous in the annals of American religion.

During this time McIlvaine preached as well, with power and eloquence, though never as flamboyantly as his peripatetic counterpart. His work proceeded within the walls of church and chapel, decently, as he thought, and in order. It too included a noted revival, at West Point, as we have seen. That revival alone, conducted amidst America's future military elite, may have affected the course of the nation as much or more than all of his other revival preaching combined. That was the view of his friend, Alfred Lee, bishop of Delaware, who touched on the matter in the memorial address he gave at the time of McIlvaine's death. As a result of the West Point revival, Lee suggested, there was "no body of educated men in our country" in which a larger proportion of consistent Christians could be found than among the officers of the army. By associating Christian faith with "all that is manly, honorable and heroic," the officers had influenced countless young soldiers in the direction of religion. "How different might have been the state of society at the present day," he said, "had our military and naval officers as a body been skeptical and profligate, spreading moral contagion among our youth!"[7] McIlvaine's achievement at West Point was followed by a successful ministry in New York City, where he preached revival to a prospering Evangelical parish. Through it all his reputation as preacher and churchman grew. He would shortly move to the West, bringing the cultivation of the East and his tempered manner of revival to the rude frontier of Ohio.

Finney's revivals moved in the opposite direction. They were, according to Benjamin B. Warfield, Presbyterian theologian and critic of Finney's work, "an invasion of the backwoods into civilization." Here was a young man, he wrote, "but two years a minister, but four a Christian, with no traditions of refinement behind him, and no experience of preaching save as a frontier missionary, suddenly leading an assault upon the churches." According to the Presbyterian revivalist Lyman Beecher, Finney's "denunciatory revivals" were designed "to stir up a commotion," [8] exciting in his audiences a measure of the uninhibited behavior mentioned earlier in connection with Cane Ridge. According to his critics, Finney preached and prayed "at" people instead of "to" or "for" them, going so far as to intercede for the sinful by name.

For its part, Finney's theology was influenced by the New Haven theology of Nathaniel William Taylor. It was, according to Charles Hodge, McIlvaine's friend, the product of a "cold, Pelagian system" attached to the "engine of fanaticism." [9] Taylor (1786-1858), professor of didactic theology at Yale University, had modified existing versions of American Calvinism by putting greater stress on human freedom and obligation, as opposed to what he considered an exaggerated view of human dependence. He stressed "reasonableness" as well, teaching that depravity corrupted the heart but left the faculty of reason unimpaired.

Pelagius, to whom Hodge referred, was a British monk and theologian resident in Rome during the early part of the fifth century. His teaching, which incurred the wrath of Augustine of Hippo, his contemporary, argued that human beings were essentially free and well-created and therefore not the victims of original sin and its attendant weaknesses and deformations. In consequence, he stressed free will in the attainment of moral purity and the overcoming of past pagan immorality. Like Pelagianism and "Taylorism," Finney's method required, by its own logic, an extremity of action on the part of penitents, who were considered fully able to deliver themselves to the "throne of grace." The principal tactic was to stir them into such a state of agitation that they were convinced of their sinfulness, willing to repent of it, and eager to come forward to experience conversion.

After seven years of revival work, concluding with a series of revivals in New York City, an exhausted Finney changed course. He devoted his efforts to the pastoring of two large congregations, one of them the Broadway Tabernacle built for him by friends in 1834. Though as many as half a million persons had participated in his revivals, and though untold numbers claimed conversion, their long-term religious state was a subject of dispute, not least by the master of revival himself. Finney admitted that many of his converts had lapsed, that the repentance and faith to which he had brought them had been in many cases temporary. He regretted that he had not urged them enough to become acquainted with Christ in a more enduring way, to learn to "abide in him" once the fires of revival were no more.

Yet Finney was irrepressible. With two careers behind him, he moved on. In 1835, he became a professor at Oberlin College in Ohio (later he would become president), where he was to spend some forty years lecturing, preaching, writing, and otherwise propagating his theological views to a wide public. He did so without the backing of the Presbyterian Church, which had pressured him to leave following publication of his *Lectures on Revivals of Religion* in 1835 and his *Sermons on Important Subjects* in 1836, each of which made it clear that he was out of step with the Calvinism of his own church.

In most details, save two, McIlvaine and Finney were opposites. The points of convergence were these: both men were converted at a revival, and both men preached revival. Yet even these likenesses were limited. McIlvaine was converted in the cultivated atmosphere of Princeton College, Finney in the frontier circumstances of upstate New York. In his evangelizing, as noted, McIlvaine worked within the structures of a liturgical church,

Finney by innovation. Moreover, McIlvaine was of genteel upbringing, educated in schools for the sons of the elite, and churched amidst the deliberate doctrine and practice of the Episcopal Church. Finney, by contrast, received a sixth-grade education on the frontier, studied law on his own, and was unchurched until reaching his mid-twenties. Theologically, McIlvaine found his home in the Evangelical tradition of Anglican and Episcopal doctrine and practice, complete with its core of moderate Calvinism; while Finney, in the words of Benjamin B. Warfield, embodied the "unordered Pelagianism of the man in the street, strengthened and sharpened by the habits of thought picked up in the law-courts." [10] McIlvaine had his own involvement with higher education, having taught at New York University and Kenyon College, where he also served as president; but the Episcopal Church, whether at the local, diocesan or national level, remained the principal venue for his work. Finney, having left revivalism behind, turned to the lecture hall, the press and the pulpit to propagate an "Oberlin theology" with all the energy he had earlier demonstrated as a traveling evangelist.

McIlvaine's revivalist and Evangelical theology was influenced by two eighteenth-century Anglican churchmen, John Wesley and George Whitefield. Although Wesley is the better known, Whitefield was his peer, or perhaps his superior, in the ability to stir listeners with evangelical fervor. If Wesley was a preacher of parts, Whitefield was a preacher of parts and a performer of genius. No other revivalist equaled him in presence and theatrical passion. He intrigued and entertained not only shopkeepers and farmers but notables as unlike as the enterprising and original Benjamin Franklin and the dour and worldly Lord Chesterfield. More important for our story, it was he who planted the seeds of Episcopal evangelizing and its insistence on the necessity of rebirth by grace, through faith, in conscious profession.

In preaching rebirth, Whitefield attacked the formalism and perceived spiritual deadness of the Church of England to which he belonged. Multitudes flocked to hear the message. They were seldom if ever disappointed by the storied preacher, from either the standpoint of religion or of entertainment. By exercising his powers to the fullest, he established a new paradigm by which to reach the unchurched, the curious, the bored, the rich, the poor. Crossing the Atlantic, he became a sensation throughout the American colonies. Yet not everyone welcomed the upstart. The Rev. Alexander Garden, the Anglican commissary of South Carolina, alongside other colonial divines, attacked the evangelist. They urged against him and other revivalists the traditions of Restoration Anglicanism, with their ceremonialism, rationalism and moralism on the one hand and their hatred of Puritan enthusiasm on the other. Consequently, the vital importance of the moment of spiritual rebirth, held by Evangelicals to be a work of God's power and grace *solely*, was displaced by an emphasis on moral and spiritual striving. Whitefield attacked the conventional view at just this point. "Justification by faith" was, he insisted, the only means of rebirth. On this principle he would not yield, as it stood at the core of his beliefs. Decades hence, McIlvaine would hold to the same principle. He would preach the same message though adhering more closely to the structures of the church. In the assessment of one historian, Evangelical Episcopalians as a whole "envisioned the forms and rituals of a liturgical, theologically rich, Protestant church enlivened by the spirit of American evangelicalism." [11]

With the consecration in 1811 of Alexander Viets Griswold as bishop of the Eastern Diocese (embracing Vermont, Massachusetts, Rhode Island, Maine and New Hampshire), Evangelical Episcopalians witnessed the raising up of a leader and soul mate to the highest levels of the church. In the years that followed, Griswold and his colleagues opposed on several points the High Church party that had hitherto dominated doctrine and practice. Predictably, the emergence of Evangelicals as an identifiable party sharpened divisions within the church. Separating the Gospel core from exclusively Episcopal worship and doctrine, as Evangelicals did in part do, was among the points of contention. High Churchmen held to an ideal of the church that was more formal and exclusive than that of their opponents. They took with utmost seriousness the notion of the visible church—their church in particular—as appointed by God to be the vehicle of salvation for believers. Thus their churchmanship demanded a direct link between the "saved" and those who were in the pews. They did not wish to dilute the distinctiveness of the visible church to which they belonged, nor had they any wish to accommodate to the conversionist evangelizing of their foes. By contrast, Evangelicals were comfortable with the notion of both a visible and an invisible church, with the latter comprising in their view all true believers regardless of the denomination to which they belonged.

Not surprisingly, charges of "enthusiasm" were leveled. High Churchmen accused Evangelicals of being too close to Methodists and Baptists in propagating their faith by highly emotional means. Evangelicals denied the charges, drawing attention to the orderly nature of their evangelizing. Though they sought to elicit rebirth according to evangelical particulars, they did not want it thought that they would do so in disorderly and unseemly ways. They—the Evangelical clergy of the Episcopal Church—tended after all to be drawn from upper-class families. (High Church clergy were mostly from the middle classes.) Thus they thought of themselves as unlikely propagators of a crude enthusiasm. By the same token, their often wealthy and influential parishioners were among the least likely to permit such excesses Yet it was their parishioners to whom the conversionist message was preached, a message more commonly—and more boisterously—preached to the less affluent sectors of the population by Methodists and Baptists. It was this simultaneously Episcopal and Evangelical approach, with its particular principles and emphases, which McIlvaine would champion throughout his life.

McIlvaine stated his revival principles in a letter to one of his parishes in his second year as bishop of Ohio. The parish, which had never enjoyed the regular services of a pastor, was clearly in need of wise and timely advice, as the teeming energies stirred by revival were producing startling results both favorable and unfavorable. With regard to the first, McIlvaine rejoiced that a "great increase of attention to the salvation of the soul" had appeared in the parish, that many members had taken an interest in prayer, and that some professed "to have been recently led to Christ, and to have obtained peace through the blood of His Cross." He expressed hope that serious inquiry into "the way of salvation" had been aroused, that members of the parish were searching the Bible, praying diligently, renouncing sin, pursuing holiness, loving one another, and seeking "to dwell together in the unity of the spirit and the bond of peace." If all these things were true, he wrote, "Indeed I do rejoice. It is the work of the Spirit." Yet he let it be known that other spirits could be at work also. Revival, he held, was a two-edged sword. The most prosperous season in a church could be the most dangerous: "The mount is the place to become giddy." He expressed his customary caution in regard to revival novelties that should have no place in the church. "Beware of all efforts to kindle excitement," he warned. "Be animated, be diligent, be filled with the spirit of prayer, but be sober-minded. Sobriety of spirit and humility of mind are inseparable." With Finney and other revival specialists in mind, he came down hard on deliberate efforts to promote emotional excess. "Let all noise and all endeavors to promote animal feeling be shunned," he said. "You can no more advance the growth of religion in the soul by excitement, than you can promote health in the body by throwing it into fever." Religion is principle, he admonished the parish, and as such can only be promoted by truth, prayer, and doing one's duty. [12]

McIlvaine also reminded the parish that the regular services of the church remained necessary—indeed, more necessary than ever—during a time of revival. Owing to the excitement generated, he warned, participants might come to believe that regular worship should be set aside in favor of irregular forms of a more stimulating character. "On the contrary," he advised, "hold on to those holy and spiritual services as your anchor, to keep you steadfast under the irregular influences to which, in...a revival of religion, all are liable." At no time, he said, does a church need a liturgy—a prescribed form of worship such as that found in the Book of Common Prayer—more than during revival. For liturgy, he said, served "against that disposition to extravagance and novelty, by which so many revivals have been deformed." [13] Moreover, liturgy was immune "to temporary prejudice; preferring to be adapted to the wants of all centuries and all people, rather than change with the times and vary with the tastes of the day." [14] In it, he declared, the Word of God was present "in purity, in fitness, and in power." [15]

McIlvaine also reaffirmed the leadership of the parish rector, with assistance only from laymen of his own choosing. "It is especially urged," he wrote, "that those who...have recently embraced religion be not put forward to take a lead." New converts, he said, brimming with energy but immature in the faith, should be among the last to be trusted with the Gospel. Yet it was all too often the recent convert, caught up in the moment, who boldly stepped forward, fervent to witness in the power of the Spirit. This should not be allowed. Rather, such should be sure that the faith "be well fixed in their hearts" before venturing forth "to bear the burden and heat of the day." [16]

McIlvaine touched on yet another concern: disunity. He had received a report that members of the parish were forming into factions. This, he confessed, filled him with alarm. Despite his exacting cast of mind and concern with doctrinal precision, he always supported the unity of the church. He was, as a bishop and a loyal churchman, a shepherd of souls as well as a theologian, and he worked tirelessly to keep the flock in harmony. Sounding like St. Paul writing to the Corinthians and Galatians of old, he made clear his distress at the news of disunity. Yet he did not ask for details, only repentance. "I ask not what [the divisions] are, whence they come, or who are concerned in them. But I say unto all, Love one another; let every root of bitterness be moved out of the way." Only Satan, he said, is the victor when a church is sundered. [17]

Much later, in his twenty-fourth year as bishop, McIlvaine provided further advice regarding revival and conversion. The advice appears in a letter written to the Rev. Noah Hunt Schenck, the new rector of Harcourt Parish in Gambier. In it, McIlvaine touched on most if not all of the themes that marked his career as a preacher of revival. They were written after many years of experience as a bishop as well as a priest and therefore sum up the mature conclusions of the man. Their measured wisdom and shrewd insight, set forth in his typically ordered manner, were applied to a variety of issues. These included the inculcation of a sense of sin, the need to stress the free grace of Christ—"his tender and boundless love"—and the danger of over-reliance on emotion. He discussed also the need for self-knowledge, the importance of Bible study, and the necessity of private devotion. He cautioned as well against doctrinal haggling in regard to the conversion event itself. This last was in the circumstances a wise piece of counsel, coming as it did from a churchman who was doctrinally astute and passionate. No one would have more gladly expatiated on the fine points of justification or the subtleties of sanctification. Yet good judgment triumphed over natural bent. [18]

McIlvaine began by urging Schenck to "aim at a deep and broad foundation, in a *thorough conviction of sin and ruin and condemnation.*" To be sure, these words have a Calvinistic ring to them, an echo of "total depravity." Indeed, they reflect the Reformed tradition that shaped Evangelical principles, and echo the Augustinian theology of the Book of Common Prayer. It was, theologically, at just this point that Evangelical Episcopalians differed from Finney and his followers. For the former held that revival was primarily a work of God's grace from beginning to end, while the latter saw it as a Pelagian affair involving the unalloyed free will of the penitent. The conviction of sin, Evangelicals held, was practical as well as theoretical, useful in both understanding the human condition and in prescribing a remedy for it. "We can know him only as we know our need of him," McIlvaine declared. In other words, one could know the vital need of being rescued from a state of sin only if one was convinced that he or she was *in* a state of sin. Only the person so convicted could find rest and joy in the rescue. "To whom much is forgiven, the same loveth much." It was considered the office of the Holy Spirit—among whose instruments the preacher of revival considered himself to be—to convict of sin and thereby awaken souls to their need of Christ. "Seek therefore," McIlvaine urged, "to bring the mind into…a sense of utter sinfulness and condemnation." Yet there was no recommendation to do this by pummeling the penitent into submission; rather, the need was for a patient but persistent application of the Gospel to the conscience of the hearer. The "mountains of self" were to be made low "and the preciousness of Christ, as a refuge and only hope, exalted." [19]

Furthermore, Schenck was to aim "at drawing away the mind [of the penitent] from seeking comfort and hope in its own experiences and feelings" and to center itself instead in Christ, regardless of cost. "Seek [in the penitent] such a frame [of mind] as will desire, not so much to get hope and consolation, as to be a Christian—and to be a Christian simply as that consists in coming to Christ, and being his, and striving to be his more and more." There were, McIlvaine well knew, words of comfort innumerable in the Christian faith. There were words for the worried, the bereaved, the fearful, the perplexed. But such were not the central focus. The center of life was to be placed in Christ. Christ was to be given sole allegiance. He was to be master, as well as guide, example and friend. "All affections, hopes, desires, motives must center there." [20]

Schenck was advised to display "the freeness of Christ…that draws the stony heart, and in which is manifested the power of

God unto Salvation." This freedom, to McIlvaine, would alone accomplish the task. The penitent must realize in his or her heart that Christ's love is not attached up front to a list of rules, rituals and ethical demands, let alone the novelties of an "engineered" revival. Free grace was the vehicle of a "perfect salvation." One must preach Christ crucified—Christ as vicarious atonement, as reconciliation, as propitiation—as "nothing else will do." Such, he said, might be "foolishness to the natural man" but not to the elect, to whom the Gospel was sent. [21]

In addition, Schenck was cautioned to avoid topics of doctrinal discussion not directly involved in the work of grace. McIlvaine warned of the dangers of the *odium theologicum*, of which there was no spectacle more repugnant in the eyes of the unconverted. "Satan takes advantage of such side issues," he said, "to lead the mind from the great question, what must I do to be saved?" [22] It was a matter of setting and circumstance. At other times, no one was more principled and precise doctrinally than McIlvaine. But when trying to win the heart of a sinner, the Gospel was to be preached directly and simply, to both convince the mind and engage the emotions. The potential convert, he knew, had no desire to split hairs on points of high theology.

McIlvaine urged that converts cultivate the life of private piety, that they place "great stress on *private* exercises of mind, in quietness, in reading, in prayer, in seeking solitary communion with God." Here he touched on a form of discipline highly esteemed by evangelicals before and after his time. The man or woman reading the Bible in solitude had been an emblem of Protestant life from the time of the Reformation, representing as it did a new form of lay piety marked not only by interiority but by literacy. McIlvaine encouraged this form of piety in others in addition to finding it vital to his own. As a corollary to this advice, he said, mistakes "are often made in having too many [religious] *meetings.*" He feared that private exercises might suffer if religious gatherings were not limited. "When meetings are so many that they encourage...a *dependence on them,* as if their *social* excitement were necessary...and so private exercises are made subordinate, and seem dull in comparison...then meetings have got into their wrong place." [23] Thus the two—private and public piety—were linked in inverse proportion, with McIlvaine anxious to preserve an important place for the former.

As a new rector, Schenck was cautioned "to institute no means which, in case the work should go on as a permanent work, could not be continued." [24] This theme was dear to McIlvaine's heart, as it summed up both his opposition to employing special means in revival and his concern to strengthen the church as an ongoing institution. When means—special "means" and "devices" peculiar to revival practice—"have to be given up because they are too many and too exacting to last, the feeling is that the work is declining...and reaction takes place, and coldness ensues." Here he observed the principle of contrast. A state of mind evoked by special means and marked by overriding joy, excitement and ecstasy—as might occur during a revival—cannot continue indefinitely. Indeed, when at last it ebbs, it leaves its subject spiritually deflated and dejected. Hence McIlvaine insisted on the priority of regular worship. Regular experience of word and sacrament in the context of a set liturgy, in the ongoing life of the church, was, he taught, necessary to the progress of the soul. To expect otherwise was to attempt to build one's spiritual house exclusively on the excitements and ephemera of occasional but soul-stirring experiences.

That being said, McIlvaine did not neglect the role of emotion in the work of revival. In a letter of 1832 to Stephen P. Tyng, his clerical friend, he acknowledged that revival "is necessarily, to some extent, a time of excitement." That excitement, however, was of two kinds. The first kind was that expressed by the soul as it received nourishment from the Word of God. Such, he held, was the *genuine* excitement of a religious revival. "But there is another," he said, "resembling it very deceitfully in color and temporary sensation....It is the fever of the mind, [to] which human nature is exceedingly prone." [25] This, he believed, should be discouraged. To him, the deliberate excitement of "animal feelings" at any point in the revival process was unseemly and unnecessary. Indeed, it could (witness Finney's own confession) elicit shallow or even false conversions. McIlvaine considered a deep and sober understanding of the Gospel message to be far superior to momentary excitement. His own conversion at the Princeton Revival, as well as later experiences, appeared to prove the point. Yet for all that, excitement was not disallowed. Indeed, there were outbursts of emotion among Episcopalians. According to historian Diana Hochstedt Butler, "violent shrieks of agony and obstreperous shouts of joy" were not unheard of among the otherwise reserved members of the denomination. [26] McIlvaine was reserved himself in giving approval to such phenomena but not necessarily opposed to it. It was partly a matter of priorities. He viewed such phenomena as of secondary importance, occasional responses to be allowed but not elicited. To promote authentic revival and avoid "fever" and "sensation," he insisted upon working within the restrictions of liturgy. The means of grace were few: preaching, Bible study, and private and communal prayer. These and no more would suffice.

In his letter to Schenck, McIlvaine included a single sentence on the Bible: "Inculcate the love of the Scriptures." [27] This too, like private devotions, was a focus of evangelical practice, and had been since Luther and the other reformers proclaimed the doctrine of *Sola Scriptura*, "Scripture alone." Although he devoted but one sentence to the subject, the fact is that McIlvaine and his fellow churchmen held the Bible to be *the* vehicle of revelation, to be God's account of himself and his relations with his creatures. It was viewed as God's own teaching and testimony in human form, as the expression, interpretation and embodiment of divine self-disclosure. Convinced it expressed God's wisdom and truth in all its parts—"the whole counsel" as it were of God's teaching, from Genesis to Revelation—Evangelicals considered the "Word written" a trustworthy guide in navigating the shoals of life. McIlvaine repaired always to Scripture as the basis of meditation, prayer and preaching.

Lastly, he advised Schenck to "seek that the work may reach with great power among all former communicants—to lead them...to begin anew to live to God." Here he expressed the hope that revival might stir the "hearts" of all students [Schenck's parish served the students of Kenyon College and Seminary] that had previously professed Christ, especially theological students and others seeking divinity degrees. He prayed they might obtain a "strength and depth of experience in Christ far beyond what they have known before." [28] He hoped, in short, to confirm or "revive" such souls in the furtherance of their ministries.

Thus, McIlvaine the revivalist remained, at heart, McIlvaine the churchman. He spurned the extraordinary means of the revival specialists. Converted in revival himself, and convinced that Scripture required nothing less than rebirth from everyone who believed himself to be a true Christian, he preached revival to the educated classes and demonstrated its relevance to a wider spectrum of believers than did most of his predecessors in the leadership of the Episcopal Church. He and likeminded clergy brought the conversion experience into play, where for more than half a century it would "win souls" in the evangelical manner and define itself against High Churchmen in a theological battle for the soul of the church.

McIlvaine's interest in working with other denominations waxed and waned. He was eager to join with non-Episcopal churchmen to promote Christian causes during his first dozen years as a priest. But his enthusiasm to promote "invisible unity" among the churches was tempered by the out-of-control sectarianism he found on the Ohio frontier. Consequently, he was willing in the 1830s to join forces with High Churchmen in efforts to evangelize, knowing that by doing so new believers would be drawn to a church with a largely unified message and a stable liturgical structure, despite its perennial push-and-pull over theology and churchmanship. He reverted to more ecumenical views—at least in part—in the 1850s, when he became convinced the nation was suffering spiritual decline. Alarmed about the growing divide over slavery, the growth of political radicalism, division within the churches, fear for the nation's viability, and what he perceived to be a national malaise, he joined clergy from other denominations to call the nation to repentance and restoration.

In this spirit, he preached to his diocesan convention in 1851 a message entitled "Spiritual Regeneration." [29] Here he focused not on the forms of the visible church—which emphasis had been a priority during his nearly twenty years as bishop—but once again on the invisible unity that held Christians of all denominations together. He urged cooperation in the work of saving sinners and, within his own church, placed renewed emphasis on the need for both spiritual rebirth and holy living. In time, the new direction bore fruit. At Pentecost 1856, Kenyon College and the town of Gambier were caught up in a revival that resulted in fifty-eight confirmations, no small thing in a tiny community. The after effects of the revival reverberated for the next two years, with similar outbreaks of religious fervor springing up throughout the diocese.

Traveling in the East to raise funds for Kenyon College a short time later, McIlvaine played a role in the "Great Revival" of 1858. The awakening, which had started in New York City in 1857, had spread to Philadelphia and other eastern cities the following year. Soon it found its way to the Midwest. McIlvaine's friend, Stephen P. Tyng, led the Philadelphia revival, and it was there that McIlvaine became involved. His first duty—a tragic one—was to conduct the emotionally charged funeral for Tyng's son, Dudley, an ardent Evangelical clergyman himself who had died following a freak mill accident. The younger Tyng had been active in leading revivals in the months before his death, and the service that McIlvaine conducted became a revival itself, with outpouring of grief and tribute. Throughout the spring of 1858, McIlvaine remained in the East, witnessing the awakening, preaching when called upon, and joining in prayer meetings. He was convinced of the authenticity of the revival, especially as it was free of "means" and "devices." It was, he was convinced, a work of God, an outpouring of the Holy Spirit. He saw it as a sign of emerging Christian union, which he viewed in turn as a sign of the coming of the kingdom of God.

Caught up in the fervor, McIlvaine's millennial tendencies were aroused. He began to suspect that the end of the world was near. When he returned to Ohio in June, he reported to the diocese on the depth and extent of the events that were sweeping the nation. His address took its text from the prophet Joel: "It shall come to pass in the last days, saith God, I will pour out my Spirit on all flesh." Based on the intensity of the revival, he became convinced that the millennium—the thousand-year reign of Christ on earth—would begin within a decade. With that hope in mind, and suffering from mental and physical exhaustion, he sailed to England in the fall of 1858. Despite his health, he was eager to spread the news. "Do not these revivals," he asked his English friend, William Carus, "stand in interesting connection with that event [the millennium]?" [30] In England, he spoke about the revival back home, penned a tract in regard to it, and encouraged prayer meetings. Upon returning to America, he was pleased to learn that revival had broken out in several parts of Britain. He saw revival in both nations as a herald of increasing spiritual unity among believers.

McIlvaine's enthusiasm for the Great Revival tempered the exclusive churchmanship he and other Evangelicals had cultivated with High Churchmen in the face of Ohio's sectarian turbulence. Thus, by the 1850s, he had returned to the interdenominational sympathies of his early years in the priesthood. Yet despite the Great Revival and its millennial portents, he saw little hope for the immediate future of the nation. As war clouds gathered, he feared revival would be followed by violence, and the millennium realized only on the heels of a great work of Satan. "Antichrist follows Christ," he predicted. "Satan's kingdom is the more awake as that of our Lord is mighty and progressive....The more manifest the spiritual blessing, the more reason to watch against the contrary." [31] When war came in 1861, his attentions turned to the struggle between North and South, and revival faded into the background. During the years in which the nation played out its agonizing drama, he would find ways to serve church and state. Not the least of these would occur early in the war, at the time of the Trent Affair, when he would serve as one of Abraham Lincoln's diplomats to Britain at a time of crucial importance. That endeavor, alongside his other Civil War activities, will be discussed in chapters eight and nine.

1. Quoted in Harold Bloom, *The American Religion: The Emergence of the Post-Christian Nation* (Simon & Schuster, New York, 1992), 60-61.
2. Quoted in Bloom, 61, 59, 60-61.
3. Lewis O. Saum, *The Popular Mood of Pre-Civil War America* (Greenwood Press, Westport, Conn., 1980), 65.
4. Quoted in Saum, 65.
5. Saum, 72.
6. Benjamin B. Warfield, *Studies in Perfectionism* (Presbyterian and Reformed Publishing Company, Phillipsburg, N. J., 1958), 16.
7. Alfred Lee, *In Memoriam: Charles Pettit McIlvaine, Late Bishop of the Diocese of Ohio* (Leader Printing Company, Cleveland, Ohio, 1873), 12-13.
8. Quoted in Warfield, 21.
9. Ibid., 34.
10. Warfield, 18.
11. Butler, *Whirlwind*, 5.
12. Carus, *Memorials*, 81-84.
13. Ibid.
14. McIlvaine, "The Present Condition and Chief Want of the Church: A Charge to the Clergy of the Protestant Episcopal Church of Ohio" (Gambier, 1836), 19.

15. McIlvaine, "Pastoral Letter of the House of Bishops of the Protestant Episcopal Church (1862)" (Project Canterbury), 8.
16. Carus.
17. Ibid.
18. Charles P. McIlvaine to the Rev. Noah Hunt Schenck, May 26, 1856 (Kenyon Archives, no. 56-05-26), 25-28.
19. Ibid.
20. Ibid.
21. Ibid.
22. Ibid.
23. Ibid.
24. Ibid.
25. Quoted in Pugh, *McIlvaine*, 82.
26. Butler, 37.
27. Schenck.
28. Ibid.
29. McIlvaine, "Spiritual Regeneration with Reference to Present Times: A Charge Delivered to the Clergy of the Diocese of Ohio" (New York, 1851), 3-7.
30. Carus, 197.
31. McIlvaine, "Bishop McIlvaine's Address to the Convention of the Diocese of Ohio, on the Revival of Religion" (Cincinnati, 1858), 18.

CHAPTER SIX

Confuting the Tractarians

In regard to the mainline Protestant churches and movements of his day, Charles Pettit McIlvaine was an ecumenist. More than the High Churchmen of his own denomination—who held an exclusivist view of their church—he was open to cooperation with Presbyterians, Methodists and others. He respected them and worked with them. There were, on the other hand, exemptions from the generally wide sweep of his irenic nature. One was Roman Catholicism; another, its half-sister, the Oxford Movement; another still, the Broad Church movement, which emerged in the last decades of his life, and which will be discussed in chapter seven.

McIlvaine's aversion to the Church of Rome was virtually an American birthright in the ante-bellum period. His attacks on that church, grounded in Evangelical and Anglican doctrine, expressed the essentials of Reformation thought. These included the reliance on Scripture as the sole basis of doctrine, as opposed to Rome's dual reliance on Scripture and Tradition, and the Protestant emphasis on "justification by faith apart from works." His attacks on the Oxford Movement, grounded in the same principles, were directed at what he saw as a betrayal of the church he loved. Predictably, human nature being what it is, there had been divisions among Episcopalians prior to the arrival of "Oxford

Divinity." In its formative years, the church had been divided among Evangelicals, High Churchmen, and latitudinarians. The latter, descendents of the Cambridge Platonists and other Anglican divines of the seventeenth century, were defined by an emphasis on reason and a relative indifference to doctrine and tradition, while Evangelicals emphasized Scripture and experiential rebirth, and were relatively indifferent to tradition and ecclesiastical exclusivity. High Churchmen, for their part, venerated tradition, were sacramentally centered, and stressed the liturgical and other distinctives of the Episcopal Church. In the early nineteenth century, the latitudinarians declined as a force even as the others became the principal parties within the church. They also became the principal competitors for power and influence. Yet their differences were largely overcome by their many shared values. Their normally cordial relations, disturbed only now and then by theological disputes or personal animosities, continued until the arrival of the Oxford Movement at the end of the 1830s.

Although Oxford divinity troubled Evangelical Episcopalians on its own merits, the fear that it was a foot-in-the-door for "Romanism" caused even greater alarm. Like many Protestants, McIlvaine and his allies feared that the Roman church—along with millions of Irish immigrants of "Romish" persuasion newly arrived on American shores—would subvert the Protestant quasi-establishment that hitherto had flourished in politics and culture. From their perspective, they had reason for concern. During the first half of the nineteenth century, Roman Catholicism in America had grown from a church of the few into the largest church in the land. Owing to this expansion and the reaction it provoked, the country experienced the most violent period of religious strife in its history. Anti-Catholic nativism at the local, state and national levels expressed the anxiety of non-Catholic Americans in the face of this shift in the nation's denominational equilibrium. As a result, "no popery" literature found a ready market and evangelical periodicals—founded initially to advance the Second Great Awakening—devoted increasing space to anti-Catholic writings. Churchmen of various affiliations joined the fray. In a pastoral letter of 1829, for example, bishops of the Episcopal Church warned against "papist perils" and the dangers they posed. Presbyterians got involved in 1834, when the renowned revivalist, Lyman Beecher, published *Plea for the West,* in which he depicted "the pope and Europe's reactionary kings, with the Austrian emperor at their head and Catholic immigrants for agents," as conspiring to take over the Mississippi Valley. A Lutheran, Samuel S. Schmucker, promoted "fraternal union" among Protestants to counter Romanist influence, and a Congregationalist, Horace Bushnell, a moderate in most matters, labored to found an Evangelical Alliance principally on anti-Catholic grounds. [1]

At times, the war of words turned to violence. In 1834, nativists burned the Ursuline Convent in Charlestown, appalling the nation. Then, in 1844, following the death of a nativist supporter at a political rally, two Catholic churches and dozens of Irish homes in Philadelphia were burned, local militia fired into crowds, and a cannon was turned on soldiers guarding a Catholic church. For three days the city was menaced by mob rule. New York City, similarly threatened, was spared a similar result owing to the pluck of Archbishop John Hughes, who stationed armed men at every Catholic Church. [2]

Frontier Ohio, soon to be the diocese of Charles McIlvaine, faced religious and ethnic tensions of its own. The Ohio Valley, settled by Catholics from France in the late seventeenth century, saw its Catholic population augmented by settlers from Maryland after the English took control in 1763. In the 1830s and '40s, Catholics from Ireland and Germany arrived to work the land and build a canal system. Protestant Ohioans, frightened by this "foreign presence," responded with anti-Catholic and anti-immigrant polemics and some persecution. In Cincinnati, in the Election Day Riots of 1855, nativist supporters attacked the city's German wards for three days. The well-disciplined defenders held their own, killing two of the attackers and wounding twenty. On the whole, Catholics were far from passive victims. In 1829, their First Provincial Council sounded an aggressive note on three fronts: proclamation of the growth of American Catholicism as a manifest priority; criticism of the King James Version of the Bible (the quasi-official Bible of Protestants), and encouragement and founding of parochial schools. In 1842, the above-mentioned Archbishop Hughes (whose name will appear alongside McIlvaine's at the time of the Trent Affair early in the Civil War) took the lead in demanding a share of public funds for Catholic schools while condemning the Protestant character of existing instruction. Other developments included the founding of the Catholic Tract Society and the appearance of Roman Catholic newspapers in major cities. As well as engaging in theological debate and polemic, these papers devoted space and energy to combat Protestant publications that demonized convents ("nunneries") as well as Roman Catholic doctrine and practice in general.[3] Within the Roman church itself, ethnic tensions added to the unrest, with French, Irish and German Catholics competing for positions of power. This, broadly speaking, was the condition in America when the Oxford Movement arrived.

The Oxford leaders or "Tractarians," named for the tracts that bore their creed, consisted of a cadre of Anglican reformers based at Oxford University. Initially, they crusaded against the intrusion of the English parliament into church affairs. But John Henry Newman, Edward Bouverie Pusey, Richard H. Froude, John Keble, and others not only reasserted the independence of the church from the state but reaffirmed ties to the Catholic tradition as they understood it. Their *Tracts for the Times* made clear their distaste for both the Protestant Reformation and the Protestant character of the Church of England. They favored instead a Catholic sensibility and doctrine, stressing tradition, sacraments, and hierarchy as major features of the church in place of alleged Protestant over-reliance on the Bible, preaching, and personal experience.

136

For a time, the American church appeared unconcerned by these writings. But that began to change in 1838 with the arrival of Newman's *Essay on Justification by Faith*, followed in 1839 by the publication of other tracts as well. Several prominent High Churchmen, among them George W. Doane, bishop of New Jersey; Samuel Seabury III, editor of *The Churchman*, and Benjamin T. Onderdonk, bishop of New York (and brother of McIlvaine's old nemesis, Henry U. Onderdonk), lent their prestige to the movement. Predictably, *The Churchman* favored publication of the tracts. Equally predictably, the *Gambier Observer* in Ohio opposed it, printing an article to that effect by the pseudonymous "Cranmer." The latter piece was reprinted in the *Episcopal Recorder*, with much acclaim by the editor. According to "Cranmer," the "poison" that had infected the Church of England was prepared "to try its force on the...Episcopal Church in this land." Tractarianism, he wrote, had been a "sore trial" for the English church, threatening to introduce "Popery within the very strongest bastions of that bulwark of the Reformation." It would, he predicted, be a severe trial for the Episcopal Church also. To no one's surprise, "Cranmer" turned out to be McIlvaine. [4]

Despite the fears of McIlvaine and others, Tractarianism posed little danger as a Roman Catholic fifth column, at least intentionally. Newman himself, in *Tract Seventy-One*, published in 1836, faulted Rome at a number of points. Principally, he charged the Roman church with committing several major errors, among them denial of the cup to the laity, the necessity of private confession to a priest, the doctrine of purgatory, the invocation of saints, and the veneration of images. He considered these practices not only corrupt but unwarranted by primitive practice. Yet, in support of McIlvaine's apprehension, one could observe that he and his colleagues were, for the most part, tepid in their opposition to Rome. Specifically, Newman tended to address "practical errors" but not statements of doctrine, such as the decrees of the sixteenth century Council of Trent. In addition, his *Tract Seventy-Two* (also from 1836) featured passages on prayers for the dead, and his *Tract Seventy-Five* included portions of the Roman Breviary for personal devotion.[5] Nine years later, as if to vindicate suspicions, he entered the Roman Catholic Church. He was, however, the only Tractarian of significance to do so. Newman's final essay as an Anglican, the audacious *Tract Ninety*, published in 1841, whipped up additional controversy within the Anglican and Episcopal churches when it sought to harmonize the Thirty-nine Articles of the Church of England with the decrees of the above-mentioned Council of Trent, the defining statement of the Roman Catholic Counter-Reformation. Delighted, outraged, or just intrigued, Episcopalians began to study and evaluate Tractarian teaching. A growing number of them liked what they read, and some began to propagate the doctrine. As McIlvaine observed in his *Oxford Divinity Compared*, his treatise on the subject, certain elements in the Episcopal Church proceeded to engage in the "most zealous efforts...to commend the peculiarities of Oxford Divinity to the diligent reading, and confidential reception, of the clergy and laity of this country."[6] Others were just as ardently opposed. Bishop Manton Eastburn, Evangelical bishop of Massachusetts, denounced the *Tracts* as the "work of Satan," as writings inspired by advocates of the Dark Ages and "followers of the Scarlet Woman."[7]

Yet the "peculiarities" of Oxford doctrine were not always easy to discern. McIlvaine himself admitted that the *Tracts* were by no means a full or systematic development of the teaching; further, they contained much that was good. "They displayed peculiarities," he said, "only here and there; in many of the earlier portions, scarcely at all, except to a practiced eye."[8] Among Episcopalians, it was McIlvaine's practiced eye that would be turned most fully upon these writings. Against them, he would marshal his talents as polemicist and theologian, activist and scholar. He would oppose Oxford amidst the clamor of church conventions and from the quiet of his study. The over five-hundred page *Oxford Divinity Compared*, his enduring monument to the controversy, testifies to the ability of an earlier Protestant apologetics, based on Scripture, traditional Anglican divinity, evidentialism, and Scottish realism, to vigorously challenge the claims of its opponents.

In spite of growing opposition, the Tractarian movement waxed rather than waned. By 1840, at a time when fourteen of the nineteen bishops of the Episcopal Church were High Churchmen, several had attached themselves to Oxfordism to one degree or another. [9] General Seminary in New York City, built up by John Henry Hobart, bishop of New York, and Benjamin T. Onderdonk, his successor, became not only the church's most prominent seminary but its principal refuge for the new movement. In the words of a convert to Rome, it was "a little Oxford on this side of the Atlantic." Its students grew in sympathy with High Church sacramentalism and Roman Catholic doctrines and practices more generally, "with the result that there was soon a considerable (but disproportionately publicized) number of converts from among the seminary students." [10] In 1841, the trend was further institutionalized when four General Seminary students, led by James Lloyd Breck, founded Nashota House in Wisconsin as a semi-monastic center for study, worship and evangelism. Breck also founded Seabury Divinity School in Faribault, Minnesota, in 1857, further perpetuating the Oxford influence.

In 1843, Bishop Onderdonk of New York helped fan the flames by ordaining Arthur Carey, a seminarian who had led discussions promoting Tractarianism and who frankly confessed his Tridentine sympathies. The ordination prompted a spate of critical pamphlets and newspaper articles. Viewing it as a provocation, Evangelicals instigated an investigation of General Seminary by a committee of bishops. Though embarrassed, the institution was eventually exonerated of all charges. Yet the inquiry did uncover a secret society with "Romish views" and two students were expelled, one of which would later become a Roman Catholic bishop. Meanwhile, Arthur Carey died in 1844 and was buried at sea en route to Havana, Cuba.

The intermittent strife of the controversy was not confined to the seminaries. Throughout the 1840s and 1850s, General Convention was the scene of ongoing disputes between Evangelicals, on the one side, and High Churchmen and Tractarian sympathizers, on the other. Despite the verbal fireworks, however, little was decided. "Official declarations of the General Convention or the House of Bishops," says historian Sydney Ahlstrom, "were necessarily compromises, and they usually only reiterated a loyalty to the Bible, the prayer book, and the traditions of the Anglican Communion." [11] Even so, Evangelicals, stirred to action by the encroachments of Tractarianism, enjoyed a sort of "golden age." During the 1840s, in a turnabout from earlier trends, their number grew to nearly half of the House of Bishops. The gain stemmed not only from the controversies surrounding General Seminary but from other Tractarian-related developments, including the conversion of more than thirty Episcopal clergy to Rome. The most prominent conversion was that of Levi Silliman Ives, bishop of North Carolina. A student of theology under High Church leader John Henry Hobart, Ives had been an Episcopal bishop for twenty-one years as well as a notable High Churchman. Strongly influenced by the Oxford Movement, he founded a semi-monastic order in 1847, an action attributed by some to Romanist sympathies. Owing to opposition in his diocese, he agreed to suppress the order the following year. Yet his drift away from the Episcopal Church was further confirmed by his embrace of Roman Catholic practices, including private confession to a priest and prayers to the Virgin Mary and the other saints. Despite discipline from his diocese, his theological convictions continued to evolve until he was no longer able to accept his denomination as a branch of the true Catholic church. Obtaining a six-month leave of absence in 1852, he traveled to Europe with his wife, and on Christmas Day was received by Pope Pius IX into the Roman Catholic Church. The following October, the House of Bishops deposed him from his episcopal office. [12]

The most publicized incidents of the entire controversy were the suspensions of two bishops sympathetic to Tractarianism and the public embarrassment of a third. Suspended were the brothers Henry U. Onderdonk of Pennsylvania and Benjamin T. Onderdonk of New York, of whom we have heard much. The third figure, George W. Doane of New Jersey, was investigated for his financial dealings in connection with two schools he had attempted to found. Though humiliated, he was never convicted of any impropriety.

The Onderdonks fared differently. Henry, a noted ecclesiastical scholar and controversialist, was the first of the two to face censure. He had become a subject of scandal owing to his abuse of liquor, specifically brandy, which had been medically prescribed to relieve the discomfort of chronic intestinal pain. Evangelicals in particular, many of whom were temperance advocates, let it be known they were alarmed by his addiction. In response, he wrote to the House of Bishops in 1844 to confess his habitual abuse of alcohol, tender his resignation, and ask for discipline. The resignation was accepted and he was suspended from all ecclesiastical duties. Later the same year, Benjamin Onderdonk was accused of irregular behavior as well. Charged with drunkenness and sexual impurity, he was tried before a court of bishops, found guilty, and suspended from all duties. Thus the careers of two of McIlvaine's staunchest foes came to an inglorious end.

The fall of Benjamin Onderdonk, in the more significant and sensational of the two incidents, began with a presentment against him by three Evangelical bishops: William Meade of Virginia, a friend of McIlvaine's; James Hervey Otey of Tennessee, and Stephen Elliott Jr. of Georgia. The subsequent trial was both scandalous and humiliating. Onderdonk, who had stirred Evangelical wrath by ordaining Arthur Carey, was accused of both public drunkenness and acts of an immoral nature. These acts included "thrusting his hands into ladies' bosoms," reaching up women's skirts to "their central parts," [13] and kissing women against their will. [14] Two of the plaintiffs were clergymen's wives and two were "young communicants of the church," both unmarried. Among the venues of the alleged improprieties were clergymen's carriages and houses. [15]

The Churchman, voice of the High Church party, rallied to Onderdonk's defense, claiming that the presentment against him—based on canon law adopted only three months earlier—was motivated by an Evangelical conspiracy to persecute and depose a strong proponent of the Tractarian movement. To be sure, it was Evangelicals who pressed the case, and it was they who were convinced of Onderdonk's guilt. In confirmation of the party spirit on both sides, Sydney Ahlstrom notes, the voting "closely followed party lines, though the formal issues were hardly theological." [16] Onderdonk expressed contempt for those who investigated the charges against him, accusing them of "reducing themselves to the low caste of informers and panders," of attempting to "seek out and scrape together [information] for the use of my inveterate enemies." [17]

Initially, Onderdonk's supporters fought the charges against him on grounds that it was unthinkable that a bishop could have acted in such a manner. Later, that tactic having failed, they suggested he had been misunderstood by his accusers. After all, he had admitted to a "warm and affectionate manner, which might sometimes be misconstrued." One of his defenders went so far as to suggest that the "jolting of carriages over bad roads" could have led to at least one such misunderstanding. This gambit, too, proved unsuccessful. How, a skeptic asked, could the bumpy movements of a carriage "jolt a man's hands into a lady's bosom or around her waist?" [18] Later still, Onderdonk's supporters observed that some of the incidents had occurred several years earlier and were therefore irrelevant by the time they were raised. It was suggested, also—by *The Churchmen* and its allies—that the women themselves were impure and dishonest and that they had encouraged Onderdonk's advances. Such calumnies did not go unchallenged. The women's character, their defenders argued, was exemplary, and the reason they had delayed stepping forward was shame and embarrassment at the circumstances of their encounters with the bishop. Charles King, editor of the *New York American*, insisted that the women were "of unimpeachable character—of delicate training—of assured position in society—all communicants of the Church of which Bishop Onderdonk is a chief minister." [19]

Onderdonk's alleged behavior was particularly offensive to Evangelicals. Such behavior, it was charged, undermined female trust in male authority in the church generally and, even more, in the authority wielded by High Church clergy under the spell of Oxford theology. Anna Pierrepont, a wealthy New York Evangelical and a friend of McIlvaine's, reported in a letter to the bishop in January 1845 the feelings of her friend, a "dear little Mrs. Batles," in regard to the scandal. In the view of Mrs. Pierrepont's correspondent, God was punishing

> an erring diocese for winking at iniquity....If indeed *all* clergymen and Bishops looked upon these acts *as unimportant in themselves no lady would sit an instant in clerical society.*...What corruption has not this affair shown! What unsoundness both in faith & practice in doctrine & morals...[New York] has long been called the Infected District—who could have believed it so much so—much blame doubtless attaches to those in the City who have long shut their eyes upon the sin they knew existed. [20]

In view of the trial and its sensational nature, even Onderdonk's supporters admitted that acquittal would have hurt the Episcopal Church. According to one historian, "No denomination—comprised of a majority of women—could afford to alienate its female communicants around such a sensitive issue." [21] The vital importance of women to the Episcopal Church in the nineteenth century, alluded to here, will be discussed in chapter eight. Following his conviction, Onderdonk retired to his home and seldom ventured out thereafter. He did, however, present a petition to General Convention in 1859, fourteen years after his suspension. In it he begged "the mercy of the removal of my sentence," conceding that his conduct may have "betrayed indiscretion." [22] General Convention did not act on the petition and, before it met again, he had died, his suspension still in place. Henry Onderdonk fared better, having been reinstated to the active ministry by the House of Bishops in 1856, two years before his death.

The fall of the Onderdonks demonstrated the clout of Evangelical Episcopalians. So too did the earlier investigation of General Seminary, in the wake of which a number of students had been either reprimanded or expelled. For McIlvaine, the fall of the Onderdonks marked the end of a long-running personal and theological feud. As becomes a churchman, he restrained the temptation to gloat over the outcome. Yet he must have felt both personal and professional vindication. After all, Henry Onderdonk had accused him in 1827 of being a "half-churchman" and both brothers had conspired to keep him out of the diocese of New York. Moreover, in 1821, Benjamin had criticized his liturgical practices in a series of letters. A decade later, he had attempted to rally opposition to McIlvaine's election as bishop of Ohio. For fifteen years, historian Diana Hochstedt Butler observes, the Onderdonks "questioned [McIlvaine's] ministry, attempted to block his appointments to churches, refused to validate his election to the episcopacy, and criticized his churchmanship." [23] With their suspension, all of that came to an end.

Whatever purported errors the trained eye might see, Tractarianism drew a measure of approval from the British public, especially in the beginning. Even some Evangelicals saw a kernel of good in it. Thus by the late 1830s, it had gained the sympathy of many churchmen, who applauded its stand on behalf of enduring religious truth and against latitudinarianism. According to one commentator, the emphases of Oxford "were generally understood by supporters to be such principles as the importance of the apostolic succession for the Church of England and Ireland, the antiquity and value of the threefold ministry, the necessity of sacraments as definite vehicles of divine grace, the interpretation of the Scriptures by the teaching of the Fathers...and opposition to liberalism in all its forms." Moreover, a number of influential periodicals, including the *British Magazine, British Critic* and *Times* newspaper, urged the spread of these "Church Principles," as they came to be called. [24]

But whatever merit this teaching may have had, McIlvaine clearly saw its animosity towards the Evangelical centerpiece of justification by faith alone. Tractarian leader Edward Pusey, for instance, argued specifically that Evangelicals employed their pet doctrine wrongly, to "sever Justification from Baptism, and make it consist in the act of reliance upon the merits of Christ only." [25] Indeed, Evangelicals *did* rely "upon the merits of Christ only" as the basis of justification by faith. Moreover, they believed baptism to be no guarantor of justification, as anyone with eyes to see could point to baptized persons who were irreligious and morally dubious. Thus the alleged abuse of the doctrine was, McIlvaine charged, the very interpretation that placed Evangelicals on the side of the Church of England historically, with its Reformation-based formularies, and Pusey on the side that was "identically Romish." [26]

In *Oxford Divinity Compared,* McIlvaine made the Evangelical case for justification at length and in detail, drawing in part on his earlier work on the subject, appropriately entitled *Justification by Faith,* [27] a 150-page treatise he had presented as a charge to his clergy at the diocesan convention of 1839. In laying the foundation, he drew on Richard Hooker (1554-1600), the seminal Anglican thinker, to identify and clarify two kinds of Christian righteousness. These were, in Hooker's words, "The one without us [justification], which we have by imputation; the other in us [sanctification], which consisteth of Faith, Hope, Charity, and other Christian virtues." This distinction—between justification and sanctification—opened the way, McIlvaine said, "to the understanding of that grand question, which hangeth yet in controversy between us and the Church of Rome, about the matter of Justifying righteousness."

According to McIlvaine's view, as related in *Oxford Divinity Compared* and his earlier charge to the clergy, justification itself could be understood in one of two ways: either it must consist of a change in a person's moral nature or of a change in a person's status before God. If understood in the first sense, it held that a person was made righteous—or *just*—before God by the *infusion* of righteousness, by the instilling or penetrating of God's grace, so that he or she would be enabled to cooperate thenceforth by willing according to God's purpose. Such was the Tractarian view. By contrast, Evangelicals held that justification was imputed by an act of God, thus changing a person's status but not his moral nature as such, although good works were the anticipated fruit of justification by way of sanctification.

According to Evangelicals, Oxford doctrine was in essence the same as that of Alexander Knox (1757-1831), Anglican divine and pre-Tractarian, and the Roman Catholic Council of Trent. McIlvaine himself, convinced that John Henry Newman agreed with Knox, sought to prove the point by quoting both Knox and the Tractarian-friendly *British Critic*. In the latter, Knox was held to be "an instance in rudiment of those great restorations which he foresaw in development. He shares with the eminent writers of the day in the work of advancing what he anticipated." Not surprisingly, among the "restorations," was the Catholic understanding of justification. "In St. Paul's sense," Knox had written, "to be justified is not simply to be accounted righteous; but also and in the first instance to be made righteous by the implantation of a radical principle of righteousness." In this, McIlvaine observed, Knox and the Tractarians, alongside the Roman church, were in agreement in viewing justification in terms of an infused, inherent righteousness. Consequently, one commentator notes, "If the doctrine of Knox and the Tractarians was the same, and if the doctrine of Knox and the Roman Catholics was the same, then obviously the doctrine of the Tractarians and the Roman Catholics was the same." It was just this, of course, that McIlvaine sought to prove. Thus, in Chapter Four of *Oxford Divinity Compared*, he claimed that the Oxford divines described the righteousness of justification as did the schoolmen of the medieval church. Consequently, their teaching was—in opposition to Hooker and other Anglican divines—a "distinctive characteristic of Popery." [28] There was, therefore, according to schoolman and Tractarian alike, a synergy of man and God in the process of justification.

Understood in the Protestant and Evangelical sense, however, as noted above, justification was held to be *imputed* without conditions, according to the merit of Christ's finished work on the cross, and by no merit or cooperation of the believer, with the exception of faith. Thus "faith alone" was the means to justification. That, Evangelicals held, was the teaching of the Scriptures and the Anglican and Episcopal churches. A friend of McIlvaine's, John Bird Sumner, bishop of Chester, stated it succinctly in his *Charge* of 1841, where he declared the following:

> The Scriptural truth is as clear as it is simple. "When all were dead [in   sin], Christ died for all"; so that "he that hath the Son hath life and he that hath not the Son hath not life". By one way alone can man possess the Son; that is, by believing in him. And therefore, faith alone can justify; faith alone can appropriate to us that remedy, which God has appointed for the healing of our plague: faith alone can give us an interest in that sacrifice which God has accepted as satisfaction for sin. Thus "being justified by faith we have peace with God through Jesus Christ". [29]

The Oxford view, McIlvaine said, linked justification and sanctification in such a way as to make the former gradual in nature, "and never complete till we are perfected in heaven." [30] In opposing this view, he urged the difference between justification, the once-for-all granting of a new status to forgiven sinners, and sanctification, the ongoing effort to increase one's holiness of life. Again, God justified sinners—by faith alone through grace alone—by imputing to them a new status, in which they were no longer guilty lawbreakers but forgiven sinners acquitted at the bar of divine justice. The merit was fully supplied, he and other Evangelicals believed, by Christ's atoning, vicarious sacrifice on the cross. Though both justification and sanctification were necessary to the Christian life, he held, they were not to be conflated into a single process, as done by Rome and the Tractarians. Justification happened once; sanctification took a lifetime.

In *Oxford Divinity Compared,* he further argued that the above flawed understanding of justification had led the Roman church and its imitator to claim an assortment of extra-biblical doctrines. Faulty Roman teaching on justification, he charged, underpinned belief in purgatory, indulgences, invocation of saints, the sacrament of penance, the sacred treasury of supererogatory merits (earned by surpassing the requirements of duty), and "all the vain intensions" of self-merit. Roman reliance on these varied means was the result, he said, of the refusal to credit God's grace, working through man's faith, as the sole requirement for the justification of sinners. Open a gap in salvation as Rome had done, he said, and it was only natural that it would be filled by extra-biblical inventions of pious but errant men. Moreover, "devices for the defense" of these doctrines produced additional doctrines—including private confession to a priest, papal infallibility, and implicit faith in the church's teaching—as further means of salvation for the faithful. [31]

In elaborating these views, McIlvaine alleged a bias on the Catholic side favoring material as opposed to spiritual sensibility and discipline. This too he linked to the justification question. He claimed the spiritually centered Protestant, convinced of the sufficiency of imputed righteousness received from Christ, by faith alone, had no need of extra or supererogatory acts of piety. By contrast, the materially oriented Catholic would always be inventing "some device or other by which God may be the more effectually propitiated and satisfied." Thus, the Catholic engaged in "those unbidden austerities and severe bodily macerations" by which he hoped his sins might be forgiven and heaven attained by merit. "In such righteousness," McIlvaine said, "there is something that seems tangible, measurable, appreciable. A man can count his penances, measure his pilgrimages, weight his gifts, and thus keep account of his righteousness." He claimed a direct tendency "to precisely such results" in both Oxford and Roman divinity. [32]

McIlvaine did not, however, think Oxford was conspiring to smuggle Roman influences into the Church of England or, indirectly, the Episcopal Church. "We suspect no such thing," he affirmed. Yet in this seeming innocence—and owing to the sterling reputations of the Tractarians—he spied a greater danger. For when they taught serious error, he said, they did so without causing alarm, and were therefore more likely to spread their creed successfully. "Men are often half persuaded already of a doctrine," he said, "when its advocate, to learning, adds evident sincerity and benevolence." Indeed, he said, history showed some "of the worst corruptions of religion" had originated among "its best and sincerest friends." Those who had most disturbed the ancient churches of Rome and Carthage, he observed, were martyrs who bore in their bodies the marks of torture. "What is now a full-grown idolatry in the Church of Rome," he asserted, "had its beginnings in the bosoms of men ready to die for Christ, and was nursed by some of the purest piety of the early Church." By and by, he said, at intervals such as to escape notice, the corruptions of the church had multiplied. "The ovum of saint-worship," he charged, "was laid, by the Serpent, in the ashes of the martyrs." In like fashion, he claimed, Oxford divinity was subtly infiltrating the church. "Because there is little change to the eye," he wrote, "no change of accustomed names; no overt invasion...no hoisting of the flag of the Pope, men may be saying, where is the fear of his coming?" But like Samson of old, he averred, the church was asleep, its strength departed, the Philistine upon it, its walls breached. "That strong bastion of our Reformed Church is Justification by Faith," he said, "erected 'upon the foundation of the Apostles and Prophets—Jesus Christ himself being the chief corner-stone.' That gone, the temple is taken, the ark is in captivity." [33]

Thus McIlvaine reached beyond the Tractarians and the Roman church of his time, back to the saints of the early centuries, back also to the schoolmen of the Middle Ages, and especially to Thomas Aquinas, the "universal and angelic doctor," whom he cast as a villain of the piece. He pointed to that earlier age as the cradle of the innovations that had most deformed Roman teaching and now, in consequence, Anglicanism by way of Tractarianism. He accused the scholastics—Aquinas prominent among them—of neglect of the Scriptures and idolatry of Aristotle. He charged them with "an ostentatious display of ingenuity, in which axioms, assumed without examination, *distinctions, without any real difference, and terms without any precise meaning,*" [34] became weapons of assault and defense in controversies over abstruse questions impossible to bring to conclusion. From these tireless debates, he said, arose opinions that appeared even at the time, to churchmen loyal to the ancient fathers, "highly dangerous and pernicious."

To a nineteenth century Protestant bishop, they suggested something also of the alien nature of a bygone age, and of unproductive and futile exercises of the mind. Like most Americans, McIlvaine was something of a pragmatist before the invention of the philosophy of that name. Although drawn to theological dispute himself, and a master of the discipline, his biblical convictions and Scottish Common Sense approach generally brought disputes to a resolution sooner rather than later, at least in his own mind. In this, his theological method was practical rather than speculative, designed more to address the here-and-now issues of life than the puzzles of metaphysical arcana. His approach to religious questions fit well the progressive, democratic ethos, which sought practical results in all things. In taking a page from the Enlightenment, he believed the Medieval period had been backward, stagnant, and superstitious, · and that its theology had followed suit. Thus he attacked what he saw as the unwarranted pride in reason so characteristic of the age, discerning in it an "emptiness of the mind," in which the church was spoiled "through philosophy and vain deceit." He said the age of the schoolmen "was singularly the age of superstition and heresies;" the age in which heretical features were introduced into and regularized by the church; features that would later be confirmed as Roman dogma by the Council of Trent. [35]

McIlvaine catalogued the "inventions of that ingenious age," some of which had found a place in both Anglican and Episcopal churches by way of Oxford, or by way of its indirect influence. Among them, he said, were sacramental confession, transubstantiation, "image worship," purgatory, and disuse of the Scriptures. (In the case of Rome, he said, Scripture was dislodged to make room for the "legends and tales of saints.") The teachings of the age introduced also the "Romish dogma" of justification against which McIlvaine would expend so much energy. In these "inventions," he found a "striking resemblance in Oxford Divinity to the mystic and subtle doctrine of Romanism in the 13th Century." [36]

McIlvaine again insisted that he was far from claiming that Pusey, Newman, and their colleagues were conscious of all the implications of their system. "We have no expectation," he said, "that they will ever get to the full advocating of Image-worship, Purgatory, &c. We speak of the tendency of their *system.*" Their system, he wrote, had found "weaker minds, and more unfixed hearts, and incautious heads, and reckless hands than theirs to work on." Hence the enduring danger was located in the "unfledged disciples" who would "suck honey and poison" out of the novelties of the teaching and then spread them abroad. [37]

In his *Oxford Divinity Compared*, McIlvaine also addressed disputes over the doctrines of "reserve," baptismal regeneration (further elaborating the justification controversy), and the "via media." The question of reserve had been raised by Isaac Williams, John Henry Newman's curate at St. Mary the Virgin Church at Oxford, in *Tract Eighty*. Williams's tract, entitled "On Reserve in Communicating Religious Knowledge," was partly inspired by admiration of his Tractarian colleagues and partly by his patristic studies, including his reading of Origen, the third century theologian who had alluded to "a mysterious holding back of sacred truth." [38] With the exception of Newman's *Tract Ninety* and Pusey's tract on baptism, no Tractarian publication was more widely condemned than this. In it, Williams accused Evangelicals of exalting preaching at the expense of obedience, an imbalance, he said, that flattered immature and worldly tempers while excluding everything that might cause them alarm, especially the "necessity of mortification and obedience on the part of man." Moreover, he chided them for offering immediate access to the full Christian life, at the expense of self-discipline and penance. Such an approach, he believed, was a betrayal of the ancient teaching of the church. Thus he advised that religious truth at its deepest levels should be communicated only to people who, by moral maturity, were prepared to receive it. To further his point, he singled out the doctrine of the atonement, or "reconciliation,"—the teaching wherein God and man, at first enemies, were reconciled by Christ's sacrifice—and the manner in which it was understood and used by Evangelicals. He charged that Evangelical preaching of this doctrine to immature Christians cheapened the understanding of God's grace and consequently minimized obedience. Teaching on the atonement, he said, should be "reserved," held back until the believer had advanced in the Christian life, at which time he or she would be less likely to separate grace from works and thereby regress from obedience.

Christ himself, Williams said, practiced a form of reserve by his "habit of concealing, in a remarkable manner, His divine power and majesty, excepting so far as persons might be found capable of receiving it." [39]

To McIlvaine and the Evangelicals, the core of Christian theology was indeed found in the atonement and the concomitant "free grace" that flowed from it. It was atonement, they insisted, when accepted by contrite sinners, which was the only sure ground for "unreserved obedience." Therefore, Christ's work on the cross was to be preached openly, not held in reserve until a particular state of obedience had been attained. To do so, they held, would be to contradict the clear teaching of Scripture. "St. Paul," McIlvaine said, "waited not till men were well initiated into Christian mysteries, before he unveiled the grand subject of atonement and justification through the blood of Christ." [40]

McIlvaine also grappled with baptismal regeneration, which teaching was found in both Roman Catholicism and Tractarianism. This doctrine, which taught that the baptized were reborn or "regenerated" in the sacrament, was anathema to McIlvaine. He, like other Evangelicals, held that rebirth—as indicated above—was linked to faith alone—*sola fide*. The opposite view had been stated by the aforementioned Levi Silliman Ives, bishop of North Carolina, in his 1849 *The Obedience of Faith*, wherein he contended that infants were baptized into "a new and heavenly nature." [41] His work met stiff resistance from fellow churchmen, and not only Evangelicals. In reviewing it, some High Churchmen held that Ives had left Episcopal theology behind, and were therefore as relieved as Evangelicals when he converted to Rome. Still, owing to High Church and Tractarian sympathy for the doctrine, the controversy persisted.

In *Oxford Divinity Compared*, McIlvaine took aim not at Ives, whose work on the subject was eight years in the future, but at the aforementioned Edward Pusey. Pusey, he said, had exceeded

Rome itself in the implications of his views. These, McIlvaine observed, insisted baptism was *not* a sign but *"the putting on of Christ*—wherefore baptism is a thing most powerful and efficacious." In opposing this, McIlvaine noted that Article Twenty-Seven of the Thirty-nine Articles of the Episcopal Church said that baptism was "a sign [not the substance] of regeneration or new birth." Yet according to Pusey, he said, baptism was *"regeneration itself*....The Church of Rome never exceeded this." As a result, he continued, the Oxford system so identified baptism with regeneration and justification "that we are not...to look to our works, our walk, our conformity with God's will...to see whether we be in faith, in Christ." [42] On the contrary, he said, according to Oxford, one need only "revert" to his or her baptism, to place all confidence in the saving grace of having been once baptized with water at the hands of a priest. In having *been* baptized, according to such teaching, one was assured that he or she was in union with Christ. Neither the good works that were said to follow upon rebirth, nor the evident holiness of one's life, were thereby considered trustworthy signs. The sacrament of baptism alone, once administered, was held up as a beacon of assurance. "Nothing," he said, "could more plainly or more impressively display the *'great gulf fixed'* between this divinity and that of the Scriptures."

Finally, regarding their place on the theological spectrum, the Tractarians advocated a middle path, a "via media," within the Church of England, one distinct—according to Pusey—from the "by-ways of Ultra-Protestantism on one side, and neither verging toward, nor losing itself in Romanism on the other." McIlvaine considered the claim bogus. The Tractarians, he said, did not pass at equal distances between Roman Catholicism at one end and Protestantism at the other. Instead, he wrote, they passed much closer to Rome, separated from it only by the papacy and perhaps one or two other doctrines. Also, he objected to the term "Ultra-Protestant." It was, he charged, little more than a Tractarian invention, a nebulous but frequently used bogeyman in Oxford polemics. It appears the term—coined by Newman and used by the Tractarians generally—was more or less what he said it was: a broad-brush polemical device applied to evangelicals in both the Church of England and the dissenting churches. As Pusey employed the term, for instance, it pertained, in McIlvaine's sarcastic words, "to whatever is in religion, or relating to it, negatively, or positively, for, or against, only excepting Romanism and Oxfordism; embracing all varieties of...doctrine and inference." In other words, it was applied to whatever in Oxford eyes was held to be extreme and especially repugnant among Protestant views. To such a loose formulation, McIlvaine lodged his protest, claiming it amounted to a caricature, had no precise definition, and served no good purpose. In sum, he said, Tractarianism represented no middle way, but was a barely disguised addition to the Roman position. "One would suppose," he said, "that a coast so undefined would afford but little guidance in keeping the middle way, except as when mariners, under fear of hidden shoals and currents...keep as far away as possible." [43] He advised keeping such a distance.

McIlvaine made it clear that he feared a counter-reformation in both the Church of England and the Episcopal Church. "The Church was once reformed away from Rome, by the powers of light," he said. "The next thing attempted will be to reform her back to Rome, by the powers of darkness." He urged the Protestant faithful to "try the spirits" and beware "angels of light" who would smuggle into the church that which might at first appear laudable. "Our Protestant Reformers," he said, "were at first Romish Priests; and when they began their work, were led by ways they knew not of....Our next Reformers may be Protestant Presbyters, reversing the work of the others." [44] In this, he was largely correct, for Newman hoped to reverse the work of the seventeenth century English reformers, Anglicans generally and Puritans in particular, who had sought to purify the Church of England from residual Roman Catholic elements. To reverse that earlier work, Newman proposed to reintroduce elements drawn from Roman Catholic doctrine and practice. Specifically, he promoted the return to fasting, penance, celibacy, and monasticism, all of which he considered beneficial practices of the primitive church and exempt from what he believed to be later Roman innovations.

In sum, against Newman and the Tractarians, McIlvaine put the Evangelical case with vigor and breadth of learning. Questions of "reserve," baptismal regeneration, and the "via media" drew both his attention and his censure. But above all, he pressed the doctrine of justification by faith alone. Relying on Richard Hooker and other Reformation figures, he asserted that the controversy over justification had been the central question in the reformation of the Church of England. Thus, in his eyes, it was not a controversy that could be separated from traditional Anglican identity. In regard to it, he said, there was perfect agreement among Protestants both in England and on the Continent. In accord with Hooker, he wrote, Luther had earlier considered justification "the article of a standing or a falling church," and Calvin that "if this one head were yielded safe and entire, it would not pay the cost to make any great quarrel about other matters in controversy with Rome." In opposition to these traditional Protestant views, McIlvaine held, there was a disquieting unity between Oxford and "the whole...maze and mystery" of Rome. [45]

When McIlvaine visited Rome in the fall of 1858, in his sixtieth year, he made a congenial discovery. "How unspeakably interesting!" he exclaimed, on observing that inscriptions on the ancient Christian tomb and catacomb relics on display at the Vatican, seemed to undermine the theology of the Roman church. "Not one," he observed, "had any Popish aspect or word." [46]

We cannot understand McIlvaine's anti-Tractarian sentiments without understanding his deep antipathy towards the doctrine and practice of the Roman Catholic Church. His remark about the catacomb inscriptions was typical of the man in his compulsion to see every fact, comment, or passing incident within the context of a theological framework, a framework that systematized point-by-point the views of Protestant orthodoxy and excoriated point-by-point the Roman views that opposed them. Yet in this penchant to criticize, he was more than an angry or prejudiced sectarian, for what he believed, taught and defended was grounded in the Scriptural and doctrinal understandings of the Magisterial Reformation, generally, and the achievements of Anglican thought and polity, specifically. He was, above all, two things: an Evangelical to the core, characterized by a rigorous theology and a passion for things of the spirit; and a man subject to severe inner divisions only partially healed. As an Evangelical, it was to him second nature to view his opponents' theology against the well-defined tenets of his own creed. As a person suffering inordinate feelings of anxiety, obsessive thoughts, and mysterious physical complaints, it was second nature to patch together the fragments of his soul with the assurances of that same unwavering creed. There was a third factor: the "anti-popery" that was prevalent among Protestants during the first half of the nineteenth century. It was a sentiment that did not leave McIlvaine un-phased. In spite of his otherwise benevolent nature, and in spite of the principled theological opposition he mounted against Rome, it appears there was in him a veiled—and probably unconscious—anti-Catholic bigotry.

There is every reason to believe that the well-traveled Ohio bishop enjoyed his visit to Rome, his "anti-Romanism" notwithstanding. Indeed, he took special pleasure in being not only present but clerically active in the city that symbolized to him so much that was anathema to the Christian faith as he understood it. In a highlight of his visit, he took the opportunity to preach, made possible by a resident artist who opened and prepared his salon for the occasion. "I knew it would not task me," he wrote to Mrs. McIlvaine, "and could not deny myself the exceeding pleasure of preaching the Gospel in the city in which Paul preached, and where reigns 'the man of sin.'" There, in the Pope's city, he delivered before a roomful of sixty worshippers an extempore message on the text, "If any man thirst." He warmed to the occasion; his soul "stirred within." "I preached the Gospel just as plainly, and simply, and earnestly as I knew how." The event, complete with singing and administration of communion, pleased the bishop very much. "It was a devout congregation," he recalled, "and I shall always remember with thankfulness and great pleasure that opportunity of preaching Christ in Rome." [47]

A visit to the Colosseum was on McIlvaine's itinerary as well, along with a tour of the Mamertine Prison. "It was a soul-thrilling thought," he said of the Colosseum, "that we stood on the very arena where, for 400 years, gladiators had fought, and where Ignatius died for Christ in the mouth of the lions, and hundreds of our dear brethren in Christ, now in glory, had been steadfast unto death." It was, he imagined, among the shades of these martyrs that he "walked, and thought, and prayed, and praised." The party moved next to the Mamertine Prison, where Roman Catholic tradition held that Peter and Paul had been imprisoned. McIlvaine disbelieved the claim in regard to Peter but was inclined to think that Paul had been indeed imprisoned and martyred at the site. Two "ecclesiastics" with torches led the visitors through the apertures, arches and chambers of the massive ruin. "We were eight Protestants," McIlvaine said, "and all, I trust, Christians." As they made their way, he sang "Come, Holy Spirit" and prayed aloud. [48]

Thereafter followed a visit to the Vatican, where McIlvaine made his comments, quoted earlier, regarding the inscriptions on tomb and catacomb fragments. He observed that the inscriptions invariably ended with the words, "in pace,"—*in peace*—or sometimes "felicissima in pace," with a symbol of Christ at the top and the words "in pace" at the bottom. These, he said, proved the faith of the early Christians was uncorrupted. Their testimony, he said, told in particular against Roman Catholic teaching on purgatory, and this in two ways: first, because none of them mentioned purgatory as an article of belief, and second, because, if they had mentioned it, they would not have written "in pace." "He who believes he goes to Purgatory to real pains, when he dies," McIlvaine said, "cannot die 'in pace.'" (According to Roman teaching, purgatory is the place of punishment where those who have died in the grace of God expiate their sins before being admitted to heaven.) Consequently, he said, the walls of the Vatican were covered for a hundred yards with "evidences against it own thunders." [49]

In these words, McIlvaine expressed no novelty in regard to his anti-Roman attitudes, for these had long been a staple of his sense of things. Nearly three decades earlier, he had spoken equally severely of the Roman church while taking a side trip to France, during a visit to England. A stay in Paris had given him a chance to observe the "shocking reality" of a Sunday "in Popish countries," and thus the impetus to sound a bit of thunder of his own. "There was the market," he observed, peering from his window, "as much studded with vegetables and crowded with business and surrounded with noise as usual." Strolling after breakfast, he found the situation no more agreeable. "My spirit seemed loaded with the daring atheism of this people," he said. "I never had such an impression of a state of general rebellion against God." With the exception that "pleasures are multiplied," he said that no one would notice any difference between the treatment of a Sunday and that of any other day. Even the ordinary labors of the people were found to be unrestrained. He saw masons at work on the walls, women binding shoes, tailors at their benches, tradesmen at their counters. It was, he said, as if Sunday "had been as literally blotted out of the memory of man, as the commandment to sanctify it has been perverted in the creeds of...Pagan Romanists." Even the worship that he chanced to witness he viewed as "nothing better than baptized heathenism." To this scene, he contrasted the "sweet Sabbath" of his own country. "Oh, how great the privileges, the mercies, the happiness, the responsibility of those, who dwell in our own Protestant country!" [50]

To retain the privileges and mercies and "sweet Sabbath" of the land and the church of his birth, McIlvaine did everything in his ability to blunt the increase of Roman Catholic power and influence. He did equally as much to halt the spread of Tractarianism. In the latter movement, he saw less of a "via media" than a "via appia." [51] Thus he labored to sound the alarm. Though his efforts were from time to time tinged with unconscious bigotry, he demonstrated the intellectual acumen required to make a clear and compelling case for the Reformation roots of the several Protestant churches, his own among them. His *Oxford Divinity Compared*, in particular, published simultaneously in New York and London in 1841, was an overwhelming success. Anglican and Episcopal Evangelicals alike embraced the book as the definitive refutation of Newman and the Oxford Movement, and the ensuing chorus of praise included encomia by noted Episcopal churchman and lawyer William Jay and Evangelical cleric and leader James Milnor, both of the diocese of New York. Jay, for his part, expressed "entire concurrence" with the book's views, while Milnor extolled its "interesting and elaborate examination" of Oxford principles and hoped for its wide circulation. [52] Periodicals in both America and Britain commended it as well. According to Charlotte Elizabeth, firebrand editor of London's *Christian Lady's Magazine*, "The Bishop has anatomized this [Tractarian] system as no other man has yet done....It [is] one of the most delightful, as well as most valuable, books we ever opened. God has not forsaken his Church." [53] McIlvaine, she added, had "more than realized the highest opinion that we could form of him by a work, the value of which it is impossible to calculate, unless we can compute the worth of Christianity itself." [54] Additional hyperbole—"the best book that had appeared since the Reformation"—came from missionary bishop and McIlvaine friend Daniel Wilson, half-a-world away in Calcutta. [55] The tome was indeed an Evangelical tour de force. Nor was its influence short-lived. It was republished twenty years later in a revised edition entitled *Righteousness by Faith* and went through several American and British editions in the 1860s.[56]

McIlvaine's labor on *Oxford Divinity Compared* not only made the definitive Episcopal case against the Oxford movement, it prepared him for the refutation of yet another foe. Unlike its predecessor, the new enemy would not draw on the mystic charm of the Middle Ages or the neo-Thomism of the Roman Catholics, but rather on the tenets of skepticism and deism left over from the Enlightenment and on the latest philosophical theories emanating from the academies of Germany and Britain. To this battle we now turn.

1. Sydney E. Ahlstrom, *A Religious History of the American People*, 559, 561, 559.
2. Ibid., 561, 563.
3. Ibid., 559, 563, 560.
4. Quoted in Butler, *Standing Against the Whirlwind*, 95.
5. Frank M. Turner, *John Henry Newman: The Challenge to Evangelical Religion* (Yale University Press, New Haven and London, 2002), 195.
6. Charles P. McIlvaine, *Oxford Divinity, Compared with that of the Romish and Anglican Churches; with a Special View of the Doctrine of Justification by Faith* (R. B. Seeley and W. Burnside, London, 1841), 2.
7. Quoted in Ahlstrom, 627.
8. McIlvaine, 3.
9. E. Brooks Holifield, *Theology in America: Christian Thought from the Age of the Puritans to the Civil War* (Yale University Press, New Haven & London, 2003), 238.
10. Ahlstrom, 627.
11. Ibid., 628.
12. David Hein and Gardiner H. Shattuck Jr., *The Episcopalians*, 231, 232.
13. Quoted in Butler, 115.
14. Charles King, "A Review of the Trial of the Rt. Rev. Benjamin T. Onderdonk, D. D., by Charles King, editor of the New York American" (Stanford and Swords, New York, 1845), 4.
15. Spectator, pseud., "Bishop Onderdonk's Trial. The Verdict Sustained at the Bar of Public Opinion; With Remarks on Laicus and Bishop Doane" (John F. Trow and Company, New York, 1845), 8.
16. Ahlstrom, 628.
17. Quoted in John Jay, "Facts Connected with the Presentment of Bishop Onderdonk; A Reply to Parts of the Bishop's Statement" (Stanford and Swords, New York, and George S. Appleton, Philadelphia, 1845), 3.

18. Spectator, 14, 8.

19. King, 4.

20. Anna Pierrepont to Charles P. McIlvaine, January 1845 (Kenyon Archives), no. 45-01-24.

21. Butler, 116.

22. Quoted in *Dictionary of American Biography*, vol. VII, ed. Dumas Malone (Charles Scribner's Sons, New York, 1934,), 39.

23. Butler, 133.

24. Peter Toon, *Evangelical Theology, 1833-1856: A Response to Tractarianism* (John Knox Press, Atlanta, Georgia, 1979), 15.

25. Quoted in McIlvaine, 52.

26. McIlvaine, 56.

27. Charles P. McIlvaine, *Justification by Faith: A Charge Delivered Before the Clergy of the Protestant Episcopal Church in the Diocese of Ohio, Sept. 13, 1839* (Columbus, Ohio, 1840).

28. Toon, 152-153.

29. Ibid., page 160.

30. McIlvaine, *Oxford Divinity Compared*, 59, 62, 57.

31. Ibid, 16.

32. Ibid., 87-88, 89.

33. Ibid., 18, 19, 26.

34. Ibid., 114 (McIlvaine cited *Enfield's History of Philosophy*, 8 vols., 502).

35. Ibid., 114, 115, 116.

36. Ibid., 116, 119, 135.

37. Ibid., 134.

38. Quoted in Marvin R. O'Connell, *The Oxford Conspirators: A History of the Oxford Movement 1833-45* (the MacMillan Company, London, 1969), 274.

39. Isaac Williams, *No. 80*, "On Reserve in Communicating Religious Knowledge," *Tracts for the Times by Members of the University of Oxford*, Vol. IV for 1836-7 (New Edition, J. G. & F. Rivington, London, 1839), 21.

40. Quoted in Steer, *Guarding the Holy Fire*, 164.

41. Quoted in Holifield, 250.

42. McIlvaine, *Oxford Divinity Compared*, 225, 394.

43. Ibid., 50, 51.

44. Ibid., 104.

45. Ibid., 16, 17.

46. Quoted in Carus, 180.

47. Ibid., 179.

48. Ibid., 180.

49. Ibid., 180-181.

50. Ibid., 51.

51. McIlvaine, 105.

52. Quoted in Butler, 107.

53. Ibid., 108.

54. Toon, page 34.

55. Butler, 108.

56. Ibid., note 75, 131.

CHAPTER SEVEN

Refuting the Rationalists

Can one prove the truth of the Christian faith? It would seem to many to be a futile exercise, given Immanuel Kant's influential critique of the traditional ontological, cosmological and teleological proofs of God's existence, as well as subsequent developments in philosophy. Yet it was not so for Charles Pettit McIlvaine. To be sure, he was never one to believe that faith in the sense of an assured personal trust in God could come to anyone by means other than God's grace. For this reason alone, the speculations of the philosophers posed little difficulty for him. Yet he did believe—putting faith as personal trust aside for the moment—that one could make a compelling case for the truth of Christian doctrine by using the methods of secular scholarship as he had learned them at Princeton Seminary. In his *Evidences of Christianity*, [1] published in 1832 and based on lectures from his academic work at West Point and the University of the City of New York, and in his *Rationalism*, [2] published in 1865 as a letter to clergy and candidates for holy orders, he made just such a case. The latter work, composed to thwart the rising influence of the Rationalist or Broad Church movement within the Episcopal Church, addressed head-on those Christian thinkers and writers who were prepared once and for all to put behind them the traditionalist, evidentiary, and Baconian approach to understanding Scripture and Christian faith.

McIlvaine's *Rationalism,* an early defense of traditional views in response to the emergence of Broad Church teachings, took aim at the ideas circulated most widely in a volume entitled *Essays and Reviews.* This book had been published in 1860 under the names of seven English churchmen of the Broad Church persuasion, all but one of whom held high office. In his rebuttal of their views, McIlvaine showed himself to be—despite advancing age—as adroit, consistent, and combative as ever. His rebuttal showed yet again that he was both objective and subjective in his thinking: objective, because he could marshal facts and ideas in logical sequences for maximum effect, and subjective, because he was moved at deep, existential levels by the need for intellectual certainty.

The emergence of Rationalism in the Episcopal Church, reported as early as 1856 by High Church clergyman John Henry Hopkins Jr. in his periodical, *The Church Journal,* drew fire from High Churchmen, Anglo-Catholics and Evangelicals alike. "A new war is at hand in the Church," Hopkins warned. "The battle, which a few years ago raged about the outer walls of ecclesiastical principles, is now beginning to be fought inside of those walls." The aging Jackson Kemper, High Churchman and first missionary bishop of the Northwest, sounded the alarm as well, warning his diocese of those who called themselves Christians but expressed "pride and arrogance, inordinate self-conceit and total want of reverence" [3] in their revision of traditional doctrines. Other churchmen joined the chorus, accusing Rationalists of being unitarians and latitudinarians—of rejecting, that is, both the Trinity and the divinity of Christ in favor of God's unipersonality.

In America, McIlvaine led the Evangelical opposition, first writing of the controversy to a group of English clergy in 1861, the year after the publication of *Essays and Reviews.* In that letter, he lamented "the alarming boldness and progress of the Rationalistic Anti-Christ in England" and expressed fear it would arrive in America in due course. "The plague will come to us if not cured by you," he warned. Just as Oxford divinity had made its way rapidly to American shores, so too would this new form "of disregard of the Scriptures." He doubted the ability of the English church to discipline those who were propagating the new doctrines. "One cannot read such productions as those of the seven essayists without asking, Is there no barrier against such evils?" [4] Yet within a decade the English church *would* discipline the essayists, although the action taken proved to be little more than a stopgap against a trend that soon proved irresistible.

Essays and Reviews had been planned and promoted by Henry Briston Wilson, fellow of St. John's College, Oxford, who had delivered the prestigious Bampton Lecture at Oxford nine years earlier. The contributors to the volume, however, wrote independently of one another. The purpose of the work, the preface said, was to illustrate the advantage to the cause of moral and religious truth of a "free handling...of subjects peculiarly liable to suffer...from traditional methods of treatment." [5] The collection, a milestone in the ascendance of theological liberalism in England, drew a storm of protest from many who were indeed content with the "traditional methods of treatment," McIlvaine among them.

In Frederick Temple's opening salvo, "The Education of the World," the author followed the philosopher and ironist, Gotthold Lessing, in maintaining there were three stages in the development of the human race, corresponding to childhood, youth and maturity. These stages, he held, were characterized respectively by rules (the Law), example (the Son of Man), and principle (the Spirit). According to Temple (who would become Archbishop of Canterbury in 1896), the third stage was at hand, with its demand that Scripture be subject to the minds of *men*, not *children*. Predictably, as Temple surveyed the past from the height of a "third-stage" consciousness, ambiguity entered his under-standing of the historicity of biblical miracles and the authority of Scripture. Moreover, the notion of progress in human history, redolent of the theory of evolution as the all-encompassing key to explaining diverse phenomena, both spiritual and material, was evident as well.

Yet more daring was Rowland William's piece on "Bunsen's Biblical Research," inspired by the work of Christian Von Bunsen, German diplomat and amateur theologian. Williams, vice-principal and professor of Hebrew at St. David's College, Lampeter, and formerly a tutor at Cambridge, adopted in the main the results of the higher criticism—as it was called—of the Pentateuch, emanating from Germany, which claimed the first five books of the Bible consisted of a much revised collection of myth, legend and history and were the work of more than one author. Williams maintained also that the book of Isaiah, chapters forty-one to sixty-six, was not the work of the prophet himself but of a later author; that the book of Jonah contained "late legend founded on misconception;" [6] that the book of Daniel was written in the second century B. C., not in the period in which it was purportedly set; that the Letter to the Hebrews was not written by St. Paul, and that the Second Letter of Peter was inauthentic. Williams' essay was indeed a provocation to an Evangelical like McIlvaine.

Other contributions to *Essays and Reviews* only added to the growing tempest, touching as they did on a handful of contentious points between conservative and liberal thinkers. In the sixth essay, Mark Pattison, tutor at Lincoln College, Oxford, prolific writer and noted scholar, who had declared that "the capital of learning is in the hands of Germans," [7] criticized the esteemed apologists Joseph ("Bishop") Butler and William Paley, and urged the revision of religious beliefs to conform to the findings of recent scientific researches. In the seventh essay, Benjamin Jowett, a classicist unrivalled in his field and Master of Balliol College, Oxford, contended that the Bible should be interpreted like any other book, an idea that suggested it might in fact *be* like any other book. The Bible, he wrote, was not inerrant with respect to historical and scientific facts, nor should it determine one's conception of divine inspiration.

Enough was enough. Low and High Churchmen alike united against the common foe. Frequently in opposition to one another, these factions were as one in finding "no good thing" in the provocations of *Essays and Reviews.* The book's bias in favor of evolutionism, as well as its plea for liberalizing the doctrine and discipline of the Church of England and abolishing the Thirty-nine Articles, roused the ire of traditionalists of every stripe. In addition, its outspoken and uncritical acceptance of scientific "fact"—as understood at the time—in preference to the "dark patches of human passion and error which form a partial crust" upon the Bible (the words are Henry Briston Wilson's), increased the consternation of all. In 1864, a synod of the clergy of the Church of England condemned the book following a lengthy trial.

McIlvaine was adamant in his opposition. In his 1865 letter on *Rationalism,* he attacked *Essays and Reviews* at a number of points, basing his critique on evidentiary apologetics, a Common Sense reading of Scripture, and Anglican formularies. He observed near the outset of his work that the *Essays* denied the traditional doctrine of divine inspiration of the Scriptures, an accusation most serious in the eyes of Evangelicals, who held to the verbal inspiration of the Bible. ("Inspiration" in the sense of *theopneustos,* Greek for "God-breathed." Verbal inspiration, as such, teaches that the very *words* of Scripture are divinely inspired.) "We do not mean that inspiration in some sense is not granted," McIlvaine explained. "We mean inspiration in the only sense worth speaking of, implying a supernatural gift of God....*That* is denied." Citing passages from the *Essays,* he said they argued against "the higher or supernatural views of Inspiration," thus denying any foundation for "any inward gift" of inspiration among the apostles or the evangelists in either the Gospels or the Epistles. The *Essays* dismissed as well, he asserted, the traditional understanding of inspiration in regard to the Old Testament. This, he charged, they had done in the face of St. Paul's remark to Timothy that *all* Scripture was "given by Inspiration of God." [8]

A further deficiency of the *Essays,* McIlvaine claimed, was that "All revelation [in addition to inspiration], in any proper or important sense," was denied. The offending authors, he asserted, held that no testimony "can reach to the supernatural;" that the belief that anything due to supernatural causes was entirely dependent on the power of faith, not reason. Thus, revelation—that is, a *"supernatural* communication" of truth—was dismissed a priori. Moreover, they insisted—on grounds of critical and inductive study of the natural world—that miracles, predictive prophecy, and other alleged interruptions of the natural order were inconceivable. Accordingly, there could be no evidence of a deity who worked miracles, or of a revelation that affirmed them convincingly. Yet such claims, McIlvaine countered, were in clear contradiction to the words of St. Peter, who wrote that "holy men of God spake as they were moved by the Holy Ghost" to communicate God's revealed truth. "With the denial of miracles," McIlvaine warned, "goes of course the denial of those two great...miracles of Christianity, the Incarnation of the Son of God and His Resurrection. And with His Resurrection goes the whole Gospel of our salvation." [9] Thus, the approach to religion found in the *Essays* would eliminate, directly or indirectly, the core substance of belief.

McIlvaine directed his attention next to claims that the dictates of every man's "natural light" had authority over the Scriptures, "to modify or reject their testimony." It was, he observed, held by William Temple to be praiseworthy of the Bible that it was hindered "from exercising a despotism over the human spirit." If the Bible demanded such authority, Temple had argued, "it would become an outer law at once," something he pronounced it not to be, inasmuch as it "imposes on us no yoke of subjection." McIlvaine could not have disagreed more. It was plain, he replied, that the *Essays*, by such teachings, laid open the way for every person "to enter upon the whole field of Scripture truth...and [to] modify, reject, or transform what is contained therein, from all natural meaning, into a mere mythical ideality." That approach he considered "but another name for rejection." To oppose it, he claimed that the covenant of grace and salvation was in fact knowable to human beings by no other means *than* by the

Scriptures, "declared unto us by the Holy Ghost." [10] Indeed, he wrote, every doctrine of the Christian faith—the divinity of Christ, the atonement, justification by faith, the personality and office of the Holy Ghost, sanctification, eternal life—have no basis in truth apart from a supernatural revelation, a revelation denied in the *Essays*.

McIlvaine then fired a broadside at the self-identity of the movement. "Its own chosen name is *Rationalism*," he said. "Its more honest name is *Infidelity*." He made the assertion in spite of Rationalism's profession of reverence for the Scriptures and Christianity in general. He viewed this as mere window dressing. Behind the "frequent use of language intended to disguise what it is more convenient to insinuate than to avow," there was—he charged—"nothing that is distinctive of Christianity." Neither in its substance, nor in its authority, nor in its necessary results, did the movement fail to subject the faith "to a most ruinous uncertainty." [11] As we have seen, certainty in theology was among McIlvaine's primary concerns. He knew that a speculative, ever-questioning, ever-evolving theology would never provide a sure foundation for a person such as himself, nor, he suspected, anyone else.

McIlvaine also insisted there was little that was new in the doctrine of the *Essays*, either as an expression of unbelief or in support of such an expression. He found its pedigree in the latter part of the seventeenth and the beginning of the eighteenth centuries. "It has," he wrote, "so much in common with the infidelity of what are known as 'the Deistical Writers' of England…that its every prominent feature is to be found…in the works of those men." Owing to the responses of learned divines, he said, those writers of a past age, "whose movement was thought, in their time, to be at least as alarming as that which we now witness," were driven from the field. But, he said, there *was* in fact something new in the *Essays*, namely, that their authors were, with a single exception, clergy of the Church of England, and one of them a bishop. Therefore, they were solemnly pledged to the formularies of the church. "One of them has since died;" McIlvaine noted, "the rest, instead of retiring from positions and duties for which they have made themselves so disqualified, continue...taking advantage of their ecclesiastical dignities, to give the more weight and currency to their evil words, and claiming, moreover, the right so to do." [12] Thus, the theme of betrayal, which had appeared in the critique of the Tractarians, appeared once again. This time, the accusation was—if possible—even more deeply felt. To object to major teachings of the church, to which one had pledged one's loyalty, was to McIlvaine tantamount to apostasy. To the mind and conscience of a man who seldom minced words, it was the height of imposture, and he let his views be known in the strongest of terms.

McIlvaine concluded with several pages in defense of the classic Anglican doctrine of Scripture. He mostly based his argument on the formularies of the Church of England, alongside the reformed tradition of early Anglican luminaries such as Richard Hooker and John Jewell. He noted yet again that the authors of the *Essays* reduced the traditional notion of divine inspiration of the Bible to something of a lesser strain. The Rationalists, he said, spoke of an "inspiration" shared not only by Scriptural figures such as Daniel and Malachi, Matthew and Paul, but by Homer and Milton and other extra-biblical figures as well, an inspiration neither infallible nor supernatural. Such an approach to inspiration was far from the one McIlvaine had in mind. By way of buttressing his view, he observed that the Ninth Article of the Thirty-nine Articles asserted indirectly the infallibility of Scripture as traditionally understood by the Church of England. The article, he noted, did so by affirming the Apostles' and Nicene Creeds because their truth could be proved "by certain warrants of Holy Scripture." They could, that is, be granted their high doctrinal status owing only to their root in Scripture, the final arbiter of sacred truth. "This was equivalent," he said, "to a declaration of *infallibility* as pertaining to the Scriptures, and consequently of the highest

Inspiration of God." By contrast, he claimed, the *Essays* undercut or even demolished such certainty. He pursued the point not only to win a theological argument but out of concern for the faithful, himself included, whose hope and comfort was in no small part dependent on holding to the Scriptures as inspired and infallible. "Of what value," he asked, "is the hope founded on the comfort of the Scriptures, when you have taken from them the authority of a pervading divine inspiration and reduced them to the level of human authority and wisdom?" [13]

In the conclusion to his letter, McIlvaine made use of a warning sounded by St. Paul in regard to the coming unbelief prophesied during the Apostolic Age itself. "The time will come," the Apostle had written, "when men will not endure sound doctrine...and they shall turn away their ears from the truth, and [it] shall be turned into fables." To counter such a development, St. Paul had urged vigorous preaching of the word of God, alongside the increased necessity of dwelling "in the things which thou hast learned and hast been assured of." McIlvaine urged opponents of the Broad Churchmen to do likewise. They were bidden to wield that "great weapon of his warfare," a weapon established for the defense and spread of the Gospel, none other than the "sword of the Spirit which is the Word of God." That word, he said, was "written for our learning to the end of the world, by which it has pleased God in all generations to shine into the hearts of lost men." [14]

In sum, in the letter of 1865, McIlvaine showed once again his ability to confront the foes of Protestant orthodoxy and Anglican tradition with "sound doctrine," in a work at once scholarly, reasoned and spirited. He showed also his penchant for theological controversy. His combination of keen intellect, extensive learning, and felt need to expound and defend a consistent and coherent orthodoxy motivated him still. In *Rationalism*, he acquitted himself ably in the eyes of those who shared his beliefs. In the eyes of his opponents, he showed himself a formidable foe. The work was indeed a solid piece of polemic, the very thing for which he had always shown talent and zeal. He had not lost his touch.

McIlvaine's critique of Rationalism grew out of the beliefs on which he based his life. The arguments he marshaled against it were the product of a lifetime of study, prayer and reflection. They undergirded the entire edifice of his Christian conviction, and were useful in opposing not only the Rationalists of the 1850s and '60s but "infidels" of any age.

The philosophical basis of McIlvaine's belief was to be found, as remarked earlier, in the Common Sense realism he had imbibed at Princeton College and Seminary. That product of the Scottish Enlightenment had been employed historically to oppose the subjectivist epistemology of Immanuel Kant, stating in opposition to Kant that truth, in the words of one historian, "was objective and available to any sincere human being of sound 'common sense.'" [15] Although Scottish realism contained an element of intuitionism, there was strong emphasis also on facts and evidence. By the use of induction, Common Sense thinkers sought to formulate general laws or principles based on facts, whether found in nature or in Scripture. To properly weigh and order those facts, a psychology of humility was cultivated. Ashbel Green, president of Princeton College and professor at Princeton Seminary when McIlvaine was a student there, cautioned especially against flagrant theorizing. Such restraint, he believed, was useful to curb what evangelicals considered the pride and impiety of non-believing philosophers.

The Common Sense view had been used in one form or another by generations of Anglican thinkers, Evangelical and High Church, to battle deists and other foes of orthodox belief. It had enabled them to reclaim natural theology—the knowledge of God obtained by human reason alone—even as they reaffirmed the centrality of Scripture and church tradition. William White, bishop of Pennsylvania, who early in the nineteenth century had put together the reading list for Episcopalian seminarians, McIlvaine among them, recommended the apologetics of such as William Paley, Bishop Butler, Edward Stillingfleet and Charles Leslie, masters all of the art of evidentialist reasoning. These and other divines argued for the veracity of the Christian religion on grounds of miracles (miracles as space-and-time *events* witnessed by human eyes), fulfilled prophecy, and inner consistency. Leonidas Polk, first bishop of Louisiana and a student of McIlvaine's at West Point, testified that his first serious understanding of Christian doctrine came through the reading of treatises on such evidences. Moreover, evidentialism underpinned the lectures and published treatises of prominent clergy throughout the ante-bellum era. [16]

The Baconian insistence on the discovery and use of "facts" (after Francis Bacon, English pioneer of empirical method) was a vital aspect of these treatises. Yet in the eyes of many post-Kantians, use of this approach in regard to theology was dismissed as illegitimate or outmoded, and seen as little more than a means by which persons inwardly unsettled by modernity were attempting to assure themselves of having objective reasons for their convictions. According to historian Karen Armstrong, the "lust for certainty" on the part of such persons "was an attempt to fill the void that lurked at the heart of the modern experience, the God-shaped hole in the consciousness of wholly rational human beings." [17] Doubtless, many sensitive and troubled souls did attempt to assuage their inner anxieties by latching onto a method promising certainty to the beliefs they held. McIlvaine may be viewed—in part—as such a person, as a rational but secretly unsettled thinker intent on filling the "God-shaped hole" in his consciousness with a certitude based on Baconian empiricism and Evangelical dogma.

Armstrong quotes from an apologetic work, *Many Infallible Proofs*, written by the American, Arthur Pierson, to illustrate the type of argument that was popular among evidentialist thinkers. Though published in 1895, the work expressed views related closely to McIlvaine's of a generation or two earlier. "I like Biblical theology," Pierson wrote, "that...does not begin with an hypothesis and then wraps the facts and the philosophy to fit the crook of our dogma, but a Baconian system, which first gathers the teachings of the word of God, and then seeks to deduce some general law upon which the facts can be arranged." [18] Though Pierson's approved method had been passé for some decades according to the mind of progressive philosophy, it had retained its devotees. Philosophical trends notwithstanding, he and others employed it as a tough-minded counter to the latest attacks on orthodoxy.

For his part, McIlvaine used evidentialism with skill and vigor, against not only Broad Church liberals but against other trends and personalities in the philosophical and religious world of his day. His lengthiest employment of the method was in the aforementioned *The Evidences of Christianity*, an apologetic based on a course of lectures he presented at West Point and the University of the City of New York. The latter course was delivered in 1831-32 to an auditory consisting largely of members of the New York Young Men's Society for Intellectual and Moral Improvement. Pleased with the warm reception it received, the university published it in book form in 1832. Several more editions followed, in both America and England. [19] *Evidences of Christianity* drew praise from McIlvaine's old Princeton professor, Archibald Alexander, and from the English divine, Olynthus Gregory, who prepared it for publication in England. The book presented to the Christian public, both lay and clerical, and to the occasional straddler who might chance upon it or seek it out, the evidentialist case for Christianity in words both forceful and eloquent. It did not, nor was it probably intended to, threaten the bastions of post-Kantian philosophy in any serious way. McIlvaine was not a formal philosopher, nor was his work likely to capture the attention of contemporary idealist or materialist thinkers. Still, as it was written early in his career, it entered an Anglo-American milieu in which

Common Sense reasoning remained a force to be reckoned with. To those persons still amenable to it, the *Evidences* carried the weight of conviction.

McIlvaine's book, in keeping to his standard approach, followed most closely the method of William Paley, the eighteenth century apologist whose pellucid work of nearly the same title *(View of the Evidences of Christianity)* was published in 1794. Along with Bishop Butler and others, Paley had taught that natural law always harmonized with special revelation. Consequently, since God was held to be author of all that existed, natural science was held to support Scripture by providing irrefutable evidence of design. This was, therefore, according to historian George Marsden, a two-tiered view, founded on an empiricist epistemology, "with the laws of nature below, supporting supernatural belief above." [20]

McIlvaine's book, for its part, opposed in trenchant fashion a number of the trends he considered dangerous and wrongheaded. For example, he defended the veracity of biblical miracles as well as the truth of prophecy, the authenticity of the New Testament, the necessity for Christians to bring forth "fruits" of the faith, the means to be used in propagating the faith, and the divine inspiration of Scripture. He put forward a detailed apologetic for each of these topics, criticizing as he did so what he saw to be the faulty understandings and unbalanced personalities of an assortment of notable skeptics.

There were plenty of targets for his criticism. Owing to the intellectual freedom of the United States and Britain, opinions in religion and philosophy were openly and loudly voiced. McIlvaine said he rejoiced to live in such an age. But, what was called the "spirit of freedom," he said, was not everywhere identical to the cause of truth and right. "There is a spirit abroad," he said, "which, under the name of freedom of opinion, would…denounce…whatever principles of moral evidence are at variance with itself. This is licentiousness; not freedom." There was in Christianity, he conceded, a great deal to offend the natural dispositions of the human race, philosophers included. It was no wonder, therefore, that reasoning persons, who were free to think and speak as they wished, so frequently reasoned against it. For the everyman of every age, he said, was proud, yet the Gospel demanded humility; he was vengeful, yet the Gospel demanded forgiveness. "Man is prone," he said, "to set his affections on things on the earth; the gospel requires him to set them on those which are above." The natural man, he continued, "is wedded to self-indulgence, glories in being his own master, idolizes himself, encourages self-dependence, boasts his own goodness, lives without God in the world." By contrast, the Gospel required that a man "deny himself, renounce all right over himself, give up his will to that of God, live for the Lord Jesus, and lean upon and glory in him alone as all his strength, hope, and righteousness." [21] In this unsparing view, it was clear the "natural heart" and the precepts of the Christian faith were directly at variance with one another. Hence, McIlvaine said, the natural man would always and everywhere search out reasons to reject it. Thus, he would paddle happily in the "Rationalistic flood."

In McIlvaine's view, nominal Christians of the nineteenth century were ill-equipped—and in most cases ill-inclined—to counter the views of Rationalists and others who would sweep away the beliefs of centuries. They were unable, therefore, to withstand the assaults of the "infidels," based as they were on modes of thought congenial not only to the man-in-the-street but to the average churchgoer as well. The deluge of naturalism and skepticism, McIlvaine claimed, easily washed "the minds of thinking men into its current, because so many have no anchorage in clearly defined…views of what *religion* is—what the Gospel is. They have nothing to *hold* them fast." Yet there was a secure point, he said, from which they could—if they would— oppose the swells and surges of philosophical speculation. That point of security, he said, was "the cross, on the elect, precious foundation-stone." [22] That alone, he said; that Archimedean point of Christian faith, would provide them all they needed, if they but knew enough to hold fast to it. Upon that foundation they would find, he believed, a religion explained and defended according to secure principles and doctrines.

Elsewhere in the *Evidences* McIlvaine contrasted the life of the skeptic and the life of the minister of the Gospel, the latter of whom, he said, strove for holiness, purity, and acts of benevolence. He admitted some clergymen were unworthy of their office, yet considered substandard specimens to be the exception to the rule. By contrast, he said, the "infidel"—the person bereft of Christian faith—*even at his best* fell far short of the virtues of piety. He did not deny there were non-Christians who led "what passes for a good moral life;" whom public opinion, social custom, respected occupations and prosperous circumstances had preserved "from the slavery of low propensities and criminal deeds." But, he asked, "what is there in such virtue, beyond a fair outside? Is it formed upon any foundation more meritorious than that of reputation, interest, and the expectation of society?" Thus, to McIlvaine, the skeptic was good, or tolerably good, largely by force of circumstance, by *accident*, as it were, whereas the Christian of sincere faith was good by conviction, by token of his or her choice of life, grounded as it was in the grace of God and the foundations of true religion. Non-believers, he held, though given in some measure to sound morals, did so contrary to the implications of their infidelity, and contrary to the character and influence of those with whom they frequently associated. "It is a general rule," he suggested, "that when you say of a man 'he is an infidel,' it is to say that he is not a moral man; not a benevolent man; not a person to engage in any self-denying labours for the purpose of doing good." [23]

In proceeding to name names, McIlvaine attacked *ad hominem* a number of well known figures of skeptical if not outright anti-Christian views, citing them as examples of the diminished life that was characteristic, he alleged, of the type. As "champions of infidelity" he named prominent deists, debunkers, and philosophers, among them Rousseau and Voltaire in France, Thomas Paine in America, and David Hume, Henry Bolingbroke and Matthew Tindal in Britain. He was especially bold in attacking Hume, the Scottish philosopher and historian, notable for his argument against miracles. To some, McIlvaine no doubt appeared to be a petulant pietist in comparison with Hume the urbane scholar; a shrimp nibbling at a whale. But McIlvaine was no shrimp. His combination of Evangelical theology and Common Sense realism, though not at the center of philosophical fashion, provided nonetheless a mooring from which to launch a vigorous assault. Among other things, McIlvaine charged Hume with holding to a contrarian morality which proposed that self denial, self-mortification and humility were "not virtuous, but useless and mischievous;" that pride and self-valuation, ingenuity, eloquence and strength of body *were* virtuous; that suicide was lawful and commendable; that adultery "must be practiced, if we would obtain all the advantages of life;" that female infidelity, when known, was a small thing, "when unknown, nothing." According to McIlvaine, Hume was a man not only of dubious morals but of dubious intellectual integrity. "Hume pretended to a great diligence in search of truth," he said, "and spent all his powers against the gospel, and yet, says Dr. Johnson, *'confessed that he had never read the New Testament with attention.'*" In censuring the philosopher, McIlvaine mentioned also the demise of the American publisher of Hume's *Essays*. The latter, who had praised Hume "to the skies," showed clearly enough "how he had profited by his favourite volume, at least by the Essay in defense of Suicide—He killed himself by drunkenness." [24]

In Hume's subversive philosophy, McIlvaine charged, little if anything could be proved. It appeared, he said, that the philosopher was a congenital skeptic, so unbalanced in the direction of doubt as to be unreliable in the generality of his views. "He was a poor, blind, groping compound of contradictions," McIlvaine wrote. To bolster this contention, he borrowed the words of a friend and admirer of Hume to describe the philosopher's turn of mind. "An unfortunate disposition to doubt everything,' Lord Charlemont admitted, 'seemed interwoven with the nature of Hume, and never was there, I am convinced, a more thorough and sincere skeptic. He seemed not to be certain even of his own present existence, and could not, therefore, be expected to entertain any settled opinion respecting his future state.'" [25]

Hume was but one of the British "infidels" to attract McIlvaine's ire. There were many others. "What gross hypocrisy and lying," he thundered, "pervade the writings of Herbert, Hobbes, Shaftesbury, Woolston [sic], Tindal, Collins, Blunt [sic], Chubb....[At one moment] they are praising Christianity, exalting Jesus, professing to have the sincerest desire that the gospel may be promoted. At another time, they are scoffing at its essential doctrines; charging its Founder with imposture; and diligently labouring to destroy it." The targets here, Lord Herbert of Cherbury, the earl of Shaftesbury, Thomas Hobbes, Thomas Wollaston, Anthony Collins, Charles Blount, Thomas Chubb, and the aforementioned Matthew Tindal, were associated directly or indirectly with deism, a creed positing belief in a Supreme Being and natural religion but rejecting revealed religion. Unflattering assertions were leveled at other deists as well, among them Henry Bolingbroke the statesman and Edward Gibbon the historian. The former was accused of sensuality and lust for power, the latter, of hypocrisy and impurity. In such manner, McIlvaine attacked both the teaching and the character of these and other thinkers. He saw, in fact, little difference between their teaching and their character. "There is not one among them," he claimed, "who would not prefer his own error to the truth discovered by another...such leaders in infidelity have...almost without exception, cultivated the coldest selfishness." [26] Despite his attack on these men, McIlvaine omitted any mention of the American quasi-deists (and founding fathers), Thomas Jefferson and Benjamin Franklin. He did, however, vent his spleen at a lesser American.

Thomas Paine—radical deist, pamphleteer extraordinaire, author of *Common Sense* and *The Age of Reason*—was excoriated in a lengthy passage of the *Evidences,* where his philosophy and life were linked to the detriment of both. Paine's first wife, McIlvaine noted, was said "to have died by ill usage," while his second "was rendered so miserable by neglect and unkindness, that they separated by mutual agreement." His third, a *companion* and not a wife, "was the victim of his seduction, while he lived upon the hospitality of her husband." There follows a litany of Paine's political involvements in England and America, with comment on their alleged irregularities, petty transgressions and expulsions. At last, lured to France by the excitements of the Revolution, we are informed that Paine resided in the house of the American minister, where his "habits of intoxication" made him a disagreeable guest. "During all this time," McIlvaine wrote, "his life was a compound of ingratitude and perfidy, of hypocrisy and avarice, of lewdness and adultery." He was reduced in the end to "drunken fits," and babbling of the immortality of the soul. [27]

Despite his charitable temper, McIlvaine could muster little sympathy for Paine. And towards others of skeptical or unorthodox views, he was equally unsparing. He looked with sober rectitude towards the judgment he believed awaited them all. "Unhappy man!" he wrote of Paine. "Neither he, nor Rousseau, nor Voltaire, is dead, except in the flesh. Their immortal souls are thinking as actively, at least, as ever. We and they will stand, on the same great day, before the bar of God." [28] Severe self-critic that he was, McIlvaine was equally severe towards those he deemed contemptible, towards those who had, in his eyes, forfeited their spiritual inheritance by dint of pride and rebelliousness.

A fair number of readers may find such criticism distasteful, and unworthy of a churchman. Yet in mitigation, one could observe that to McIlvaine the vital questions of philosophical discourse—especially where they touched on religion—were issues of life and death, blessing and curse. He believed these matters too important to be left in the hands of "infidel" philosophers. He neither accepted their conclusions nor trusted their motives. These learned men, he was convinced, knew in their hearts of the existence of God, despite their clever denials and subtle evasions. They were guilty therefore of betrayal and, by such reasoning, entitled to little sympathy.

If Voltaire was the prince of scoffers, Hume was the prince of skeptics. Hume's role as "original champion" of the principle that no conceivable amount of testimony could prove the truth of a miracle singled him out for close and critical examination. His essay, *On Miracles*, opened with a boast: "I flatter myself, that I have discovered an argument...which, if just, will, with the wise and learned, be an everlasting check to all kinds of superstitious delusion, and consequently, will be useful as long as the world endures." Hume based his argument on three things: the "laws of nature," the uniformity of experience, and the unreliability of human testimony. A miracle, he claimed, would violate both the laws of nature and the uniform experience of those laws. If, for instance, a dead man should come to life, it would be a miracle, but such a miracle, he claimed, had never been observed "in any age or country." Such, he asserted, was the uniform experience of the human race. Hence, "there is here a direct and full *proof*, from the nature of the fact, against the existence of any miracle; nor can such a proof be destroyed, or the miracle rendered credible, but by an opposite proof, which is superior." In consequence, he said, no testimony was able to establish a miracle unless its falsehood was deemed to be more miraculous than that which it was attempting to prove. [29]

Despite the evident logic of the argument, it depended for its affect on brushing aside the possibility of historical evidence for miracles. This, McIlvaine was not prepared to do. He was, however, prepared to match wits with the philosopher. To him, Hume was an "infidel" whose boldness presented an irresistible target. Though McIlvaine may or may not have waded into the minutiae of the philosopher's works, there is every reason to believe he had studied them enough to grasp the essentials of the system. For him, this was enough. According to his friend, Alfred Lee, bishop of Delaware, McIlvaine was particularly skilled at tracing principles to their conclusions. "Various adjuncts and fruits" of a system of thought, Lee said, "were regarded by him not as isolated and immaterial fragments, but in their necessary connection as parts and outgrowths of the whole." [30] In assailing Hume, he put this skill into operation.

Nor did he mince words. To McIlvaine, Hume's assertions about miracles were an "absurdity," an approach to the subject "so mystified with the drugs of false philosophy, so disguised under the dress of logical forms and ceremonies, and so followed…with the influence of one of the chief names in modern skepticism, as to perplex many minds unaccustomed to the entanglements of sophistry." He admitted the popularity of Hume's argument. He asserted, in fact, that it had been early adopted by many less ambitious skeptics as a means of justifying their own unbelief. By such as these, he said, a "labour-saving machine" had been sought to silence at once the inconvenient variety and troublesome multitude of Christian evidences. "Hume invented it," he said. "Anybody can work it." And what was the "machine" he invented? Just this: a verbal device making it unnecessary to study the Bible in order to refute its claims. "He [the aspiring skeptic] may never have seen [the Bible];" McIlvaine said, "but if he can only retain in his memory these few talismanic words, 'No testimony can prove a miracle,' it is enough. At the rubbing of this marvelous lamp, the fabric of Christianity passes away." [31]

From first to last, McIlvaine held that miracles were a proof of divine revelation. To attack miracles, therefore, was to attack revelation, which in turn was to attack the heart of Christian faith and authority. Hume had the temerity to do so, but by means that McIlvaine found refutable. To convince others of the same, he devoted seven pages of his *Evidences* to a carefully reasoned attempt to destroy Hume's case. In regard to miracles, he said, "The argument of Hume, with all its assumptions and false statements, and equivocal expressions...prove[s] not only that miracles cannot be proved by testimony, but that they cannot be proved at all." [32] To the contrary, he believed they *could* be proved, and he set out to do so.

According to McIlvaine, a miracle was an extraordinary event in the physical world, surpassing human or natural powers to explain. In this, if nowhere else, his view was close to Hume's. Such alleged occurrences as walking on water, turning water into wine, multiplying loaves and fishes, healing by word or touch— these were miracles. Owing to their intrinsic improbability, they had been traditionally ascribed to a supernatural cause. That all persons of ordinary intelligence and learning should understand a miracle to be just this, McIlvaine took to be axiomatic. No one, he said, would mistake the restoration of sight to a blind man by a medical procedure—no matter how wonderful and complicated the procedure had been—to be a miracle. The result, though astonishing, would clearly be according to the "laws of nature." By contrast, no one would mistake the restoration of sight to a man born blind by the mere word of another—without any intervening natural cause—to be anything less than a miracle. Such was McIlvaine's view of nature and supernature in regard to the miraculous.

In building his case, McIlvaine sought to establish a rationale for the working of biblical miracles. In doing so, he put forward the following proposition: "There is nothing unreasonable or improbable in the idea of a miracle being wrought in proof of a divine revelation." There was, in other words, nothing inherently unreasonable about a divine being having chosen to intervene supernaturally, by miracles, in the course of history. Indeed, how *but* by miracles, he asked, could God have attested to the revelation that he was purported to have given? Moreover, those who had been charged with communicating that revelation must have needed to prove their mission by some credentials. What better credentials, he asked, could there be but miracles? "Now the idea of a revelation from God," he said, "and the idea of a miracle to attest the divine commission of those who make it, are essentially connected." Thus, miracles were the "seal of God;" [33] miracles attested to the authenticity of the ambassadors sent from God.

McIlvaine put forward a second proposition: "If miracles were wrought in attestation of the mission of Christ and his apostles, they can be rendered credible to us by no other evidence than that of testimony." Here it was a question of the type and validity of evidence generally. In the course of defending the proposition, he set forth the several means of evidence common to the human race: the evidence of the senses; the evidence of mathematical demonstration; the evidence of testimony. Each of these was appropriate to a particular department of subjects. A question of morals, for instance, could not be demonstrated by mathematics, or proved by the senses. Neither could a question of historical fact—be it a fact of natural or supernatural history—be settled by anything but testimony. "It might as well be put to the tests of chymistry," he said, "as to have applied to it either the evidence of mathematical demonstration, or of the senses." As there was a separate department for each of these species of evidence, he said, each was sufficient, in its appropriate sphere, for the complete establishment of truth. "We are," he said, "just as certain that such a man as Napoleon once lived, as that any proposition in geometry is true—though one is a matter of testimony, the other of demonstration." He proceeded to argue that miracles—like the existence of Napoleon—were capable of being proved. "I return to the proposition that if miracles were wrought by Christ and his apostles, they can be rendered credible to us, of the nineteenth century *by no other evidence than that of testimony.* Mathematical evidence is evidently inapplicable to the question. It is a matter of fact belonging to another century, and therefore intangible by sense. Nothing remains but testimony." [34]

Thus there was an obsession among the skeptics, McIlvaine charged, to render testimonial evidence questionable or inadmissible. He set himself to expose and refute this tactic. Hume's argument, he noted, had two major points: that a miracle was a violation of the laws of nature, and that testimony to prove a miracle could not surmount that fact. "Hence the reasoning is," he said, "that a miracle being, in the author's estimation, contrary to experience, [it] opposes and contradicts the very foundation of its evidence, and therefore destroys itself." Now this reasoning, McIlvaine suggested, "is very conclusive, provided we admit its premises." This he would not do, for "The grand hinge of the whole is this, that our belief in testimony is founded on no other principle than OUR EXPERIENCE OF THE VERACITY OF HUMAN TESTIMONY." [35] Upon this principle, expressed in a flurry of capitals, McIlvaine anchored his argument. Hence, the veracity of human witness regarding well-attested events of the past—in this instance, Scripture events—could be shown to have a high probability of truthfulness.

In opposition to this view, he conceded, Hume and his fellow skeptics had pressed their case with sagacity. "The adversaries of the gospel," he admitted, "have had wit enough to see that either the evidence of miracles must be overthrown, or they must surrender the contest." He charged, therefore, that Hume and his followers had laced their arguments with evasions and false premises. They did so, he said, not because of the facts of the case, but because of a desire to evade the facts. "The pains which all skeptics have taken to escape from being shut up to the faith of Christ," he wrote, "adopting every other conceivable method than the one simple…plan of refuting the direct evidences of Christianity, should [prove] that there is a force in those evidences which their enemies dare not encounter face to face." [36]

McIlvaine held that the Christian church, in its earliest phase, witnessed the events recorded in the Scriptures. Indeed, he believed that the church's principal institutions had been founded on those events. "Our New Testament books are its records," he said, "which, like those of any other institution of past ages, have been handed down from generation to generation. The members of the Christian church have died from age to age, but the church, the society, the living keeper of these records, the librarian of the scriptures, has never died." Though Hume and others denied these records, McIlvaine argued, there was no sound scientific or philosophical reason for doing so. To the contrary, he maintained, skepticism itself could be undermined by the common sense collecting, ordering and interpreting of facts, and by the weight of the "solid mass of testimony by which the miracles of the gospel are defended." [37] To this end, he dedicated his intellect and his vigorous, forceful pen.

1. Charles Pettit McIlvaine, *The Evidences of Christianity, in Their External, or Historical, Division: Exhibited in a Course of Lectures* (Smith & English, Philadelphia, 1852).
2. McIlvaine, *Rationalism, As Exhibited in the Writings of Certain Clergymen of the Church of England, A Letter to the Clergy and Candidates for Holy Orders of the Protestant Episcopal Church, in the United States* (C. F. Bradley, Cincinnati, 1865).
3. Quoted in E. Clowes Chorley, *Men and Movements in the American Episcopal Church*, 306.
4. Ibid., 307.
5. Quoted in O. W. Heick, with contributions by J. L. Neve, *History of Protestant Theology*, Volume Two of *A History of Christian Thought*, by J. L. Neve (The Muhlenberg Press, Philadelphia, 1946), 220.
6. Ibid., 221.
7. Quoted in Ieuan Ellis, *Seven Against Christ: A Study of 'Essays and Reviews,'* Volume XXIII of *Studies in the History of Christian Thought*, edited by Heiko A. Oberman (E. J. Brill, Leiden, The Netherlands, 1980), 286.
8. McIlvaine, *Rationalism*, 6, 7.
9. Ibid., 7, 8.

10. Ibid., 9, 10, 12.
11. Ibid., 14.
12. Ibid., 14, 17.
13. Ibid., 22, 24-25.
14. Ibid., 27, 28, 29.
15. Karen Armstrong, *The Battle for God* (Alfred A. Knopf, New York, 2000), 141.
16. E. Brooks Holifield, *Theology in America*, 243.
17. Armstrong, 141.
18. Quoted in Armstrong, 141.
19. Loren Dale Pugh, *McIlvaine*, 70.
20. George M. Marsden, *Understanding Fundamentalism and Evangelicalism* (William B Eerdmans Publishing Company, Grand Rapids, Mich., 1996), 131.
21. McIlvaine, *Evidences*, 29, 34-35.
22. Quoted in William Carus, *Memorials*, 238.
23. McIlvaine, *Evidences*, 331.
24. Quoted in McIlvaine, 333-334, 335.
25. Ibid., 141.
26. McIlvaine, 336, 337.
27. Ibid., 340, 341.
28. Ibid., 341.
29. Quoted in Ernest Campbell Mossner, *The Life of David Hume* (Oxford University Press, 1980), 287-288.
30. Alfred Lee, "In Memorium," 19-20.
31. McIlvaine, *Evidences*, 133, 134.
32. Ibid., 139.
33. Ibid., 128, 129, 130.
34. Ibid., 131, 132.
35. Ibid., 134, 135.
36. Ibid., 128, 144.
37. Ibid., 147, 144.

CHAPTER EIGHT

Social Issues

The involvements of Charles Pettit McIlvaine reached well beyond church politics and theological debate. He was also involved in the social issues of his time, contributing characteristic energy and acumen to matters relating to the Civil War, voluntary societies and the role of women. Most significantly, he served Abraham Lincoln as special envoy to Britain at the start of the Civil War. Owing to the success of that mission, he played a critical role in the subsequent unfolding of the war. He also cut an imposing figure in the drawing rooms of society, both American and British, from the days of his young manhood until his death at the age of seventy-four. His wisdom, rectitude and charm caused him to be sought out by political figures, social reformers and benevolent societies alike.

In all of these matters, he demonstrated the serious intentions and humane views that characterized his work in church affairs. He demonstrated the importance of "meaning it" at all times, in both personal relations and institutional commitments. Though he may have fallen short in pressing the agenda of abolition, as we shall see, he acquitted himself admirably in regard to helping people of color who fell within his personal orbit. Though he expressed an anti-Catholic bias, as we have seen, he showed himself on the side of the angels when it came to doing his duty on behalf of his fellow citizens. He was not motivated by political or social ambitions in the larger public sense, but he was quick to respond, out of Christian charity and a sense of noblesse oblige, to those whom he could assist in personal ways.

The personal touch was evident in his relations with persons of every background and station, whether rich or poor, black or white. He treated others as not only equals but as immortal souls of eminent worth. People of color more than once felt his personal care and concern at moments of crisis. Women, too, experienced his good nature as they served with him as co-laborers in the church. Even the single greatest contribution he made to his country in the secular sphere, his diplomatic mission during the Civil War, reduced itself in the end to his impeccable integrity and personal charm. In the eyes of Abraham Lincoln, such qualities equipped him for this most delicate and important undertaking.

Although the Civil War mission was his greatest single act of public service, McIlvaine's labors extended also to zealous participation in voluntary benevolent societies. These, in turn, were closely connected to his work as a churchman, although they reached in many instances beyond the direct sphere of the church. The principal goals of these societies, to improve morals both personally and socially, were millennial in nature. They were, that is, performed in anticipation of the prophesied thousand-year-reign of Christ on earth prior to his Second Coming, at which time He was expected to gather up his saints and return to heaven. It is not surprising that McIlvaine warmed to these efforts, for his doctrine contained more than a pinch of millennialism. Evangelical benevolent societies aimed at bringing the "kingdom of God" into the world, into the lives and within the reach of citizens of all backgrounds, denominations and attainments. This commitment of the churches, though spurned by the exclusiveness of High Church Episcopalians, was a hallmark of evangelicals in general and of McIlvaine in particular.

"Christians are rapidly learning, while they differ in opinion upon subordinate subjects, to differ in heart upon none," he said in his address of 1826 to the American Tract Society. Such a statement, from a master of theological detail, shows how eager the young clergyman was to set aside secondary doctrinal matters in the interest of reaching people for the kingdom of God. How wonderful it was, he said, to see churchmen of many denominations "and advocates of as many varieties of secondary opinions" joining hands in common purpose, "delighting to forsake the arena of sectarian...controversy, to mingle their minds, and hearts, and labours." [1] He saw Christian unity as promoted by the voluntary societies as a herald of the increase of Christian love in the "latter days." The societies, he and other evangelicals believed, were doing something the visible churches could not do: through charitable cooperation, they embodied the notion of the "invisible church." This notion, of a body of authentic believers as distinguished from the multitude of nominal believers, was vital to the evangelical paradigm and its expression in interdenominational initiatives. Because evangelicals transcended in principle the distinctions between Protestant denominations, they were in practice eager to cooperate with fellow members of the invisible church, regardless of whether they bore the label of Episcopalian, Presbyterian or Methodist. They gladly joined in common works of charity, education and reform.

By the same token, Evangelical Episcopalians and fellow members of the invisible church were impartial, religiously speaking, in regard to the country of which they were citizens. Patriots they were, with the normal quotient of love of country. Nonetheless, they measured their country by the same religious and moral standards as they measured others. They never proclaimed America to be a "chosen" nation, beloved of God in any singular sense. They believed the millennial kingdom would transcend nations, though they assumed that America would share in that kingdom. To the extent the nation welcomed the spread of

Christian faith and virtue, to that extent it would participate in the glorious millennium.

As in other aspects of McIlvaine's life, his interest in benevolent societies extended to Britain. Already a veteran of such societies—Sunday school, Bible, tract, temperance, and others—on this side of the Atlantic, he came to know their counterparts in Britain in 1830, when one of his periodic collapses sent him abroad in search of rest. Though this allowed him escape from his labors as pastor of St. Ann's Church in Brooklyn, he did not lapse into indolence. In the company of his friend and fellow clergyman, James Milnor, he traveled about England for eight months, visiting Charles Simeon and other evangelical leaders, both Anglican and non-Anglican. He addressed seamen's and Sunday school societies and attended the Islington Clerical Conference, an annual meeting of British Evangelical clergy. He met Hannah More, the religious writer and educator of the poor, and attended meetings of the British Anti-Slavery Society, where he met William Wilberforce, the statesman and abolitionist. "This visit laid down a pattern of cooperation between the evangelical societies of the two countries that would remain in place throughout the nineteenth century," observes historian Diana Hochstedt Butler. "For McIlvaine, Britain was as important to bringing forth the millennium as was America." [2]

Much later, in 1866, McIlvaine was named to serve as a member of the Peabody Trust. The benefactor of the trust, William Peabody of Massachusetts, whose generosity had benefited the poor in both Britain and the United States, selected McIlvaine for his "wisdom, ability, and integrity." As a member of the trust, he served alongside Ulysses S. Grant, just a year out of uniform following the end of the Civil War, and R. C. Winthrop, former Speaker of the U. S. House of Representatives. "Mr. Peabody," McIlvaine wrote to his friend William Carus, "who gave so largely to the poor in London, is going on in his largesses in this country. He has given upwards of £250,000 to various educational and charitable institutions, since...last autumn." He noted that Peabody was not only giving large gifts to public causes but that he had also distributed generous portions of his fortune to relatives and other family connections. Peabody was not waiting "for a *will* to be executed after his death," he wrote, "but giving the money now. He is thus not merely disposing of his income, but of his principal—his own executor. What a good example of a rich man!"[3] Peabody had succeeded, he suggested, in threading his camel through the eye of a needle.

McIlvaine, alongside countless other clergymen, supported efforts to encourage temperance in the use of alcohol. The temperance movement, like others mentioned above, expressed his ardor to improve the lives of others. As a natural reformer and duty-bound tender of morals, he had no difficulty in making common cause with the multifaceted temperance movement of the ante-bellum period.

Although most of the early attacks on alcohol were based on a civic or hygienic rationale, a strong moral element had been added when Presbyterian revivalist Lyman Beecher began to formulate in his mind a crusade against not only intemperance but Sabbath-breaking and profanity as well. "Our vices are digging the grave of our liberties," Beecher cried, "and preparing to entomb our glory."[4] Owing largely to his efforts, the Connecticut Society for the Reformation of Morals was organized in 1813. The crusading zeal soon spread, gathering about it an evangelical spirit that transcended party bias as it grew in power and influence. A similar movement was launched in Massachusetts by Jeremiah Evarts, a lawyer associated with the foreign mission cause. His group, the Massachusetts Society for the Suppression of Intemperance, soon spawned local auxiliaries, as did Beecher's. Following a hiatus during the War of 1812, the crusaders returned to work with added fervor. Timothy Dwight, the Congregational theologian and latter-day Puritan, took the lead in turning the movement from one of opposing intemperance to one of enjoining abstinence, even though the word "temperance" remained associated with the cause. In 1826, Beecher took the same route in his *Six Sermons.* That volume presented a "strong and persuasive case for temperance," according to historian Sidney Ahlstrom,. "It was many times reprinted and constantly quoted by other temperance leaders."[5]

Associating moral rigor with the temperance crusade became a recurring theme, especially among Protestant clergy. In the year Beecher's *Six Sermons* was published, the movement was further strengthened by the founding in Boston of the similarly inclined American Society for the Promotion of Temperance. Its founders, not surprisingly, were men active in the missionary movement also. In 1829, reformers in Connecticut followed Boston's example. Within a year, its temperance society reported 172 branch societies with twenty-two thousand members. In 1836, a boost to the crusade was given by the founding of the American Temperance Union, which, contrary to its name, was formed on a total abstinence platform. Meanwhile, state societies remained active in the cause. The Maine Law, passed in 1846, was the first statewide prohibition measure. When revised in 1851, it became a model for numerous other states, among them Vermont, Rhode Island, Michigan and Connecticut, as well as the Minnesota Territory.[6]

To assist the movement, McIlvaine took pen in hand and produced at least one rather curious document—curious both in tone and style. Although his prose, generally, was a bit prolix after the manner of the age, it was notable for its grace, balance and sweeping cadences. Yet in a piece for the American Tract Society in the early 1830s, entitled *Address to the Young Men of the United States, on Temperance,* [7] his language turned purplish. It appears that he believed his effort to dissuade young men from the abuse of alcohol would best achieve its aim by graphic portrayals of the evils of excess. One cannot help notice a certain, doubtless unintended, comic effect in the tract, especially as he warmed to his subject. "How," he asked, "with a refinement of cruelty almost peculiar to itself, does [excessive drink] fly in the face of its victims, and hold their quivering eye-balls in its fangs till they abhor the light and swim in blood!" How indeed? The imagery, if no more, was likely to remain fixed in the mind of the reader. "Mark that carbuncled, slavering, doubtful remnant of a man," he continued, assaying the habitual drunkard and his sorry state of life. Watch him, the clergyman advised, "retching and picking tansy [an herb used for curative purposes] before sunrise—loathing his breakfast—getting his ear bored to the door of a dramshop an hour after—disguised before ten—quarrelling by dinner time and snoring drunk before supper." He ruminated on the inevitable course of such a man. "Think of his thus dragging out months and years of torture," he advised, "till the earth refuses any longer to bear such a wretch upon its surface, and then tell me if any Barbadian slave was ever so miserable." Think of it. That was McIlvaine's intent, to have every young man who chanced upon his tract think deeply of the man hopelessly enslaved to alcohol. Though for him the style was atypical, the message captured the reforming impulse of the young clergyman and the times in which he lived.

McIlvaine's relationships with women in the field of religion were by all accounts cordial and respectful. Among the ordained ministry, it was of course a man's world. But the presence and influence of women in carrying out much of the practical business of the church, as well as their role in teaching the faith to the young, was routine in many quarters. Thus, McIlvaine's attitude towards women in the church was largely customary. Yet his deep and emotional relationships with his mother, wife and daughters were palpable, and doubtless influenced the pattern of his relationships to females generally. That this feeling of easy relationship extended to the women of the church is not surprising.

The importance of women in most churches—and not in the nineteenth century only—cannot be overestimated. In contrast to Orthodox Judaism and Eastern Orthodox Christianity, there had been for centuries a strong feminine influence in both Protestantism and Roman Catholicism. So disproportionate were women among the churched, and so active were they in church work, that clergy—though grateful for their service—expressed frequent concern about the imbalance between male and female members. In doing so, they emphasized the need to convert more men and, when such occurred, found it a time for celebration. So out-of-balance had this state of affairs become that religious journalist Leon J. Podles was able to assemble a book's worth of anecdote and analysis on the subject in his recent *The Church Impotent: The Feminization of Christianity*. The book investigates a pattern that had, by McIlvaine's time, been present in the western churches since the early modern period, if not earlier. In nineteenth century New England, according to one historian, ministers of prominent churches tended to be "hesitant promulgators of female virtues in an era of militant masculinity." Thus it was not unusual for a wife to attend church while her husband partook of the symbolism, ritual and camaraderie of the Masonic lodge. By contrast, "Ministers found the most congenial environment not in business, political clubs, or saloons, but in the Sunday school, the parlor, the library, among women and those who flattered and resembled them." [8] By the end of the century, the alleged effeminacy of the mainline Protestant clergy had become a subject of satire. A Catholic novel, *The Lost Rosary* by Con O'Leary, offered a scathing, unbalanced, portrait of the typical minister of the day. "He was," the book charged, "a Methodist, a Revivalist, a Baptist, an advocate of women's rights, an earnest worker in the field of missionary labor, provided said field consisted in gliding here and there to nice little evening parties, shaking hands—or, more properly speaking, finger tips—with ladies whose age forbade the custom of whole-hand shaking....Mild tea drinking, a little sherry, claret occasionally." [9] Podles observes that Catholics, too, had their shortcomings, "if we may judge by the repeated efforts to get Catholic men to attend to their religious duties." [10]

One can perhaps close one's eyes and picture McIlvaine, in youth and age, sipping his cup of tea, attending "nice little evening parties" and otherwise savoring the joys of refined society. But the man was hardly captive to the caricature sketched in *The Lost Rosary*. He was, after all, a leader of men in an ongoing ecclesiastical struggle, the bishop of a rough and ready diocese, the determined president of a men's college, a reliable provider for his family, a fighter for the causes in which he believed, and a man unafraid to speak or write his mind. Furthermore, he faced the existential realities of life—unpredictable circumstances, the threat of disease, the certainty of death—with unblinkered eyes and unwavering courage. Moreover, his male friendships were hearty and healthy; he held his own in the company of such as Abraham Lincoln and John C. Calhoun, and he preached extempore before large crowds and congregations. Yes, he was "neurotic," in today's parlance; yes, he brooded about death; yes, he suffered periodic collapses of health. Yet these were but testaments to the humanity of a fully masculine figure.

That being said, it is a fact that women—especially Evangelicals—were heavily engaged in the work of the Episcopal Church in the nineteenth century. They served in voluntary societies, mission work, revivals, prayer meetings, and, of course, Sunday school teaching, all vital aspects of the Evangelical program. Moreover, they were allowed responsible positions of leadership owing to the flexibility of Evangelical clergy, a status not afforded them by High Churchmen. According to Diana Hochstedt Butler, "They [Evangelical women] made up most of the work on a lay level." [11] In addition, Episcopalian and Presbyterian women, as members of increasingly well-to-do churches financially, used their churches "as an important means of establishing a pecking order within the community." [12] Though barred from ordination and thus unable to engage in the institutional debates of the church, women were not uninterested—nor quiet—in regard to larger church issues. Emily McIlvaine, Bishop McIlvaine's wife, was outspokenly Evangelical in her churchmanship, and other women took serious interest in church debate and conflict as well.

McIlvaine's early success in Sunday school organizing, which took place when he was a student at Princeton Seminary, was not attained without the help of the pious women of St. Mary's Parish in his hometown of Burlington. In a history of the parish, he "and others" are credited with organizing the school. After careful preparations, the hometown lad—then hardly more than seventeen years of age—and five other teachers welcomed forty students to the first session in the spring of 1816. Of the teachers, four were women. Their names, otherwise lost to history, were Mary Wallace, Rachel Wallace, Susan Sterling and Bertha S. Ellis. McIlvaine's lone male colleague was one Thomas Aikman, who was not even an Episcopalian. He was, in McIlvaine's words, "a very good Scotch Presbyterian."[13]

McIlvaine's attitude towards people of color as individuals appears to have been exemplary. His views regarding questions of race in general appear to have leaned in the same direction, with emphasis on personal relations and a sense of decency, and a de-emphasis on institutional cure-alls. Yet he had devoted time to the latter also. As early as the 1820s, he and William Meade, later bishop of Virginia, worked with the American Colonization Society, with a view to returning emancipated slaves to Africa as a means of ending slavery. When later developments rendered the plan untenable, McIlvaine shifted towards a more aggressive—though still restrained—position. His growing militancy was influenced by contacts in Britain in the 1830s with William Wilberforce, Hannah More and other Evangelicals, as well as by his friendship in the 1840s and after with William Jay, the best known Evangelical Episcopalian antislavery activist.

In the 1840s and '50s, Evangelical Episcopalians generally began to involve themselves in antislavery agitation and related political matters. This fomented a rift with the High Church, as the latter espoused separation of church and state, the traditional Episcopal position. High Churchmen were reluctant to condemn slavery itself. Despite the dubious morality of their stance, it strengthened them as a party. While northern and southern Evangelicals split over slavery and thereby weakened themselves, the High Church held together. The post-bellum expansion of Anglo-Catholic and Ritualist tendencies—extensions of the Tractarian movement of an earlier decade—was due in part to this increased High Church power and unity.

Although he joined the Republican Party when it was formed in the 1850s, McIlvaine remained shy of taking an overt role in efforts to end the South's "peculiar institution." Thus, in 1858, he declined to sign a resolution adopted at an antislavery convention in Cincinnati, even when asked to do so by a friend, Salmon P. Chase, United States senator from Ohio and later President Lincoln's secretary of the treasury. "I suppose," he wrote to Chase, "that in the abstract question of slavery and its chief circumstance, there is little difference of opinion between myself and many that will sign the paper....I do not think that good such as is sought is likely to result from such a convention, and therefore must respectfully decline signing the call." [14] That said, he did support the policies of Lincoln both before and during the Civil War.

McIlvaine's good-heartedness towards people of color, whatever his shortcomings in regard to institutional measures to secure their freedom, is revealed in a pair of incidents from his years as bishop. The first incident occurred during a near fatal steam ferry mishap in January 1855, as he and two-hundred other passengers—along with omnibuses, wagons, and horses—attempted to cross the Ohio River. Having concluded a visit to Louisville, McIlvaine was planning to link up with the Jefferson railroad and return to Cincinnati. As recorded in the February 5 issue of the *Western Episcopalian*, the ferry, while crossing the Ohio, became lodged in a mass of ice in the middle of the river. Unable to move forward or backward, it drifted slowly towards a waterfall, where it was feared it would to be crushed to pieces and its passengers lost amidst the freezing waters. In the harrowing hours that followed, McIlvaine

A Born-Again Episcopalian

acquitted himself admirably, facing death with courage, showing care and concern for others, and praying as one would expect a clergyman to pray. A temporary respite occurred when the ferry— "was it not God's guiding in answer to prayer?" the Western Episcopalian queried—struck a hidden reef at the start of the rapids and was at least for the moment held safe from the falls. As the ferry held to the reef, several small boats from the Kentucky and Indiana shores made their way to the stranded craft, where their crews began to remove passengers in threes and fours. Women were first, with "coloured women...as kindly cared for as the white." Moreover, "One or two coloured men were allowed to go in the skiff with their wives." When McIlvaine was urged to enter the boat with a young woman in his charge, the daughter of a fellow bishop, he "resolutely refused," though "all seemed anxious to accord [him the privilege owed] to his age and character." Such gallantry did not go unrewarded. In timely fashion, a flatboat arrived to remove McIlvaine and fifty other men from the ferry. Yet the peril had not passed. The captain of the flatboat made it clear that his craft would "take the falls," and thus he ordered all on board to remain silent while he focused on his duties. As the passengers awaited their fate, the *Western Episcopalian* reported, McIlvaine "sheltered a poor shivering coloured boy under his cloak, and commended himself and his fellow-voyagers, with composure and confidence, to his covenant Lord and Saviour." In the event, the boat slid safely through a chute in the falls and, despite scraping a reef at two points, broke free and was saved, as were all who rode her. In a follow up account, McIlvaine corrected a single detail, noting that he had not tended to the boy until after the flatboat had passed the falls, not having seen him until then. "It was after we had passed the falls the little coloured boy was found almost frozen," he recalled in the *Western Episcopalian*. "He had no overcoat. The omnibus-man was moving him about to get his blood circulated. I took him under my cloak, which was long and warm, and held him to my body to get its heat; in that situation he became quite comfortable." Despite the racial divides afflicting the country, the incident stands as tribute to the small decencies and courtesies that characterized McIlvaine's—and the omnibus man's—behavior. [15]

The second incident, recounted by his daughter, occurred in 1859, on McIlvaine's return from abroad. When he stopped at Gambier to visit his son, who was a student at Kenyon College, a friend told him that "the place was much agitated" owing to the treatment of a "colored man" named William Alston. Although the man was a seminarian at Bexley Hall, the chaplain refused him Holy Communion with the rest of the students, who by custom presented themselves after the clergy had communicated. Instead, he was told to remain in place "until the whole white population of the place had partaken." At that point, "the solitary colored man" could come forward. Upon being apprised of the situation, the bishop said to his friend, "Let no one know that you have spoken of this to me." The next day, refusing to preach in the morning and purposely leaving his prayer book behind, McIlvaine went to the chapel and took his place by the side of Alston, who was seated apart from the rest of the students. He requested that he be allowed to look over Alston's prayer book. "When the time for the administration of the Lord's Supper came," his daughter recalled, "my father waited until the clergy of the place had communicated, and then, stepping forward and bidding Alston follow him, advanced and knelt at the chancel, placing the colored man by his side." She added: "It is needless to say that with this ended the matter, except in the gratitude of his companion." Alston went on to complete his studies and to be ordained, graduating with the class of 1859. [16]

McIlvaine, in his sixties at the time of the Civil War, suffered agonies of soul throughout that costly, protracted conflict. Like countless others, he mourned the loss of friends, among them the president of the United States and a brother bishop who took up arms against the Union. At the beginning of the war, he remained moderate but troubled in his views of the situation. By war's end, he was angry and bitter at the cost in lives, fraternal good will and disruption of civil society. As a Christian and a bishop, he was a man of peace. Yet war had come and swept all before it. War had enveloped the world he knew and changed it forever, supplanting the frontier and agrarian society of the ante-bellum period with a Gilded Age of industrialization and rapid urbanization. Near the beginning of the war, at the time of the Trent Affair, he would perform an act of diplomacy that would help mitigate the severity of the conflict in a manner generally unsung by chroniclers of the war. In addition, during the darkest days of the fighting, he would tender advice to political and military leaders, and extend pastoral care to soldiers on both sides.

Despite his wide sympathies, McIlvaine was a staunch Union man. "There is," he said, in addressing his diocesan convention in June 1861, "no such thing as being neutral in this controversy, unless we would live in a land over which the Constitution of the United States claims no authority. There is no middle ground between loyalty to its government and disloyalty." [17] He expressed also the sadness he felt in regard to separated brethren who found themselves, by choice or circumstance, on the other side of the divide. He thought, no doubt, of Leonidas Polk, his brother bishop and former student, and the course he had taken. In addition to being bishop of Louisiana, Polk had become a pillar of Southern society, and owner of a sugar plantation with three hundred slaves. At the outbreak of war, he was appointed a major general in the Confederate army, an honor that would eventually cost him his life in battle.

At the triennial General Convention of the Episcopal Church in 1862, McIlvaine introduced a draft resolution on the floor of the House of Bishops strongly supporting the Union and opposing the southern bishops—Polk among them—who had met in July 1861 to form the Protestant Episcopal Church in the Confederate States of America. The draft referred to Polk as having set aside the "exalted spiritual duties of an Overseer of the flock of Christ" to "exercise high command in such awful work [the war]."

Bishops could not, the draft said, "as Overseers over the same flock...refrain from placing on such examples our strong condemnation." [18] In typical fashion, he placed principle above personality, and stood firm for the unity of the church even as he stood firm for the unity of the nation. The resolution passed. At the same convention, the House of Bishops, with ten southern bishops "temporarily absent" owing to the formation of the Episcopal Church in the Confederacy, approved a pastoral letter strongly supporting President Lincoln's leadership and the Union's position in the war. This action represented a shift in thought and sentiment on the part of the bishops, who earlier had stood aloof from the political issues facing the nation, asserting their station as church leaders as reason for doing so. Now, all had changed. In a letter to Lincoln of October 1862, McIlvaine told the president of the pastoral letter, unabashedly informing him that he, McIlvaine, had been the author. [19]

Although he chastised Polk for his secessionist views and his participation in the war, McIlvaine participated in the war himself, though in ways more fitting to a clergyman's calling. During the course of the war, he visited and preached at Union camps; worked for both the interdenominational United States Christian Commission and the United States Sanitary Commission (the forerunner of the Red Cross), to raise funds to help supply the soldiers; corresponded with military leaders (including George McClellan, commander of the Army of the Potomac during the first part of the war); secured commissions for friends and relatives, and offered advice to political leaders, including President Lincoln and Secretary of the Treasury Salmon P. Chase. His sympathies and activities were associated mostly with the Christian Commission, a private social agency founded in New York in 1861 by leaders of the Young Men's Christian Association and the American Tract Society. The organization, which was evangelical in outlook, worked to meet special needs and provide comforts not supplied by the federal government to its armies, including additional food and clothing, medicine, prayer books, devotional tracts, newspapers, and other books. [20] In addition, he labored to elevate and clarify the role of the chaplaincy in the Union army. This effort, though largely unsuccessful, indicated his desire to help in ways that drew on his area of special competence. Also, upon being elected president of the American Tract Society, he spread pro-Union and pro-emancipation propaganda, the opposing southern members having left the organization.

McIlvaine displayed interest also in matters more properly of a military nature. This friend of generals and former West Point chaplain and instructor was not about to allow his office as bishop to keep him totally uninvolved in the clash of arms. In June 1861, for example, in the early days of the war, while in Washington to confer with the president, he rode with Lincoln in his carriage to inspect the test firing of new rifled cannon. He endeavored also to visit the battlefield, a desire not uncommon in those early days of the war, when ladies and their beaus from Washington society spread their picnic blankets within sight of the fighting before being chased back to the capital a step or two ahead of the Rebel advance. Also in June 1861, he received clearance and assistance from General Winfield Scott ("Old Fuss and Feathers") to visit and preach before two Ohio regiments at outposts near Washington. While visiting the Ohioans, he "went with a scouting party a mile and a half 'in the advance' to the lines of the most extended units, two regiments from Connecticut." [21]

On July 22 of the same year, he was in Washington again, where he was houseguest of treasury secretary Salmon P. Chase, a longstanding friend from Ohio. The Battle of Bull Run, the first major engagement of the war, had taken place in Virginia the day before, and the shattered Union army was streaming back into the capital. Hot and sultry weather and hours of rain provided a fitting complement to the mood of the defeated army. Chase's daughter, Nettie, standing at her window, witnessed an endless, clattering procession of "gloomy-looking vehicles"—supply wagons, gun batteries, and black-curtained ambulances. Inside the house, Chase and an elder daughter, Kate, assisted by McIlvaine, tended to "eight or ten" wounded soldiers. "Tall, slender, and with chiseled features," a Chase biographer writes, "the bishop was a commanding presence as he assisted...in comforting the wounded." Nettie Chase recalled one young soldier provoking him unintentionally with a spate of curses. "Just let me swear a bit, it helps me stand the hurting," he exclaimed. Undaunted, the bishop admonished the young man. "Learn to pray instead," he urged. "God can help you much more than the devil can."[22]

May 15-25, 1863, nearly two years later, McIlvaine was active again among the troops. In this period, he was present with the Army of the Potomac under General Joseph Hooker, two weeks after the stinging defeat at Chancellorsville, ministering among the soldiers at the front lines. A year later, in May 1864, as Ulysses S. Grant launched his massive war of attrition against the South, he was near the action yet again. As battle raged in the wood and swamp of the Wilderness, he wrote to his wife[23] from the house of the Christian Commission in Fredericksburg, Virginia, where he was among two to three hundred delegates praying and laboring on behalf of the soldiers. The brief letter provides a vivid account. He observed, among other things, that 12,000 to 15,000 wounded soldiers had been brought into town. "Think of it," he wrote, "every house filled. What a scene. Battle yesterday 12 miles from here." The battle must have been that of Spotsylvania, fought May 8-20. Despite the "fresh suffering" all about, he told his wife that he was "truly glad" that he had come. He noted that he had bivouacked on the floor of a deserted house "penetrated with the shot of the battle last year," a reference to the engagement in which Ambrose Burnside's Union forces had been severely punished by Robert E. Lee's well-entrenched Confederates.

As part of his duty, McIlvaine noted that he had "addressed and prayed with" eight-hundred Rebel prisoners "drawn up in a line." Seated on a horse, he had spoken to them not of condemnation but of reconciliation. "Not one word was said to wound their feelings," recalled George H. Stuart, president of the Christian Commission and a witness to the event. "On the contrary, the Bishop took special pains to conciliate the men, by telling them that he spoke to them as an ambassador of Christ and not as their enemy. He besought them, in the hour of their misfortune and sore trial, to look to him [Christ], assuring them that in him they would find help in this, the time of their need." Stuart said the men were deeply affected, and many of them brought to tears.[24]

McIlvaine was moved by the experience as well. "I have," he wrote, "seen & learned a life lesson—a life history in a day." In trepidation, he looked forward to developments in the military situation. "A great battle expected today," he wrote in the same letter to his wife. "We are near enough to hear the sounds of it take place. But…where will the wounded be put—all is full." In reflecting on the war, he said: "Never the Gospel seemed so precious—never the awful course of the Rebellion so horrid. Don't be anxious about me. I am very well—not depressed in spirit." Always one to be at the center of events, he said he expected "to go to [General] Grant's Headquarters tomorrow." When faced with the immediacy of death and dying, he was at his best. "Not depressed in spirit," he acquitted himself superbly in serving others in trying circumstances, even as he had done so earlier in a cholera epidemic in Brooklyn and in the steam-ferry mishap on the Ohio River. Where others might flinch, the bishop always rose to the occasion.

Even as the war sundered McIlvaine's friendship with Bishop Polk and other companions of the cloth, his devotion to President Lincoln grew. The two had been on cordial terms for some time, and he wrote admiringly of the president in a letter to William Carus, in February 1865. He observed that Lincoln had "grown in his ability by experience. He is a plain man in appearance and manner, though nothing like in the latter, what many who have heard of his humble birth suppose." He was also, he said, "remarkably kind, and almost invincibly adverse to severe measures toward individuals who deserve severe punishment." [25] Owing to acquaintance with the president, he had been assigned more than three years before to the most important duty he would perform at any time during the war. He had performed that duty impeccably, and as a result had rendered the catastrophe of the Civil War something less than it might otherwise have been.

McIlvaine's foray into diplomacy had stemmed from the concern of Lincoln and his cabinet that Britain might enter the war on the Confederate side. Thus the president, by personal invitation, and with the agreement of Secretary of State William Seward (the instigator of the plan) and Secretary of the Treasury Chase, had proposed to McIlvaine that he go to England and, in McIlvaine's words, "without seeming to do so...endevour [sic] by conversations to influence the English mind as to our cause." [26] The invitation was a timely one, for southern agents were active in Britain, seeking support for the Confederacy. Sympathies between the British—especially the upper classes—and the southern planter aristocracy had long been cordial, and the English textile industry was dependent on the region's greatest export, cotton; hence the importance of McIlvaine's mission.

Known for his achievements and rectitude, alongside his convivial ties with Englishmen of note, McIlvaine was an ideal choice for the assignment. His many tea parties, church services and countryside excursions in the mother country had, it would seem, prepared him for a task he could never have envisioned. Though at first he was reluctant to accept the assignment, owing to its secular nature, the strong support of his diocesan clergy helped him decide to accept. He was, in fact, to be one of three members of the initiative, the others—friends of one another—being Thurlow Weed, New York newspaper publisher and Republican party boss, and John Hughes, Roman Catholic archbishop of New York and pugnacious champion of the Irish immigrant community. In a letter to Secretary Chase, McIlvaine wrote that his role in England would necessarily "require as much mixing with the higher classes as possible, which involves a higher tariff for expenses." Thus it was agreed that he would be allocated $480 plus a credit balance of $500 at the Evans and Company Bank in Cincinnati. [27] Archbishop Hughes was to travel at government expense also, but Weed, owing to his controversial anti-slavery views, was asked to provide his own support. With arrangements in place, McIlvaine and two of his daughters, Nan and Anna, departed Cincinnati for New York in November 1861, where they and Hughes took passage to England aboard a Cunard steamer. Weed, for his part, sailed to Catholic France, accompanied by the aging General Winfield Scott, who planned to feel out the diplomatic situation while seeking treatment for vertigo. In the event, Scott returned to the United States shortly thereafter when it seemed to him that an Anglo-American war would follow the Trent crisis and that the French might join the British. Meanwhile, McIlvaine and Weed conducted diplomacy in England, although Weed initially assisted Hughes, who had sailed from England to France.

Each of the envoys had carefully defined areas around which he was to focus his attention. McIlvaine was to make his appeal to British bishops, deans, lesser clergy, and influential persons in government. Weed, once returned to England, was to utilize his journalistic abilities and connections to wage a campaign against Confederate propaganda in the columns of the London Times. Hughes was to convey the Union position at the courts of Napoleon III and Pope Pius IX. The envoys were not to supplant but rather to supplement the efforts of the American ministers in London and Paris. Charles Francis Adams, American minister to London, realized immediately that such endeavors in the hands of less sensitive men might well be hazardous, with conflicts and contradictions all too likely between the more or less autonomous agents. It is a tribute to the wisdom and discretion of the envoys that no such problems arose. Adams, with whom McIlvaine met frequently during the winter of 1861-62, informed Secretary Seward in December that the bishop had "already...been of material use—will be of still more hereafter if peaceful relations should be preserved." [28]

Just eight days after the mission had been proposed, its importance was enhanced by what has become known as the Trent Affair. That series of events began when the Confederacy sent two agents, John Murray Mason, former U. S. senator from Virginia and proud grandson of the American patriot and founding father, George Mason, and his former Senate colleague, John Slidell of Louisiana, on a diplomatic mission of its own. Mason was entrusted to plead the Confederate cause in Britain, while the French-speaking Slidell was to do the same in France. After eluding the Union blockade, the two men reached Cuba and transferred to the Trent, a British packet. On November 8, 1861, the packet was intercepted by the San Jacinto, a sloop of the U. S. Navy, under command of Captain Charles Wilkes. Wilkes gave the order to fire across the bow of the Trent, after which the craft was boarded and Mason and Slidell taken prisoner. Though the captain was hailed as a hero in the northern states, the reaction in Britain was one of outrage. The British began at once to prepare for war, calling up reserves, putting factories on overtime and dispatching troops to Canada.

McIlvaine arrived in Britain on December 7, 1861, in the midst of the prevailing war fever. Immediately he arranged to meet with government leaders to exchange views on the incident. Among them were Sir Henry Holland, the Queen's physician extraordinary, whom McIlvaine had met in Cincinnati a year earlier; Arthur F. Kinnaird, a philanthropist, banker, humanitarian, and Liberal member of the House of Commons, and Lord Shaftesbury (Antony Ashley Cooper). Following these meetings, McIlvaine penned a twenty-two page letter to convince Washington that the British were ready to go to war if the matter was not adjudicated promptly. He recommended among other things that Mason and Slidell, who were being held at Fort Warren, near Boston, be released. He based his recommendation on both expediency and principle, having concluded that the American action against the Trent had violated international law. Weed seconded the opinion in a letter the following day. In the meantime, Lincoln and his cabinet had for several days studied the official protest from Lord Palmerston (Henry J. Temple), the British prime minister, and his foreign secretary, Lord John Russell. On January 8, 1862, Washington's reply to London stated—to the relief of Americans and Britons alike—that the envoys would be released. The reply, which had been delivered by Secretary Seward to the British ambassador, Lord Lyons, on December 27, claimed that Captain Wilkes had been justified in seizing Mason and Slidell but conceded that he had erred in releasing the Trent instead of escorting her into port for adjudication in a prize court. The crisis was thus defused and war fever began to abate. Mason and Slidell, who for a dollar a day had been feasting on duck, terrapin, oysters and turkey (even as they enjoyed Havana cigars, afternoon toddies, and innumerable games of whist),[29] were sent packing to the South.

Despite the initial threats of war, McIlvaine reported from Britain that sermons expressing strong aversion to hostilities had been "preached all over the land" and that prayer meetings with the same object had been many. "Indeed," he reported, "almost wherever you hear a prayer *that* comes in."[30] Among the meetings had been a gathering of four thousand persons at Exeter Hall in London, drawn together by the English Evangelical Alliance to pray for peace. McIlvaine had preached at the event. The influential Peace Society and the Society of Friends had preached and prayed for peace as well. As quickly as it had come, it seems, the war fever had broken.

McIlvaine remained in England another six months, working to sway opinion in favor of the Union and reminding the British of their solid anti-slavery sentiments. While he engaged in a preaching tour in the English countryside and visited fellow bishops and lower clergy, Weed for his part cultivated influential

Londoners, pleading for moderation and peace, and planting conciliatory articles in the press. At the same time, both men sought the good will of English pacifists and their circles. Weed, who considered McIlvaine "devoted and wise," wrote to Seward that his fellow envoy had been "visiting bishops and clergy, and doing good wherever he goes." In another report, he informed the secretary that McIlvaine "is doing vast good, in and out of the city [London], and in influential quarters." [31] For his part, Secretary Chase, who had been outspoken in cabinet meetings during the crisis, expressed gratitude to McIlvaine for "doing a great work and a good one." [32] The archbishop of Canterbury was complimentary as well. "Few men living," he said, "have done so much to draw England and the United States together." [33]

Thus, McIlvaine's mission to England did not end with the Trent Affair. He continued to move in prominent social, political and ecclesiastical circles, informing his listeners of the Union cause. At Hursely Park, the country estate of McIlvaine's longtime friend, Sir William Heathcote, he was introduced to Spencer Horatio Walpole, former secretary of state of the Home Department and, McIlvaine noted, "a very reasonable person to our side." Later, he spent a week at Farnham Castle as the guest of another longtime friend, Charles R. Sumner, bishop of Winchester, where he had further opportunities to meet influential members of church and state. He then visited additional bishops before returning to London in early February, where Parliament was debating American affairs. There, at Fulham Palace, Archibald Campbell Tait, the bishop of London, hosted McIlvaine and introduced him to a number of highly placed persons, as did Lord Arthur Fitzgerald Kinnaird, Lady Gainesborough (Francis Noel), and the Duke of Argyll (George Douglas Campbell), keeper of the Privy Seal. McIlvaine offered his views to a number of members of Parliament and to at least three members of the prime minister's cabinet. He was able to report to Secretary Seward on February 21 that his opportunities had much exceeded his expectations and that "everybody sees the change in public opinion, or expressions of it recently." As a prominent American bishop, McIlvaine was a celebrity figure as much as a special envoy, preaching at both Oxford and Cambridge and impressing Britons both great and small. Never one for false modesty, he stated in a letter of January 14 to Bishop Gregory Bedell, his assistant in Ohio, "that there is no doubt, I have been instrumental in keeping down a great deal of the froth that was rising, certainly I could not have a warmer welcome or a wider field." Writing again to Bedell a month later, he made it clear he knew his own worth. "I have the greatest consolation in knowing that I am serving our dear country, and hence Ohio, and the Church, by being here, as (pardon me) no one else of America could, for no layman could go where I go, and no clergyman of our land has the acquaintances and the entrée among clergymen of all positions and religious laymen of all ranks, which God has given me." [34]

Historians have praised the success of the mission. In the view of a nineteenth-century observer, the presence of McIlvaine and Weed in Britain "was an advantage to us in the storm that arose on the news of the capture of Mason and Slidell....They were able...to contradict the stories which were widely circulated and eagerly believed, that the secretary [of state, William Seward] had the utmost animosity to Great Britain, and a serious purpose of bringing on a war between the two countries." [35] A more recent commentator agrees that the mission "performed a real service." He writes: "Weed's abilities in the field of political adjustment were brought into full play, both in England and France....McIlvaine did good work with the English clergy and laity." [36]

McIlvaine, one could say, did "good work" in most everything he undertook, both before the diplomatic trip and after it. His care for others in need, be they people of color or members of his own race; his Evangelical appreciation of women's service; his dedication to social reform; his empathy with the suffering soldiers of the Civil War, and, of course, his hand in the successful mission at the time of the Trent Affair, all testify to his steadfast

CHAPTER EIGHT – *Social Issues*

character and abundant gifts. His religion did not end at the church door. It extended into a larger world of social issues, a world in which it found additional scope for spiritual and material service. But the church—its life, its teaching, its mission—was the center of his life. Everything he did beyond the church emanated from his primary calling. In the next chapter, we will look again at McIlvaine the churchman: at the principal role to which he dedicated his life. It was a role he fulfilled ably, energetically, and militantly, for more than fifty years, to the praise of friends and the consternation of foes.

2. Butler, 49-50.
3. Quoted in William Carus, *Memorials*, 284, 285.
4. Quoted in Sydney E. Ahlstrom, *A Religious History of the American People*, 426.
5. Ahlstrom, 426.
6. Ibid.
7. American Tract Society, New York, 1833.
8. Quoted in Leon J. Podles, *The Church Impotent: The Feminization of Christianity* (Spence Publishing Company, Dallas, Texas, 1999), 5. Quotations from Barbara Welter, "The Feminization of American Religion: 1800-1860," in *Clio's Consciousness Raised*, ed. Mary S. Hartman and Lois Banner (Harper and Row, New York, 1974), 22, 43.
9. Ibid., 5.
10. Ibid., 6.
11. Butler, xii, 11.
12. Barbara Welter, *Dimity Convictions: The American Woman in the Nineteenth Century* (Ohio State University Press, Athens, 1976), 87.
13. Quoted in George Morgan Hills, *A History of the Church in Burlington*, 383.
14. Charles P. McIlvaine to Salmon P. Chase (Kenyon College Library Archives), no. 58-03-29.
15. Quoted in Carus, 159-164.
16. Quoted in George Franklin Smythe, *Kenyon College: Its First Century*, 265.
17. Quoted in Loren Dale Pugh, *Bishop Charles Pettit McIlvaine*, 60.
18. Ibid., 122.

19. James B. Bell, "Charles P. McIlvaine," *For the Union: Ohio Leaders in the Civil War*, ed. Kenneth W. Wheeler (Ohio State University Press, 1968), 252-253.
20. Ibid., 251.
21. Pugh, 110.
22. Quoted in John Niven, *Salmon P Chase: A Biography* (Oxford University Press, New York, 1995), 260.
23. Charles P. McIlvaine to Maria McIlvaine (Kenyon College Library Archives), no. 65-05-19.
24. Quoted in Maria McIlvaine, *Obit Book*, 1873.
25. Quoted in Carus, 251.
26. Quoted in Pugh, 114.
27. Bell, 243.
28. Quoted in Bell, 242, 250.
29. Norman B. Ferris, *The Trent Affair: A Diplomatic Crisis* (The University of Tennessee Press, Knoxville, 1977), 31.
30. Quoted in Ferris, 157.
31. Quoted in Frederick W. Seward, *Seward at Washington, as Senator and Secretary of State: A Memoir of His Life, with Selections from His Letters, 1861-1872* (Derby and Miller, New York, 1891), 30, 32, 58.
32. Quoted in Bell, 251.
33. Quoted in Butler, 164.
34. Bell, 248, 249, 235.
35. Thornton Kirkland Lothrop, *William Henry Seward* (Houghton, Mifflin and Company, Boston and New York, 1896), 350.
36. Glyndon G. Van Deusen, *William Henry Seward* (Oxford University Press, New York, 1967), 307.

CHAPTER NINE

Churchman

Charles Pettit McIlvaine was the energetic leader of a movement, the conscientious shepherd of a flock, and a militant intellectual. Even as he led his fellow Evangelicals to their greatest prominence in the Episcopal Church, he served as the tireless bishop of a diocese, a responsibility that required not only preaching, teaching, pastoring and confirming but handling also a myriad of administrative details and visiting far-flung parishes in days when travel taxed even the heartiest of men. He was also an ardent ecumenist in his relations with other Protestant bodies, and a loyal and affectionate friend to churchmen both inside and outside his own denomination. Yet his irenic stance did not prevent him from upholding the distinctive doctrines of the Episcopal Church, and speaking on their behalf when he thought it necessary to do so. Through it all, as we have seen, he established himself as a writer of eminence: as a cultivated expositor and polemicist in matters ecclesiastical and theological.

Although the Evangelical party he led was never able to gain a decisive majority in the House of Bishops, after 1840 it represented for a time the church's most swiftly growing parishes. It also gave strong support to Episcopal home missions and served prominently in many interdenominational voluntary associations. [1] The party enjoyed a sort of "golden age,"

215

represented as it was by strong bishops like William Meade and John Johns of Virginia and Stephen Elliott of Georgia, and a little later by the likes of Alfred Lee of Delaware, Manton Eastburn of Massachusetts, Henry Lee of Iowa and Thomas Clark of Rhode Island. Earlier notables included Alexander Viets Griswold, bishop of the Eastern Diocese and first leader of the party, and Philander Chase, McIlvaine's predecessor as bishop of Ohio. The number of Evangelical clergy doubled during the 1840s and the party was invigorated by the entry of formerly non-Episcopalian ministers into the church. As Bishop Clark of Rhode Island said of this period, "The growth of the Church was very much in the Evangelical direction, and it looked as if [the] party might soon attain a decided ascendancy."[2]

For all his willingness to work with other churches, McIlvaine was a staunch proponent of a strong Episcopal Church. This was especially so after his arrival as bishop of Ohio, where he witnessed the need for firm institutions amidst the flux of sectarianism and revivalism. "If we would promote the spirit of vital godliness in the world," he said in his charge to the Ohio clergy in 1836, "we must promote...the Church...as the earthly house of its tabernacle in this wilderness." People may as well, he said, expect their minds to be in health while their bodies were diseased, "as that the spirit of religion will flourish, while the body of religion, the visible Church, is disordered." A strong church, he continued, would provide a bulwark against false doctrine, predatory revivalists and the introduction of theological novelties. The Episcopal Church, he said, owing to its bishops, its liturgy and its educated and settled clergy, provided such a church. It was a "haven," a civilizing force amidst frontier chaos. He praised the Episcopal Church for remaining undamaged by innovation, free of prejudice, adapted "to the wants of all centuries and all people," and steadfast in refusing to "change with the times and vary with the tastes of the day." It was, he said, guarded from novelty by two things; first, by holding to the "old paths" marked out by the Reformation, and, second, by serious attention to the administration of the sacraments and especially of the "apostolic institution" of confirmation.[3]

Despite such principles, McIlvaine retained an ecumenical outlook throughout his career, rejecting the exclusivism of the High Church party. As a result, he worked amicably with representatives of other Protestant denominations on matters of mutual concern. He considered their common undertakings to be based on shared truth, on spiritual "unity" rather than organizational "union." His preferred vehicle was the international Evangelical Alliance, organized in London in 1846, which held views congruent with his own in resisting institutional union or denominational consolidation while promoting unity on the basis of shared theology and evangelical experience. The paradigm was well stated by Bishop Bedell, McIlvaine's assistant: "Unity does not depend on organic union....Protestantism, indeed, is not a church. Evangelical Christianity is not a form of organization....They are systems of positive truth, characterizing many churches."[4]

Despite their disagreements on doctrine and worship, Evangelicals and High Churchmen made peace for a time in the 1830s. Although suspect because of his earlier views and activities, McIlvaine won approval from at least some High Church bishops owing to his stand in Ohio against revivalist excesses and sectarian strife. He further pleased his erstwhile opponents by preaching more often than previously on the external merits of the Episcopal Church. He would continue such preaching for nearly two decades, before the threat of civil war and a sense of national malaise would draw him back to more revivalistic and interdenominational themes.

Also in the 1830s, Evangelicals and High Churchmen reached a compromise on missionary efforts. The compromise, agreed to informally by McIlvaine and the High Churchman George W. Doane, bishop of New Jersey, assigned domestic missions to High Churchmen and foreign missions to Evangelicals. Unwittingly, by entering the agreement, McIlvaine sowed the seeds of long term Evangelical decline. "In 1835," historian Diana Hochstedt Butler writes, "the division appeared fairly even. [But] over the next twenty years, the country grew rapidly by western expansion, and the High Church party had become more aggressive and 'Romanized' in its views. All the new domestic missionary positions created in the west were going to bishops and priests of High Church sentiments." [5] Although Evangelicals would reach the peak of their power and influence in the 1840s, long-term trends worked against them. By contrast, the High Church party—despite the buffetings of highly publicized controversies and scandals—was at the beginning of a period of expansion.

In addition to their advantage in domestic missions, High Churchmen found themselves invigorated by the birth in the 1850s and '60s of Tractarianism's offspring, Ritualism (or Anglo-Catholicism). Ritualism drew heavily on medieval and Romantic influences, quite unlike the Tractarianism of a generation earlier, which had looked to the early church to inform its theology and liturgical practice. Proponents introduced a raft of innovations, among them Eucharistic vestments, incense, crucifixes, genuflexion, vested choirs, choral services, elevation at communion of both bread and wine, invocation of saints, and prayers for the dead. Ritualists held that the English Reformation of the sixteenth century had never intended to rid the church of these forms.

The movement was given its theory and program most forcefully in *The Law of Ritualism* by John Henry Hopkins, bishop of Vermont. Published in 1866, the book argued in favor of ceremonialism on biblical grounds, pointing to the use of incense, vestments and ornament in the Old Testament. It noted also that some Ritualistic practices were supported in the first Prayer Book of Edward VI. Although the arguments had a measure of cogency, Evangelicals—feeling threatened by the incipient "Romanism" of the movement—were not about to accept them. According to

McIlvaine's *Righteousness by Faith,* published in 1864, it was ritual such as that promoted by Hopkins and others that was a foot-in-the-door for everything Evangelicals opposed. The Ritualists, he wrote, threatened "to promote a taste for a ceremonial sensuous religion…to introduce and make fast the whole Sacerdotal system of Priesthood, Sacrifice, Altar, and the *opus operatum* of Baptismal efficacy….All this, of course, is of the very essence of Popery." [6]

"Baptismal efficacy," yet again, was at the center of conflict. It had been the primary issue dividing Reformers and Roman Catholics in the sixteenth century and Evangelical and Tractarian Episcopalians in the 1840s. Should baptismal efficacy (or baptismal "regeneration") be conceded, Evangelicals held, the Episcopal Church would be replaced by a system of sacramentalism and the mediation of priests. In other words, if the means of regeneration should come to be focused on the sacrament of baptism alone, as opposed to faith alone, the Episcopal Church would be repeating the error of Rome. Even Bishop Hobart, McIlvaine argued, patron of the High Church in days gone by, had separated baptism and regeneration. In January 1867, McIlvaine and twenty-three other Episcopal bishops, High Churchmen among them, signed a declaration condemning Ritualism as an innovation. The strong support for the declaration, which represented nearly half of the House of Bishops, gave the normally vigilant McIlvaine a false sense of security. As a result, he showed little interest in subsequent attempts to revise the prayer book as a counter to Ritualist inroads.

Prayer book revision, pushed by the Rev. Benjamin B. Leacock of Harrisburg, Pennsylvania, and other Evangelical clergy, represented a new tactic in the churchmanship debate. It was based on the view that both the shortcomings of Reformation-era theology and the prayer book itself were accountable for present-day problems in the church. According to Leacock's *Prayer Book versus Prayer Book,* "We have every reason to [believe] that the antagonism existing between these two systems [between, that is, Evangelical and Ritualist views], must be found in the Prayer

Book also." [7] Leacock and his colleagues believed the prayer book was a "friend of both parties" and therefore a major source of church strife. Only revision could expunge "sacerdotalism" from the Episcopal Church.

In November 1867, at the annual meeting of the Protestant Episcopal Evangelical Societies in Philadelphia, clergy and laity alike issued a declaration calling for both prayer book revision— especially in regard to baptism and regeneration—and increased cooperation with other Protestant evangelical bodies. The second point, which aimed at the perceived failure of the Episcopal Church to respond adequately on its own to the "subversion" of Ritualism, argued the need to recognize other Protestant churches in the effort to preserve evangelical religion in America. Although feelings ran high and talk of schism was in the air, cooler views prevailed. These latter were expressed by bishops Manton Eastburn, Alfred Lee, and McIlvaine. Despite their sympathies with much of what they heard, they saw their principal responsibility as preservation of the church. McIlvaine, who refused to sign the declaration, did agree to support prayer book "relief" but not revision, a subject to which we shall return.

The question of Protestant interdenominational cooperation had simmered for decades in the Episcopal Church. Evangelicals promoted it, High Churchmen opposed it. The issue was inflamed in the 1860s when Evangelicals developed a renewed interest in working with other churches to curb Ritualism. As before, High Churchmen would have none of it. This was made clear in 1868, when the Rev. Stephen H. Tyng Jr., rector of Church of the Holy Spirit, New York, tested their patience by officiating at a Methodist church in New Brunswick, New Jersey. For doing so, he was charged with violating the canon that prohibited officiating in another church without express permission of his superiors. In a much-publicized trial, he was found guilty and publicly admonished by Horatio Potter, bishop of New York and successor to Benjamin Onderdonk.

Another case, involving the Rev. John Wesley Cracraft, was of more immediate concern to McIlvaine. Though canonically resident in the diocese of Ohio in 1864, Cracraft had visited Galesburg, Illinois, where Grace Episcopal Church was on the lookout for a new rector. While there, he had preached at a Congregational church. The latter, as a hotbed of abolitionist and pro-Union sentiment, was congenial to Cracraft, an Evangelical and an abolitionist himself. Henry J. Whitehouse, bishop of Illinois, a Democrat and a Southern sympathizer, was not pleased. Not only was he upset by Cracraft's interdenominational activity, he was displeased with the priest's abolitionist sentiments. In 1868, he lodged a presentment against him before the standing committee of the Diocese of Ohio, charging him with "preaching in a Congregational church, without using the Prayer Book or vestment." Following deliberation, the committee found in favor of Cracraft, concluding his actions were "not considered a ground of presentment." [8] In a turnabout of events, he and McIlvaine accused Whitehouse—a controversial Anglo-Catholic—of prejudice against Cracraft's Evangelicalism and preaching sermons on questions involving the Civil War. Such was the thrust-and-parry on interdenominational cooperation, a dispute complicated by tensions of the war and its aftermath.

In addition to their interest in interchurch cooperation, some Evangelicals continued to press their concerns about the prayer book. At the 1868 General Convention, "relief" but not revision was sought. L. W. Bancroft, professor of church history at Bexley Hall in Gambier, along with Benjamin B. Leacock and others, presented a petition to the House of Bishops asking permission to omit expressions in passages of the prayer book that the petitioners believed to be contrary to Scripture. The bishops denied the petition. Yet in 1869, McIlvaine and ten other Evangelical bishops followed up the request, urging in a letter to their colleagues that clergy "burdened and distressed" by certain prayer book expressions regarding infant baptism be allowed to use alternate phrases. This "measure of relief," they hoped, would be "of great importance to the peace and unity of the Church." Bishop Potter of New York immediately berated the communication in a pastoral letter to his diocese, arguing there were a "hundred reasons lying upon the very surface" that called for immediate rejection. [9] As with the previous initiative, the proposal failed. Yet again, in 1871, prayer book revision was addressed at General Convention. Again, the bishops dug in their heels, concluding after four days of deliberation that revision was not in order. They did, however, declare that the church needed to clarify its position on baptismal regeneration. In doing so, they declared—with but one dissenting vote—that the language of the prayer book should not be used to determine the doctrine that moral change occurred in baptism. The language should not be construed, that is, to mean that a moral change was wrought in the recipient of baptism; that he was, in other words, regenerated by the rite itself.

McIlvaine interpreted the vote as a victory for Evangelicals. By it, he believed, "the whole Tractarian and Romish *opus operatum* is denied, the inseparableness of the sign [baptism] and the grace signified [regeneration] is denied, and the utmost latitude for the evangelical views of the efficacy of baptism is acknowledged." [10] But George D. Cummins, bishop of Kentucky and a proponent of revision, was less sanguine; and Cummins proved to be the more prescient of the two. Within weeks, the declaration—owing to its ambiguous language and to polarized factions within the church— began to unravel. The hydra of baptismal regeneration was far from dead. The declaration was criticized by numerous Evangelicals, among them two members of the Bexley Hall faculty in Gambier as well as McIlvaine's assistant, Gregory Bedell. Although McIlvaine defended the declaration stridently, radical Evangelicals found themselves increasingly at odds with the document's ambiguity. They saw it as allowing Evangelicals and Ritualists to interpret baptismal regeneration in their respective ways, and thus as ineffective in stemming the Ritualist tide.

Although sympathetic to the notion of "relief," McIlvaine was convinced that the prayer book as it stood was adequate to the Evangelical position. He and others cited articles twenty-five and twenty-seven to uphold their view that baptism was a sign of regeneration but not the means of it. At the same time, they realized the language of the rite itself ("seeing now dearly beloved brethren, that *this Child* is regenerate and grafted into the body of Christ's Church") indicated that the person baptized *was* regenerated. Consequently, a literal reading of the baptismal rite introduced ambiguity into the logic of the Evangelical view. To counter this, Evangelicals held that baptism and other doctrines should always be interpreted by the articles, which clearly stated Protestant principle, and not by the poetry of the liturgy. In addition, McIlvaine believed the prayer book should be understood in its historical context, according to the view of its framers, and not according to those who faulted its lack of clarity. Relations between Ritualist and Evangelical militants continued to worsen in the early 1870s. At length, Cummins decided to leave the Episcopal Church. His stated reasons were three: first, his conscience was troubled by having to preside as bishop at Ritualistic churches in his home diocese of Kentucky; second, he had lost all hope that Ritualism could or would be eradicated by the national church; and third, the controversy over interdenominational cooperation made it clear that his real affinity was with like-minded evangelicals rather than with Episcopalians. On December 2, 1873, in opposition to the views of most Evangelical Episcopalians, eight clergymen and nineteen laymen, led by Cummins, organized the Reformed Episcopal Church. McIlvaine, who had died nine months earlier, was spared the sight of the schism.   .

The reality of sin, justification by faith alone, and the experience of conversion stood at the center of the Evangelical movement. Evangelicals stressed also the authority of Scripture over tradition in deciding issues of importance, and they were decidedly less elaborate in their worship than High Churchmen. Writes historian

Sydney Ahlstrom: "Extemporaneous prayer, special night meetings for devotional exercise, and occasional revivalism were permitted, sometimes even encouraged." [11] Of course, in McIlvaine's case, revivalism represented something far beyond an occasional concession. It was implicit or explicit in virtually every worship service he led. Early in his priesthood, in Georgetown, he set aside a congregational day of prayer and fasting for the purpose of religious revival. The act was characteristic of things to come. He himself had been converted at a revival; he wished others to have the same opportunity. Revival was always at the center of his thoughts.

In McIlvaine's day, it was customary for Evangelicals to attend both Morning and Evening Prayer on Sundays, with sermons scheduled at both services and Sunday school prior to Morning Prayer. Sermons were long and largely doctrinal in nature. Such preaching was typical of Protestants in general, for whom the sermon tended to be the focus of worship. Unlike Catholic bodies, where the liturgy built toward a climax in Holy Communion, Evangelicals built their worship around the Word written and the Word preached. In addition, vestments tended to be simple, with the minister wearing only a surplice during worship except during the sermon, "in preparation for which he would typically withdraw behind a screen to change into [an academic] gown." [12] Moreover, among Evangelicals, the "Real Presence" in the elements of bread and wine was not asserted, the Agnus Dei (a triple chant preceding the communion in the Catholic Mass) was not sung, Holy Communion was celebrated but once a quarter, and altars were shunned. Altars were anathema to Evangelicals because they symbolized the necessity of the continuous sacrifice of Christ as represented in the Catholic Mass. They held instead that Christ's death on Calvary was a finished work, sufficient in itself for the atonement of sins, a once-for-all act that had brought to an end the ages-old system of blood sacrifice. McIlvaine, as we know, subscribed to this view. In his diocese, altars were absent lest a parish wished to incur the displeasure of the bishop, and a simple table was used instead.

The architectural style that accommodated an altar drew the ire of Evangelicals. For an altar, a more or less elaborate affair carved in marble (and always and everywhere, McIlvaine insisted, fashioned in the likeness of a tomb) was positioned against a wall in the sanctuary, requiring the celebrant to turn his back to the people in the nave. Evangelical clergy, who preferred to face the laity while officiating at the Lord's *Table*, saw a hierarchical, anti-democratic bias in the opposite practice. In addition, in favoring use of a table, they stressed the memorial aspect of sharing the symbolic body and blood of the sacrificed savior rather than the mysterious and partially hidden reenactment of his death.

McIlvaine recounted in a letter to his friend, William Carus, in 1866, a pair of incidents involving altars, both of which underscored the bishop's unswerving views on the subject. He had for some time, he wrote, made clear his determination not to consecrate a church with an altar. "In one of my churches," he observed," a cross of wood was put on such a structure. I would not enter it till they took the cross away, and I did not consecrate it till the structure was changed." The second incident involved a parish to which he had written prior to his visitation. Owing to his letter, he assumed he would find no difficulties in regard to the use of an altar. An hour before worship, he visited the church to assure himself that all was in order. "Lo! Such a structure," he exclaimed. "I said at once, I cannot consecrate the church. The rector entreated. As there was no time to make a change, and the congregation would soon be there, I consented on the condition that what was there should be covered out of sight, and a table substituted as soon as possible, which was done." [13]

Suspicious as they were of Roman Catholic influences, Evangelicals displayed in their churches and public worship an austerity at times bordering on the puritanical. The pulpit, symbol as it was of preaching, dominated the Lord's Table, even as crosses and candles were all but banished. Neo-Gothic architecture, although its popularity grew among Episcopalians during the ante-bellum period, was suspect for its connections to Roman innovations of the late Middle Ages. As mentioned in the Introduction, Evangelicals preferred the basilica style dating from the early centuries of the church. In that style, there was an *apse*, a semicircular or polygonal space at the eastern end of the chancel, approached by a long hall, or nave. The chair of the bishop was placed in the center of the apse, with seating for fellow clergy arranged in a semicircle behind him. During the Liturgy of the Word, the people stood or sat in the nave; during celebration of Holy Communion, they gathered about a simple wooden altar in front of the bishop. Over time, as the liturgy became more formal, the altar was recessed into the apse, away from the people, creating a sacred space called a sanctuary. "Eventually," one historian observes, "the sanctuary was accessible only to clergy, and the altar was raised and made of stone." [14] The momentum behind these innovations was reversed by Protestants in general and Evangelicals in particular, as they removed altars wherever they found them and replaced them with Communion Tables, fully accessible to the people. A church of basilica design, congruent with McIlvaine's views, was built on the campus of Kenyon College several years before his death, as noted in the Introduction.

McIlvaine, who lacked all sympathy for mere ritual observances, used his authority as bishop not only to oppose altars but to limit processionals, surpliced choirs, musical innovations, pious postures, crosses and vestments; in short, to oppose all that "general display" which seemed in his eyes to replace the necessary interiority of genuine faith with showy externals that flattered the natural appetites. In his view, worship was to be God-centered, not man-centered, deep and heart-felt, not superficial and sensually oriented. These principles he attempted to inculcate in all of his parishes.

In keeping with such notions, he encouraged congregational singing in preference to the use of trained choirs. His views on this and other aspects of church music received their clearest statement in his pastoral letter of 1855, written in response to concerns expressed in church periodicals. Of congregational singing, he remarked, "How little we have of it!" There was, he said, plenty of singing *to* congregations, "But what a poor substitute it is for that singing of the praises of God *in* the congregation and *by* the congregation, which our service contemplates." He encouraged the clergy and laity of his diocese to "unite in vocal praise of God" as a matter of duty, pleasure and spiritual profit, in the absence of which, "the best music that man ever executed can make no amends." Hence, choristers and organists were not to use the church as a concert hall. Nor were they to allow the place of music to overstep its bounds, as some believed it had. There had been complaints that music was taking up too much of the service, owing to long interludes between hymn stanzas and repetitive singing of the *Gloria Patri* and other doxologies. Predictably, McIlvaine opposed such "vain repetition," smacking as it did of Ritualist ceremonial. Yet another concern was the selection of tunes. In this, he advised his clergy to choose mostly familiar pieces, those that were simple and easily learned. He cautioned against adding new music "without the least regard to the rights of the congregation." It would be wise, he urged, to consider "the devotional feelings and profit of the people." Thus he advised clergy to suppress the selection of unfamiliar tunes in favor of tunes that had been sung for generations. Additions, he said, were permissible "now and then, if additions are really needed, as the people…may reasonably be expected to learn." [15]

Despite vigorous opposition to High Church and Tractarian views, Evangelicals were largely allied with their fellow churchmen on at least two points: in their gratitude for the threefold ministry of bishops, priests and deacons, and in their genuine love for the Book of Common Prayer. As to the first, they viewed it as a pillar of order and a proper reflection of governance in the early church. They had no wish to question its importance or legitimacy. Yet their agreement was not complete. They did not, for instance, accept the "apostolic succession"—a key aspect of the tradition—in terms agreeable to Anglo-Catholics or High Churchmen. Unlike these others, they emphasized the spiritual as opposed to the institutional succession. Even so, McIlvaine's view on the permanency of the apostolic office, expressed in a sermon in 1839, was enough to trouble the Presbyterian theologian Charles Hodge, when it was reprinted many years later. In reply to his friend's concerns, McIlvaine affirmed his view as representative of "the usual low-church doctrine" of his denomination. Moreover, he claimed, low-church Episcopalians and Presbyterians understood apostolic succession in the same way, to wit, "that a *certain part* of the authority committed to the Apostles was intended to continue in the ministry to the end of the world, and, has continued—such for example as the power of ordination." The difference between Episcopalians and Presbyterians, he said, was that "the latter hold the descent to have been in the line of Presbyters, the former in the line of diocesan Bishops." Thus, the spiritualizing tendency of McIlvaine's thought was clear, even as the instrumental utility of the episcopate was affirmed.[16]

As to the prayer book, Evangelicals found in its poetic and stately language a guarantor of ordered and dignified worship, in the conduct of both Sunday services and revivals. Indeed, McIvaine went so far as to find in it a partial substitute for the absence of a pastor. Such absences were not uncommon during the Civil War, as many clergy served as chaplains in the army. In such circumstances, he urged, congregations should "take advantage of the great privilege of having our Book of Common Prayer, whereby a Church without a Pastor may still have its public worship and the Word of God, in fitness, and in power." At such times, he advised congregations to meet together regularly, to "have the Morning and Evening Prayer, and some approved published sermon, read by one of your number." Thus, the congregation would "have much to enjoy, though not all you need and desire." [17]

McIlvaine testified to his love and respect for the prayer book early in his career, even as he recognized the need to modify its use under some circumstances. In a letter to his bishop, James Kemp of Maryland, written in 1821, he declared that he yielded to no one "in attachment to our Church and particularly in attachment to its liturgy." Yet in the same letter, he said there were times—when presiding before largely non-Episcopal gatherings, for instance—when use of the liturgy would be a "difficult and lame operation." In such circumstances, he said, "we ought to use that method of worship by which we can avoid the most difficulties and embrace the most of the liturgical excellencies." He noted that the Thirty-fourth Canon of the General Convention allowed for such variations. [18]

In a second letter to the bishop, written the following year, he observed that he had been appointed chaplain of the U. S. Senate, a duty that required him to preach occasionally to the U. S. House of Representatives as well. Despite his wish to use Episcopal liturgy at such times, the congregation was "always extremely heterogeneous, entirely without prayer books." Thus, he found it expedient to adapt the service to its participants, by using portions of the liturgy in such a way as to encourage responses from worshippers but not to confuse them. "I hate irregularities," he wrote, "and if I have ever been chargeable with any, it has always been on account of a conscientious belief that they were justified by circumstances." [19]

In their loyalty to the episcopate, the threefold ministry and the Book of Common Prayer, McIlvaine and his colleagues— however inclusive their views—kept some distance from evangelicals of other denominations. Although an Evangelical to his fingertips, he was first to last a lover and devoted servant of the Episcopal Church.

There has always been in the office of bishop an undeniable measure of dignity. There has been also a large measure of selfless burden-bearing. In McIlvaine's case, there was not only the customary pastoring of clergy and lay people, with all the care and concern that that entailed, but the need to serve them in a frontier environment in which travel was often difficult. The idealized image of a bishop—of a blessed figure trailing clouds of glory—was replaced often by a man with dust on his coat and mud on his boots.

McIlvaine showed his mettle by facing head-on the challenges of the Ohio frontier. In defiance of the calendar, he embarked in late November 1832—shortly after his arrival from the East—on a tour of the diocese, an exhausting round of visiting, preaching and lecturing. His travels on horseback took him from Zanesville to Newark and from Mount Vernon to Gambier, then to Berkshire and Delaware. He preached daily and often nightly, and returned home in January 1833. Although a lover of home and family, he would keep up a vigorous pace of visitation throughout his years as bishop.

In a letter to his mother of October 1839, seven years after coming to the diocese, McIlvaine found himself in the midst of a five-week separation from his family, having had to attend the diocesan convention at Steubenville as well as visit parishes. He admitted that, owing to his traveling, preaching, talking and attending to other duties, he was thoroughly fatigued, and said that he could do nothing more than throw himself on his bed at night. "I think it would amuse you, mother," he wrote, "could you see me in all my varieties of posture and work during a visitation, especially if you think of me, as I can hardly help thinking of myself, even in the most dignified duties, as *a mere boy of some eighteen years."* His circumstances, he told his mother, varied from the most "refined society of the State, perhaps next to the most uncultivated," and his duties varied as well. At one stop he would find himself delivering a charge to the clergy, at another scolding "some parish in the woods" for allowing abolition lectures in the church, or for protracted meetings, or for perfectionism, "the last thing, one would suppose, to be scolded about." Often contenting himself with no more than a bowl of milk and a piece of apple-pie, he would depart one parish and be off to the next. [20] Fifteen years on, he was "roughing it" still. In a letter to Carus in May 1854, he noted that in the three weeks since he had left home he had preached twenty-five times in twenty-three days, "besides the confirmations and addresses and talking and traveling." He confessed to feeling weary in body and mind, a little tired "of the worldliness of the world," and to a longing to join Carus and others across the sea. It was, he wrote, the longing for England—and all that that meant to him in terms of relaxation and spiritual renewal—that had prompted him to write the letter. He had barely found a moment to write, he said, as he had had "to preach twice today, confirm once, and drive twenty-five miles over a not very *English* road." [21]

McIlvaine further told Carus, in this letter of 1854, about a singular incident in which he managed to find a bit of humor in spite of the discomforts he had endured. It seems the train had set him down some seven miles from a small Welsh-origin parish, where he had scheduled a visit. He had expected to be met by "some conveyance" dispatched to take him from the station to the parish. Owing to a misunderstanding, however, this was not to be. Nor could he find a horse for hire in the village. "So," he wrote, "I shouldered my baggage, which was not light, and overcoat (the day was hot and the road very rough and hilly) and trudged on the *seven miles*, occasionally sitting on a log, and taking a book to read, till I had rested my arms from their load." By and by, he entered the village, "to the consternation of the Welsh pastor and his wife." The only ill effect of this misadventure, he wrote, was a severe cold and cough, which lingered even as he was writing to Carus. "Such is our dignity sometimes in Ohio!" [22]

In April 1857, in a letter to his wife, the fifty-eight-year-old bishop described yet another spell of rough travel. Having left Medina, at six-thirty in the morning, he had ridden twelve miles "in an open buggy through awful roads—was almost frozen." He arrived at Strongville, his destination, "just in time to get a little thawed," before entering the church to preach and confirm, and to consume a quick dinner. "Then rode seven miles in a driving snowstorm, right in the face, to Columbia. Had five minutes to get warm; preached and confirmed; got tea, rode three miles to the station and got to Cleveland at ten at night." Despite the rigors of the journey, he celebrated the fact that he had neither caught cold nor developed a sore throat. Although wearied by the exertion, he wrote, he was feeling a sense of growing refreshment. In fact, as his mood lightened, he drew a lesson from the experience, vindicating his calling and service. "What hard work it is," he wrote. "I sometimes ask myself what is my self-denial and self-sacrifice? I answer, *in all this;* for whatever it might be to some others who have not such love of home, and quiet, and order, and retirement, and all that they bring with them, it is to me a very great sacrifice." [23]

The burden of being a bishop was more than physical. In a letter to his son, Charles, in March 1866, McIlvaine described the emotional weight of the office. "I have so much care and burden," he wrote, "my mind is such a depot of all the troubles, and weaknesses of those over whom I am placed, that I often say to myself, 'Well, I shall go away soon.'" Alarmed by the allusion to his demise, he quickly recanted. After all, who was he to pine for earthly departure and grumble about the duties of his calling? He reminded himself to be aware of his obligations—"Take care lest you be not weary of the Master's will"—and of his love for his wife and children, and the melancholy thought of being separated from them. Still, he said, "If ministers, who desire to be made Bishops, only knew what the place is...they would hope that whenever an election is to take place, it may be forgotten that they are in existence." [24]

The arduous nature of McIlvaine's travels and visitations was tempered in some measure by stolen moments of privacy between worship services. Indeed, these intervals afforded him a break in routine unable to be enjoyed even at home. At such times, he wrote his mother in May 1841, "I escape into the woods, where no ear hears, or man's eye sees....Recently I have had many such forest interludes." He wondered if such sylvan moments, laced with fond memories, did not accompany him into the pulpit from time to time, "and give a tinge to my thoughts, or a certain life to my feelings, in which thoughts of dear mother and times past, from youth up, have much share." [25]

Party struggles between Evangelicals and High Churchmen dampened McIlvaine's response on occasion to events that would have otherwise excited his attention and energies. This would appear to have been the case in 1867, when he was invited to Lambeth Palace in London to attend the first-ever worldwide gathering of Anglican bishops. Colonial bishops and Anglo-Catholics had sought the conference to resolve issues of authority and oppose Rationalist heresies. Matters had come to a head on both counts in 1863, when John W. Colenso, bishop of Natal, was excommunicated for heresy by the Metropolitan of South Africa. Undaunted, he had appealed to the Crown and the judgment was reversed. Thus, the authority of the South African Church was in question.

About this time, the aging McIlvaine confided to his journal that he was "greatly tried, and often depressed." Yet he insisted the truth was "more precious" to him than ever. Moreover, his trust in God was intact. "Lord, give me patience to wait and pray, and work, and contend, and watch. Let me not be *weary!* Still in my declining years make use of me." [26] In the event, he was made use of at Lambeth.

It would be McIlvaine's sixth trip to England, and the thought of another long journey—despite his love for the mother country—

must have weighed heavily on him. In addition, he was wary of the conference owing to its promotion by Anglo-Catholics. On the other hand, that it might address the Rationalist heresy surely piqued his interest. As to misgivings about the conference generally, he made them clear in a letter to Carus. He did not think, he wrote, that such "a variety of minds...could get in three days to any very important conclusions, and it is questionable whether the manifestation of an outward union...would be of much spiritual interest or benefit." Nor was he pleased with the opening declaration, the first draft of which had been sent to the bishops in July. Writing to Carus on August 17, he said it was "most empty, cold, timid, reserved." [27] Moreover, he said, it contained too many references to church councils and tradition and not enough to Scripture. Also, he disliked its statement on Christian reunion.

The document had been written by Robert Gray, Metropolitan of South Africa, the very prelate who had excommunicated Bishop Colenso. To be sure, it expressed Anglo-Catholic emphases, speaking favorably of the primitive and undivided church and the historic episcopate. It stressed also the vital nature of the first four general councils. [28] Though unhappy with it, McIlvaine thought it a document of importance, and worth improving. His good friend, C. R. Sumner, bishop of Winchester, agreed, and McIlvaine set about to make changes. "I took the paper to my room," he said, "and to a great extent re-wrote the first resolution, going as far as I dare, with any hope of its acceptance." [29] In its revised state, it highlighted Scripture, mentioned the Thirty-nine Articles, and asserted that any hope of reunion would demand, among other things, the "diligent searching of the Scriptures, with humble reliance on the Holy Ghost." [30] Although it was submitted to Archbishop of Canterbury Charles T. Longley prior to the conference, it was not accepted as written.

When the conference convened on September 24, seventy-six bishops were present (150 had been invited), including approximately thirty Evangelicals, four Broad Churchmen, and forty-two High Churchmen and Anglo-Catholics. At least forty-three of the attendees were from the colonies or the United States. At the same time, others excused themselves from attending, some from old age, some from the expense of the journey, some from pressing diocesan business. Still others, mainly Evangelicals from the York and Canterbury provinces, and several in the Irish part of the United Church, refused to attend because they doubted the legality of such a conference. Indeed, as late as the 1890s, there remained leading bishops who refused to attend Lambeth because they saw it as a supranational synod usurping the powers of Queen and Parliament.

In his 1867 welcome, Archbishop Longley reminded the delegates that they were present to confer together on topics of mutual interest and to discuss, in particular, the situation of the colonial churches. He reiterated that the conference was *not* a general synod capable of enacting canons, but an assembly to discuss issues and pass resolutions that would be a guide for future action. Following the archbishop's welcome, several memorials were presented, including one from Edward Pusey and the Anglo-Catholics, who sought discussion of reunion with the Roman Catholic and Orthodox churches. Their proposal was not acted upon.

Meanwhile, McIlvaine and his colleagues were busy revising the opening declaration, and by day's end had completed a new draft. In it, the notion of the faith of the primitive and undivided church was given a Protestant accent, by asserting that it had been affirmed by the Fathers of the English Reformation. Largely satisfied with the day's work, McIlvaine wrote to Carus that the document was "considerably improved; some of my suggestions substantially adopted. It is certainly a good deal better than the former." [31] Nevertheless, some Evangelicals remained unsatisfied. Among them was Francis Jeune, bishop of Peterborough, who had refused to attend the conference. In his view, the revised draft still accorded the general councils too high a place relative to Scripture. Neither was he happy with the claim that the English Reformation was a return to the faith of the primitive and undivided church. Moreover, he regretted the absence of any mention of the Thirty-nine Articles, which the confreres had deleted. On the other side of the divide, the Anglo-Catholics were dissatisfied that only the first four general councils were mentioned.

With displeasure on all sides, additional revisions were proposed. Initially, the Evangelicals appeared on the way to victory, for they obtained deletion of references to the undivided church and the general councils altogether. For his part, McIlvaine argued against mention of the councils because the Thirty-nine Articles did not recognize them as independently authoritative. To the extent they were, he said, it was because they agreed with Scripture. In this, he gained the support of Archibald Tait, bishop of London and a Broad Churchman, who believed that any reference to the councils as definitive bodies would be the same as adding a new article to the rule of faith. Also, by adding the words "in visible Communion with the United Church of England and Ireland," Evangelicals focused attention on the national church and its Protestant roots. Alarmed by the turn of events, Anglo-Catholics named a committee to deal with the final section of the declaration, and succeeded in reinserting language affirming the undisputed general councils, hence putting emphasis again on the early church and episcopate. Finished at last, this third draft was adopted by the bishops.

Owing to the final status of the declaration, to the collegiality of the participants, and to the strong words of a resolution regarding Bishop Colenso's teachings (which, the bishops declared, had "deeply injured" the communion and created "scandal" in Natal), McIlvaine departed satisfied. "The feeling of the whole meeting," he wrote to Carus, "the bearing of all towards one another, the decidedly high tone of manners and spirit, were truly delightful. I could heartily unite in the last resolution of thanks to God for such a meeting, as all did. How little did I expect at one time to be able to do so." [32]

As an ecumenical churchman, McIlvaine was especially open to working with Presbyterians, with whom he had been educated at Princeton and with whose evangelical leanings he resonated. In regard to this enduring relationship, a touching incident occurred in November 1867, the year that witnessed the first Lambeth conference. The incident was recorded in detail by A. A. Hodge, son of Charles Hodge, McIlvaine's former classmate. It so happened that delegates to the National Presbyterian Convention and members of the Protestant Episcopal Evangelical Societies had gathered in Philadelphia at the same time. The latter body, of which McIlvaine was a leading member, expressed its ecumenical spirit by asking for a blessing on the Presbyterian convention. When it came to the attention of the Presbyterians that a prayer had been said on their behalf, a committee "was deputed to carry the salutations of the representatives of all branches of the Presbyterian Church to their Episcopal brethren." The following day, an Episcopal delegation, consisting of McIlvaine and four other dignitaries, brought in turn "the salutations and blessings" of their brethren to the Presbyterians. "They addressed the Conference in warmly affectionate language," A. A. Hodge wrote, "and offered extemporaneous and eloquent prayers in their behalf, and pronounced upon them the Apostolic benediction. Such a scene has no parallel." [33]

Charles Hodge, the venerable Presbyterian theologian, was brought forward to respond to the generous words of the Episcopalians. "We wish to assure you, sirs," he said, "that your names are just as familiar to our people as to your own! That we appreciate as highly your services in the cause of our common Master, as the people of your own honored Church." The good will so expressed, evangelically understood, was a testimony to "unity" and not to "union." It bore witness to shared unity of heart, experience of conversion and reverence for Scripture, as

A Born-Again Episcopalian

opposed to the notion of formal union of diverse church bodies based on doctrinal compromises, always anathema to evangelicals. Hodge then addressed McIlvaine directly, recollecting the experiences they had shared. "You and I, sir, were boys together in Princeton College, fifty odd years ago," he recalled. "Often at evening have we knelt together in prayer. We passed through...the baptism of that wonderful revival in that institution in 1815. We sat together, year after year, side by side, in the same class-room. We were instructed through our theological course by the same venerable teachers." Though the two had gone their separate ways to serve their own churches, Hodge ventured to claim that their views had remained those of brothers in Christ. "I do not believe," he said to McIlvaine, that "you have preached one sermon on any point of doctrine or Christian experience, which I would not have rejoiced to have uttered. And I feel fully confident that I never preached a sermon, the sentiments of which, you would not have publicly and cordially endorsed." With scarcely "a dry eye in the house," his son reported, the elder Hodge continued: "And now...here we stand, gray-headed, side by side, for the moment representatives of these two great bodies of organized Christians. Feeling for each other the same intimate cordial love, and mutual confidence; looking not backward,—not downward to the grave beneath our very feet,—but onward to the coming glory." In suggesting there was a providential purpose in this unplanned meeting between Presbyterians and Episcopalians, Hodge drew attention to the similarities of the two churches in regard to origin, creed and experience. "Does it not seem to indicate, sir," he concluded, "that these churches are coming together? We stand here...to say to the whole world, that we are one in faith, one in baptism, one in life, and one in our allegiance to your Lord and to our Lord." Of course, the two churches never became one. Yet Hodge's words testify to the attraction between persons who shared a robust evangelical theology and a traditional Protestant piety. These two, Hodge and McIlvaine, symbolized that ecumenical unity. They were indeed one in faith, one in

238

baptism, one in life. They fully believed they would be one in "the coming glory," as well. [34]

McIlvaine was convinced he would find himself, following death, in a far better place than that of his earthly trials and travails. As we have seen, he had meditated periodically in his journal on the afterlife in regard to himself as well as the members of his family and his friends. Heaven, to McIlvaine, was no vague possibility but an absolute certainty, a place where he would join those whom he had loved. Thus, following the death in battle of his former student, Leonidas Polk, bishop of Louisiana and a major general in the Confederate army, he meditated once more on issues of life and death. Again, he pondered the loss and measured the gain. Though sundered in their earthly loyalties by the Civil War, their greater loyalties had remained intact. "I never doubted his rectitude of purpose and motive, because he was as he was," he wrote of Polk. "But my dear and venerable brother, you are now at rest; your warfare is accomplished; you are freed from the tribulations that beset us here; you see all things in the light of God; you are *with Christ.*" Such considerations transcended earthly disagreements, and put in perspective McIlvaine's opposition to Polk and the other southern bishops during the war years. Despite the bitterness of the war, he spoke with affection of his fallen comrade. "He [Polk] was a wise man, a devoted man, a holy man," he said, "a spiritually enlightened man…eminently a sincere and pure and honest-minded man." Two bishops, he said, could not have been more of one mind in all the associations, works and views they shared, excepting the terrible division that had rent the nation. Indeed, the men continued to pray for one another notwithstanding. Although he would live another decade, McIlvaine, in ruminating on the death of Polk, anticipated his own death might come soon. "How short the time before I shall depart also!" he wrote. "I hope, indeed, to be found in Christ, as I doubt not he [Polk] was. Then shall I go where he has gone before, and where union is forever, 'joy unspeakable,' holiness without spot— where Jesus is." [35]

In a letter of Christmas 1862 to William Carus, McIlvaine was even more explicit in regard to the future state. "Dear Carus," he said near the close, "to think of eternity together, and all the glorious communion of saints, before God and the Lamb. To know Christ—this seems to grow on one more and more; to enter further into the Holy of Holies; to see more into the Ark—and the glory!" [36] He expected to exchange the paltry glories of earth, sporadic and unsatisfying as they were, for a glory unalloyed and without end. He was prepared for that spiritual translation to take place at any time. At that moment, he believed, the angels would snatch him from the earthly church he had served so well and carry him in the blink of an eye to the real and heavenly church, where he would pass through the veil into God's eternal sanctuary.

High Church, Tractarian and Rationalist churchmen had provoked McIlvaine to take up the cudgels against his fellows at various times during his career. In doing so, he followed the example of Charles Simeon, the Anglican Evangelical introduced some chapters ago, whom he had met on his first trip to England. Simeon too had opposed the views of his fellow churchmen, while putting forward the Evangelical principles he held dear. McIlvaine venerated Simeon's character, his doctrine and his labors and sought to emulate all three. Owing to the grace of God, he said, Simeon had been "a most single-minded, unwearied, undaunted, patient, wise, successful minister of the Gospel." [37] McIlvaine might have been describing himself. In following his master, he had nurtured a churchman of like abilities and inclinations.

Like Simeon, also, he had kindled the ire of those who were committed to other forms of churchmanship. Simeon had been branded an "Ultra-Protestant" by the High Churchmen of his day, and McIlvaine was branded with epithets of a similar kind by the High Churchmen and Tractarians of his own. Was McIlvaine an "Ultra-Protestant?" Not in his own eyes. As indicated earlier, he considered the term to be one of abuse, designed to arouse feelings, not to clarify thought. He viewed himself as he had viewed Simeon, as a consistent follower of the Reformation and as an upholder of the Thirty-nine Articles, no more, no less. For these and other reputed "offenses," as well as for "holding forth Christ, and not the Church, as the sinner's refuge," he, like Simeon, was held in "utter aversion" by partisans of the High Church. [38] Yet despite opposition—no doubt, in large part, because of it—he was, like Simeon, able to develop his gifts and character to the fullest. Embroiled in controversy throughout his career, loved by many and reviled by some, he remained through it all, again, like Simeon, a dedicated churchman—and more than a churchman. He was a "true believer," an authentic Christian who "meant it," a man without guile or irony. Principle, duty and piety guided his every move, excepting only those occasional slips common to us all.

During the post-Civil War period, there was something of an easing in his circumstances. In those later years, he could look back on a life filled with faithful witness and ahead to an eternity filled with glory. In a letter to an unidentified clerical friend, written in January 1870, he said "our time is almost over—we shall be taken from great evils to come, probably greater trials of faith and patience to the people of God than have ever been known since the Reformation." He seemed little troubled by the likelihood of such "great evils." Perhaps he was relieved that he would not have to endure them. For his part, he would continue to live as he had always lived, under the aspect of eternity, his bags packed, ready for departure. He wrote to the same friend: "We 'look to that blessed hope and the glorious appearing of our great God and Saviour,' and we need not be on the earth then to rejoice in his Advent." [39]

Poor health, exacerbated by the death of his son, Joseph, in 1870, more than ever convinced McIlvaine that his own time was short. Yet another mission was yet to be carried out. In November of the same year, the Evangelical Alliance had named him to a delegation to visit the Emperor of Russia, on behalf of the persecuted Protestants of the Baltic provinces. At first he declined. By the following spring, however, he had changed his mind, "being greatly urged" to participate and concerned by the effects on his health of the early heat in Ohio (ninety-one degrees on May 29, he noted). He sailed on June 17 aboard the *City of Brooklyn,* arrived in Britain on June 27, and departed for the Continent shortly thereafter. He was in the company of forty delegates, led by Philip Schaff, the German-American theologian and church historian. Initially scheduled to meet the emperor himself, the delegation—consisting of "distinguished philanthropists" from America, England, and "all parts of Europe"—attained eventually a ninety-minute audience with the czar's prime minister, Prince Gortschakoff, at Friedrichshafen, on the German side of Lake Constance. A pleasant exchange followed, with assurances by the prince that the emperor would take into consideration the views expressed. McIlvaine was numbered among those who spoke on behalf of the delegation. [40]

The following year, in June 1872, McIlvaine set foot in England for the last time. He was welcomed by the Prince of Wales (later King Edward VII), introduced to the royal family, and invited to dine aboard the royal yacht on the occasion of a visit by an American squadron at Southampton. Over lunch, Queen Victoria personally acknowledged McIlvaine's hospitality a dozen years earlier when the prince and his entourage had visited Cincinnati. [41] So improved did McIlvaine feel during this visit, that by the New Year he was eager to set out for Italy in the company of his good friends, Canon and Mrs. Carus. After several weeks of touring, the party arrived in Florence on February 16, 1873, whereupon McIlvaine fell ill. After lingering for nearly a month, he died on March 13.

Yet more worldly glory was to come. McIlvaine's body was transported to England, where funeral services were held at Westminster Abbey. Tributes poured in from all quarters. After being returned to America, the body was interred in Clifton, near Cincinnati, which had been the seat of the diocese of Ohio for more than twenty-five years. Additional tributes were heard, as a multitude of persons touched by McIlvaine's example grieved at the loss. When the diocese convened in May, Bishop Bedell commented that for "the first time in its history of fifty-six years, the Diocese is bereaved of a bishop by death. Through forty years of the most difficult stages of its progress, Bishop McIlvaine has been its leader and guide. It is fitting that we should now commemorate his influence, for we are reaping the blessed results of it." [42]

Preacher, pastor, writer, controversialist, amateur diplomat, Evangelical; above all, churchman: McIlvaine's achievements were recognized and praised by people of all stations. In the language of St. Paul, he had run his race; he had won the imperishable crown. A life of purpose, discipline and grace had come to an end. Though family, friends and colleagues grieved, he had died as he would have wanted: at peace in the Lord whom he had served all his days.

1. Sydney E. Ahlstrom, *A Religious History of the American People*, 625.
2. Quoted in E. Clowes Chorley, *Men and Movements in the American Episcopal Church*, 132.
3. Charles P. McIlvaine, *The Present Condition and Chief Want of the Church: A Charge to the Clergy of the Protestant Episcopal Church of Ohio* (Gambier, 1836), 3-4, 6, 16-18.
4. Quoted in Diana Hochstedt Butler, *Standing Against the Whirlwind*, 189.
5. Butler, 142.
6. McIlvaine, *Righteousness by Faith, or the Nature and Means of Our Justification Before God* (Protestant Episcopal Book Society, Philadelphia, 1864), xii.
7. Quoted in Butler, 198.
8. Quoted in Chorley, 277.
9. Ibid., 403-404, 405.
10. Quoted in Butler, 205.
11. Ahlstrom, 625.
12. Loren Dale Pugh, *Bishop Charles Pettit McIlvaine*, 89.
13. Quoted in William Carus, *Memorials*, 259.

14. Rebecca Lyman, *Early Christian Traditions* (Cowley Publications, Cambridge, Massachusetts, 1999), 98.

15. Quoted in Jane Rasmussen, *Musical Taste as a Religious Question in Nineteenth-Century America*, Volume 20 of *Studies in American Religion* (The Edwin Mellen Press, Lewiston, N. Y., and Queenston, Ontario, Canada, 1986), 59-60, 221-222.

16. A. A. Hodge, *The Life of Charles Hodge*, 414-416.

17. McIlvaine, *Pastoral Letter of the House of Bishops of the Protestant Episcopal Church (1862)*, Project Canterbury.

18. McIlvaine, letter to Bishop Kemp, February 26, 1821, Christ Church Georgetown archives.

19. Ibid., December 17, 1822.

20. Quoted in Carus, 121.

21. Ibid., 155.

22. Ibid., 156.

23. Ibid., 168-169.

24. Ibid., 260.

25. Ibid., 123-124.

26. Ibid., 267.

27. Alan M. G. Stephenson, *The First Lambeth Conference*, 1867 (S. P. C. K., London, 1967), 214.

28. The first four councils were generally accepted by both Evangelicals and Anglo-Catholics, while Anglo-Catholics accepted the fifth and sixth councils also, and some even the seventh.

29. Stephenson, 214.

30. Ibid., 214-215.

31. Ibid., 216.

32. Ibid., 301.

33. A. A. Hodge, *The Life of Charles Hodge*, 505.

34. Quoted in Hodge, 506, 506-507, 507.

35. Quoted in Carus, 236.

36. Ibid., 239.

37. McIlvaine, editor, *Memoirs of the Life of the Rev. Charles Simeon*, xii.

38. Ibid., xiii.

39. Quoted in Pugh, 124.

40. Carus, 309-314.

41. Ibid., 328-329.

42. Quoted in Pugh, 126.

CHAPTER TEN

Facing Death

If, as Plato said, the practice of philosophy is a preparation for death, then Charles Pettit McIlvaine was a philosopher par excellence. By vocation and temperament, he was drawn to the subject of death in life, to the hope of life in death. From his earliest years in the ordained ministry, he meditated upon his own death and wrote often about it. He pondered as well the deaths of family members and friends, believers and skeptics alike. Behind every earthly joy and every pleasure, he detected the pall and the churchyard—followed by glory! He wished to die after the manner of his hero, Charles Simeon, whose heroic sanctity was described in earlier chapters. In the end, he got his wish. He died as he had lived: as a devout Christian, as a true believer, at peace. He died, ironically, under the skies of Roman Catholic Italy, far from his beloved family. Nevertheless, he died well, having prepared so thoroughly for those final weeks and days and moments.

In his introduction to the *Memoirs* of Charles Simeon, McIlvaine directed readers "very particularly" to the passage in which Simeon's final hours were the subject of the narrative. He urged readers to be alert to the "aged pilgrim" and "good soldier of Christ" as he stepped "into the valley and shadow of death, fearing no evil, leaning on the staff, and guided by the rod of the Good Shepherd." Simeon had been composed, filled with hope, and child-like in his trust of God, ready and waiting for the moment of departure. "Never," McIlvaine wrote, "have I read the narrative of a Christian minister's last hours, with more disposition to say, *'let my last end be like his.'*"[1]

In hoping for a not dissimilar death, McIlvaine was a man of his time. For the notion of a "good death," far from being the anomaly of an introspective churchman, was common among Americans of the ante-bellum period. Historians debate the reasons for this. A principle reason would seem to have been the revival of religious sentiment generally, a circumstance focusing the mind more pointedly than before on the eternal destiny of the soul. The Romantic influence in literature and art was likely another factor, owing to its reassertion of passion and imagination in contrast to the classicism and rationalism of the eighteenth century. Romanticism elevated the importance of the individual and his or her experiences in life and death, encouraging preoccupation with personal destiny. Finally, there was the carnage of the Civil War itself. All of these factors, in an age when childhood mortality remained high, surgery was fraught with pain and risk, and antibiotics were unknown, inclined people to brood upon death. Death could come at any time: on the farm, in the mill, from an epidemic. People of an inward turn of mind prepared for it. Deathbed scenes were a staple of both life and literature in McIlvaine's America.

In addition, there survived in that era residues of the Puritans' earthly pessimism and cosmic optimism, alongside a substratum of folk belief touching on life and death. The dying, a fair number of them at any rate, took comfort in noting that afflictions sanctified—made holy—those who suffered. According to the 1855 edition of *Webster's Dictionary,* suffering helped a person in "detaching the affections from the world and its defilements." Thus the Puritan patrimony continued to provide a framework in which people could find meaning and purpose, even in death and dying. Others, generally among the poorer classes, found a measure of meaning and purpose in superstition, where recourse was had to the palliatives of faith healers and "cunning folk," and where signs and portents played their role in life. Yet, despite the ministrations of conventional piety and folk magic, the laws of nature reaped their annual toll. The laws on which the grower of corn depended brought a harvest of death also. Thus pious and thoughtful folk took note, and prepared for a "good death." Above all, they feared "dying hard;" of suffering physically or mentally in their final days or, even worse, of being unwilling to die, of lacking composure and clinging to life when all was lost. [2] Much better it was to have a good death, to depart in faith and tranquility.

Ante-bellum Americans understood death and dying against a backdrop of literary fashion as well as personal experience. Writers of the period reflected the preoccupation in a variety of ways, from the philosophical to the sentimental to the macabre. In his essay, *Fate,* delivered as a lecture in the 1850s but not published until 1860, Emerson spoke of the dignity of facing death heroically, of accepting fate after the manner of the "hindoo, under the wheel," or as the Calvinists of an earlier generation, who "had something of the same dignity [and] felt that the weight of the Universe held them down to their place." Melville, in *White Jacket,* said much the same but more bluntly: that acceptance of fate "relieves men from nervous anxieties." Thus the fatalist, viewing his end as providential, as part of the overarching pattern of meaning, was enabled to confront with a measure of hope and dignity the death that would arrive at some unpredictable moment in all of its inevitability.

Death from consumption (tuberculosis), in particular, sounded a distinct note of tragedy and loss in ante-bellum literature. Indeed, according to Lewis Saum, it became "a hallmark of the Romantic sensibility grown morbid." Young women, especially, their lives ebbing away, added an element of wistful poignancy to this prevalent form of death. Their beauty "was heightened as the disease progressed. Bodily deterioration lent alabaster pallor to the skin...fever gave luminous intensity to the eyes and brightly contrasting red spots on the cheekbones."[3]

It was the era also of Washington Irving, Edgar Allen Poe and Nathaniel Hawthorne; of fictional corpses, specters and graveyards; of headless horsemen, telltale hearts and gloom-laden sagas. It is not surprising that Mark Twain, writing later in the century, should have created, in *Adventures of Huckleberry Finn*, the mournful, ante-bellum figure of Emmeline Grangerford. This girl, who pined away at fifteen, had spent her days in writing funereal verse, drawing romantic pictures of grieving ladies, and pasting into a scrapbook her collection of "obituaries and accidents and cases of patient suffering...out of the *Presbyterian Observer.*"[4]

Life imitated art. Emerson was given to periodic visits to the graves of Ellen, his first wife, and Waldo, his first son and namesake. During these visits to the family mausoleum, he would open their coffins, months and years after burial had taken place, and brood upon his loss. [5] Abraham Lincoln, some years later, would mourn the death of his young son with a like intensity. "I dream of my dead boy Willie again and again," he told a colonel at Fort Monroe. He felt "sweet communion" in those dreams, though convinced of their unreality. [6] Lincoln himself embodied mid-nineteenth century melancholia and his untimely death by assassination seemed, in retrospect, somehow fated. McIlvaine officiated at a service in honor of the slain president when Lincoln's funeral train arrived at Cleveland. "The dear martyr," he said of his friend, "his face uncovered, was just before me as I spoke, and every time I opened my eyes I saw him lying in death. After the service, began the constant procession on both sides, two parallel lines of people, each looking as they passed at the discoloured face."[7]

In 1872, a year before his own death, McIlvaine remembered that an aisle of the church in which he had been raised, St. Mary's,

Burlington, accommodated the graves and gravestones "where two or three of the former generations were buried." Thus he was raised in a church where the dead and the living maintained a physical proximity as well as a spiritual one. The dead were present among the living, the living among the dead. The temporal and the eternal intersected. Personally, he recalled, when writing to the Rev. George Morgan Hills for a history of St. Mary's, four generations of his family were buried at or near the east end of the church. These and other remains had been relocated from within the structure earlier in the century. He noted too that his father and a brother, Bloomfield, had died in the house opposite the church in 1826, "in adjoining rooms, and on two adjoining days—and were placed in one grave." He singled out for special mention the grave of his wife's elder sister, Maria Coxe, "whose Christian character and life were as precious ointment at the Saviour's feet, whose good works were as well known in Burlington as those of Dorcas, at Joppa." (The beneficent Dorcas, who appears briefly in the Acts of the Apostles, was known for making clothes for the poor.) [8]

There were other precious graves. In a letter to his brother, Henry, in September 1833, McIlvaine observed that his "pleasure in Burlington for a long time has been in a great measure among the dead, in association with the thoughts of those who were, but are gone." He confessed that he loved "to steal into the beloved garden, changed as it is, and meditate and pray and anticipate." He described his visits as a "feast" and the graveyard as "all life, as well as death." [9] One is reminded of the practices of the early church, when Christians celebrated "festivals of resurrection" at the tombs of the martyrs. [10] During his visits, McIlvaine ruminated on his father, whose "dust" lay side by side with Bloomfield's. "My heart bleeds yet at the name of that most precious, most affectionate father," he wrote. "To this day I cannot think of him without feeling, as if my heart would break with gratitude, for all he did and felt, and desired to do for us, and the thought that I can do nothing now for him." [11]

Four years later, in 1837, he wrote to another brother, Joseph. In this letter, too, attention is given to death and eternity, alongside gratitude for Joseph's tentative steps towards sanctity. Joseph, who was serving in the Pennsylvania legislature at Harrisburg, was urged to be "about this work"—the work of Christ—"obeying the clear light that is in you; following the strong convictions which God has wrought upon your mind and heart." Now thirty-eight years of age, McIlvaine suggested neither he nor Joseph could expect to be long lived. This conviction of approaching death appears, in part, to be an evangelical commonplace, delivered by habit; a reflexive gambit to keep one's mind fixed on death, judgment and eternity. "We have but a little while before we go hence," he wrote. "The time ahead seems very short." In the event, he was correct in regard to his brother's death. Joseph's untimely demise was little more than a year away, although there was no indication at the time of the letter that he was ill. "I look beyond the present," McIlvaine said. "....We are far on the way. The end draws near, we have a great work to do—a work that ought to have been long ago begun, and should be now far advanced." He encouraged Joseph to look beyond "this little valley of life," to secure "the glorious boundless life of a ransomed soul forever." He admonished his brother to engage himself in God's service, to take refuge in Christ, to be a man of constant prayer. "How [such habits of piety] would set you up in peace and prospect, how [they] would fill up many a void in the present, and banish many a cloud from the future, and raise your spirit, and make you feel what you are as an immortal being." In January 1839, he commemorated the first anniversary of Joseph's death. His brother had been depressed near the end, it was said, and yet it was said also that he was set to abandon political and worldly pursuits to lead a new life and prepare for the ministry of the Gospel. He had told his friends as much. The aborted redirection of his brother's life, the state of his soul, and his post-mortem condition filled McIlvaine's thoughts. "I cherish the fond hope," he wrote, "that you are with Christ in glory—that I shall meet you there. Farewell till I die—it may be very soon." [12]

In fact, his death was thirty-four years distant. Yet its palpable presence shadowed his days and his nights and preserved him under the aspect of eternity. It reminded him of his dependence on God, of the brevity of his days, of the need to be active in God's service in the here and now, not by and by. On the occasion of his birthday, it was his habit to enter, in his journal, reflections on his spiritual state and anticipations of death in the year ahead. According to his friend, William Carus, "He regarded each year as he entered upon it as not unlikely to be his last. The result of this habitual expectation of death was a calm and constant preparation for it; so much so, that it may be truly affirmed that he always so lived as to be ever ready to die." [13] His inward turn of mind and his faith as a Christian inclined him in this direction, to be sure, but periodic bouts of illness confirmed him in it. As we have seen, these illnesses date from his time at Princeton Seminary, when a collapse in health cut short his stay and caused him to complete his studies at home.

By the time he was rector of Christ Church, Georgetown, his obsessive concern over his health in general and periodic collapses in particular had become publicly evident. Vestry minutes record times where he was "too weak to consider or continue" his duties, thereby requiring him to be granted extended periods of absence to recover himself. [14] These absences did not prevent a most successful ministry, nor did they appear to disquiet his parishioners. In part, the mindset of the time tolerated a fair amount of worry over health matters; in part, the members of Christ Church were impressed by their eloquent, polished and kind rector. Therefore they were disinclined to be critical of his health-related eccentricities. Some years later, during his tenure at St. Ann's, Brooklyn, similar collapses occurred. Owing to these bouts of ill health, he sailed to England in 1830, there to recuperate. Ironically, the symptoms that led to the trip arose as the young rector was entering in his journal an account, just received, of the "happy effects" on a listener of a sermon he had preached on prayer. "Suddenly," according to Carus, "his health failed from neuralgia of a violent kind, and entire rest and a voyage became necessary for his recovery." In preparing for the journey, he experienced considerable apprehension. "So uncertain my days," he wrote in his journal. "I sail to-morrow, and expect to be gone five or six months. I embark upon the great deep. I go among strangers. I know not that I shall ever behold my precious family and dear people again. O my God, help me with childlike submission to leave myself perfectly in Thy hands!" [15] The hiatus would result not only in recuperation but in making personal contact with notables of the English church, as well as lords and ladies, who would be of service to him in future endeavors. These contacts, as observed in earlier chapters, would influence the course of his career in many and varied ways.

Two months after leaving home, McIlvaine wrote his wife that he had improved rapidly and markedly, although residues of ill health remained. "The disorder had taken a deeper hold than I supposed," he said. "It is broken, but the eradication of its seeds will be gradual. I have had two bad turns since I got here, but they were short." He proceeded to describe the regimen he followed in the attempt to recover his health. "I must," he wrote, "have patience—be very quiet—read nothing—write as little as possible—eat very plain food—sleep much—and by the goodness of God I shall return to you and my dear people in health. I am much stronger, and look better than when I left you, but my head is easily disordered." [16]

Sixteen years later, in 1846, he experienced again a "disordered head." As described, the symptoms indicate a mild stroke. Mrs. Anna Pierrepont of New York, a friend of the family, wrote to McIlvaine's son-in-law, the Rev. George Washington DuBois, to inform him the bishop had "been seized with a total loss of memory after he had taken a bath." During the seizure, she wrote, "everything seemed like a dream to him." But once a doctor had administered a "powerful medicine," recovery began. "The confusion of ideas had left him," Mrs. Pierrepont continued, "but he still felt weak and did not remember well." When he visited the following day, he appeared languid and complained of continued weakness, which he blamed on the medicine from the day before. He suggested that the attack might have been linked to an earlier one in his back, a form of "nervous affection." Mrs. Pierrepont served him a biscuit and a glass of wine before sending for a carriage and riding with him to a ferry for departure. [17]

Despite his apparently fragile health, McIlvaine had, by the time of the Pierrepont letter, been serving the diocese of Ohio as bishop and Kenyon College as president for nearly fifteen years. Although the physical rigors of the frontier as such seem to have affected him little, anxiety and interruption of domestic life related to his work appear to have caused him much distress. "The physical labor I think little of," he wrote. "It is the care, anxiety, connected with such a charge; with all the breaking up of one's home relations and parental offices; the almost impossibility of carrying on any process of mental improvement." In 1858, the diocese—long aware of his proneness to anxiety and illness— granted him an eight-month leave to go abroad in search of respite. As his condition had not greatly improved by the time of his return in February 1859, the convention elected an assistant bishop, the Rev. Gregory Bedell, to help lighten his duties. "The convention was concerned about the health of the bishop," Loren Pugh writes, "particularly fearing he might suffer a stroke of apoplexy." Occasional "loss of memory, the confusion of ideas, and other symptoms validated their concern." [18]

On his final trip abroad, in 1872-73, McIlvaine's health seemed to improve. Hence, he planned to sail for home in November, to resume his work. But Bishop Bedell and other friends urged him to extend his trip into the New Year, noting that premature returns had in the past caused him to relapse. With some reluctance, he agreed to stay on. "So here I am till April next at least—perhaps May," he wrote to his daughter, Mamy. "I have so much improved in health that I have good reason to hope that by spring I shall be able to go home & stay at home—& be of some use." [19] The letter was written in his seventy-fourth year. Four months later, he would be stricken with his final illness.

To the modern reader, McIlvaine's periodic trips to Europe to remedy his ailments might appear to be an unnecessary indulgence. Could he not have found, one might ask, equally effective treatment at domestic hot springs and spas? By traveling to England, he removed himself for months at a time from his family and his diocese. Perhaps that was the point. His travels were not for recuperation only but for a measure of personal enjoyment as well. They were perhaps a kind of "coping mechanism" (as it would be called today), as suggested in chapter two, a means of maintaining mental equilibrium by escaping not only the pressure of clerical responsibility but family burdens as well. Correspondence indicates the bishop's wife accompanied him on a trip to Britain in 1853, and on other occasions one or more daughters joined him on his travels; beyond these instances, it appears he traveled alone or with friends. Despite his deep affection for his wife and children, he was able to leave them for extended periods. Arguably, he was a bit selfish in all of this, but perhaps forgivably so, given the responsibilities that weighed upon him, his severe diligence in fulfilling his duties, and the melancholic temperament with which he struggled.

In addition to the illnesses that were so much a part of his life, McIlvaine more than once faced the specter of death from forces outside of himself. While rector of St. Ann's, Brooklyn, in 1832, he acquitted himself courageously during a cholera epidemic that ravaged the community. Despite the danger posed by the highly contagious and often deadly disease, he endeared himself to many by going door-to-door to visit the sick and comfort the bereaved. He showed courage as well during the steam-ferry mishap on the Ohio River in 1855, at which time he had remained composed, attended to his duties as a cleric and a gentleman, and waited for what appeared to be almost certain death with a prayer on his lips, as recounted in chapter eight.

Yet another brush with death occurred in August 1868, in his seventieth year. In a letter to William Carus, [20] he described the incident in detail. It occurred as he drove his buggy in the vicinity of Cincinnati, with his wife, Emily, and the Rev. G. T. Fox as passengers. Unaware that a railroad track was at the top of a steep rise, he had driven halfway to the summit before his wife spotted an oncoming train and called a warning. There was no signal from the train itself, he recalled, and from "the sound I could not judge where it was—how far off. It seemed distant." As the narrowness of the road made it difficult to turn about, he drove forward to get a look at the train and decide his course of action. "In a few moments I saw it only a hundred yards off, and at full speed. My road lay directly across its track—on the same level." Though the whistle sounded at last, the buggy had by then nearly reached the crossing. "To stop there," McIlvaine said, "was the certainty that the horse, frightened by the train rushing right past his face, would back us down the steep side of the road, some thirty feet." There was barely a moment for decision. "I saw," he said, "there was nothing to be done but *press across*....If the horse should hesitate at the track, I knew we were to be destroyed." For an instant, it appeared the horse would indeed shy from the danger. "I had not time to seize the whip," McIlvaine said. "I shook the reins and ordered." The horse leaped across the track, even as "the train rushed behind us, and I do not think there were more than six feet between it and the hind wheels." In assessing the incident, he called it "a marvel of deliverance! What if the horse had hesitated but two or three seconds! What mercy! What interposition of God's hand!" Mrs. McIlvaine, the first to see the train, sat silent until the danger was passed; "but the retrospect almost unnerved her."

In such instances, the inwardly anxious McIlvaine showed himself to be courageous and resolute in the face of danger and possible death. Nebulous fears of daily happenstance and chronic thoughts of an early demise appeared to be absent at times of immediate danger and unexpected testing. At such moments, his steely core showed through. His inner strength, evident in the long years of leadership and controversy and in the face of illness and anxiety, was equally evident in these incidents. He faced them as he had faced more quotidian events, with an underlying faith in the God whom he trusted at all times to do the right thing, according to his mysterious purposes.

Death, McIlvaine believed, presented a far different aspect to believers than it did to unbelievers. To the one, it was the entrance upon blessedness; to the other, the end of all expectations. "The religion of heaven is the religion of believers on earth," he wrote, "but with both its robes, its sanctification as well as justification, made perfectly white in the blood of the Lamb." By contrast, neither a desire for heaven nor an inkling of its reality was to be found in the non-believer. "How impossible," McIlvaine said, "that a man should be happy in heaven, were he even taken thither, who has never learned to partake in the happiness of religion." [21]

In musing alike on the destinies of believer and non-believer, McIlvaine recounted the pathos of the last days of "infidels." His account of the demise of Thomas Paine was presented in chapter seven. He wrote of the death of Voltaire also, and touched on Thomas Hobbes and his final "leap in the dark." "The question is," he said, "does infidelity sustain and comfort its disciples in the hour of death?" He proposed to show, in his *Evidences of Christianity*, that it did not. He took as an example the death of the philosopher David Hume, the religious skeptic and debunker of miracles. Hume's companions held that their late friend had died "the death of a philosopher," a death both admirable and worthy of emulation. Using the narrative they provided, McIlvaine turned the tables on them. "He knew his end was near," he wrote of Hume. "Whether he was to be annihilated, or to be forever happy, or for ever miserable, was a question involved on his own principles, in impenetrable darkness. It was the tremendous question to be then decided." But Hume avoided the question. Though he knew death was near, he voiced no curiosity as to his posthumous state. Instead, McIlvaine observed, he spent his time *diverting* himself. And with what? "With preparing his Essay in defence of *Suicide* for a new edition; reading books of amusement; and sometimes with a game at cards." When weary of these, the sage turned to other activities. He was found "talking silly stuff about Charon and his boat, and the river Styx! Such are a philosopher's diversions, where common sense teaches other people to be, at least, grave and thoughtful." In Hume's case, as McIlvaine construed it, puerile pastimes were the deliberate means of turning his mind from death. "Was he afraid," McIlvaine asked, "to let his mind settle down quietly and alone to the contemplation of all that was at stake in the crisis before him? Whatever the explanation of his levity, it was ill-timed…an affected piece of over-acting, intended for posthumous fame….He died 'as a fool dieth.'" [22]

According to a footnote in the *Evidences*, he died miserably as well. McIlvaine's source was the philosopher's longtime housekeeper, whose account was published in the *Christian Observer*. The details, McIlvaine insisted, had never been called into question, although they contradicted earlier versions given by Hume's friends. (These earlier versions had been questioned by others also, among them John Wesley and other clergymen, who—not surprisingly—doubted claims of the philosopher's peaceful end.) According to the housekeeper's account, Hume endured a death neither peaceful nor pleasant. When he had been with friends, she agreed, he had been cheerful and seemingly unconcerned about his approaching demise. At such times, he "spoke of it to them in a jocular and playful way." But when he was alone, it was a different story. "He was," she said, "anything but composed; his mental agitation was so great at times as to occasion his whole bed to shake. He would not allow the candles to be put out during the night, nor would he be left alone for a minute." She claimed to have seen "disturbed sleeps and still more disturbed waking …

involuntary breathings of remorse and frightful startings....[These] continued and increased until he became insensible. I hope in God I shall never witness a similar scene." McIlvaine believed there was evidence to support the woman's testimony. After all, he said, according to Hume's own words, the future state carried with it terrors of darkness and uncertainty. Thus Hume had known, he insisted, "that his ALL, FOR EVER, was at stake; and that he was unconcerned, unanxious, *when not diverted*, is incredible." [23] As in the case of Thomas Paine, McIlvaine appears to have felt little sympathy for the dying infidel. As in the earlier instance, this too may perplex today's readers. Yet, as with Paine, so with Hume: McIlvaine considered him knowingly guilty beneath the air of polite doubt. For such a one, he could summon little compassion. Compassion, after all, is an emotion, a sentiment. To McIlvaine, compassion was reserved for the poor, the sick, the widow, the orphan, not for arrogant skeptics. In Hume, celebrated figure though he was (and is), he saw a creature of pride and rebellion, a victim of his own sophistries, yet all the more guilty for that. In Hume, he saw the embodiment of ceaseless doubt; therefore, an offender against revelation, faith and commitment; in sum, an enemy of all those things in which he himself believed.

"This is my birthday. I have now attained to *seventy years of age*. The Lord's goodness, and love, and grace, and mercy, be praised." Thus McIlvaine opens his journal entry of January 18, 1869. From his earliest years as a priest, he had made such entries on the date of his birth. In these dozens of entries he had assessed his health both spiritual and physical, praised the Lord whom he served, and censured himself for falling short in the duties he attempted with such diligence to fulfill. Every year, it was a summing up of all that he had done and left undone, of all that he had hoped for, of all that he had received. He never failed to express gratitude. He made sure always that he ascribed the good things in life to powers that were beyond his own. "My whole soul praises Him for what He has saved me from…during these years of such great immeasurable unworthiness." [24]

McIlvaine "reviewed with wonder and humiliation unspeakable" the story of his life, beginning when he had "first turned to the Lord," while in college at Princeton, in his seventeenth year. "Grace has abounded indeed," he wrote. "Most heartily and thankfully can I say…'By the grace of God I am what I am.'" He praised God for the grace that had sustained him through illnesses, trials and failings, and affirmed his trust that grace would see him through, grace "made perfect in weakness." He looked for grace to sustain him *especially* at the gates of death. "He will provide for that time of need," he assured himself, "as He has provided for all times past. But faith is often weak. I cannot anticipate that time without some uncomfortable apprehensions." So he asked to be strengthened. "Lord, increase my faith. Give me the victory. Enable me to glorify Thee by my trust and peace in the presence of that last enemy." [25]

Midway through 1869, he sensed once more the approach of death. He seemed to have become more reconciled to dying, better prepared for parting with the good things of creation. "This world," he wrote, "much as I love its beauties of nature, and most precious as my dear family are to my heart, I have no unwillingness to leave. My affections, I believe, are on my blessed Lord, and *where He is*." As providence would have it, he lived on. The day he turned seventy-two, he made note of health worries, family deaths and church concerns. Even a hint of millennialism entered in. Through it all, through "great mercies…and much sorrow," he declared abiding trust in God. In that season of loss, a son, Joseph, had died, as mentioned in the last chapter. "My health had previously begun to fail," he wrote. "My son's death caused it to sink rapidly, so that I could do nothing that required any mental effort." A month earlier, Charles Bloomfield McIlvaine, a grandson, had died too, a little boy of "sweet" disposition. In consequence, the bishop sailed to England, partly to seek "reinvigoration" of his health, partly to visit his favorite daughter, Mamy, who lived in London. "Is it not very likely," he asked, predictably, "that this year will be my last on earth? That before its months are come and gone, I shall have known what it is to be out of the body? In that case, 'present with the Lord,'— present before Him with my precious Joe, and the dear children who went before him—present with all that multitude of the blessed who make the 'Communion of Saints' in Heaven!" He expected an increase of tribulation until the coming of the Lord, who would bring "restitution of all things." Despite declining health, he remained a warrior in the ecclesiastical wars, if only in his prayers. "Remember, O Lord!" he asked in the same entry, "Our American Episcopal Church—send labourers, put down the Romish superstitions...and doctrinal corruptions that now assume so much boldness." He prayed for a halt in the "progress of the Rationalistic evil," [26] and interceded for those who would remain in the world to carry on the fight after he was gone.

But the arrival of death was delayed yet again. Hence, we find McIlvaine, a year later, writing to his daughter on his birthday, meditating once more on the anticipated approach of the end while expressing surprise at his longevity. "I have," he wrote, "been permitted to attain an age greater than that of any of my family, parents included." He recounted how, in his boyhood, he was thought to have the "least vigorous" constitution of anyone in the family. Yet here he was, alive, in his seventy-fourth year, having outlived all his siblings. "Through a life of constant, exacting labour and great tension of mind," he wrote, "having had much mental trial and bodily exposure, and having suffered many dangerous accidents and encountered many critical dangers, by care, and goodness, and merciful forbearance of my Heavenly Father I am brought to this day." Reverting to form, he added: "My darling, I have little reason to expect another birthday." But he was not troubled. "It is not a sorrowful thought....It has *feeling*—of tenderness and solemnity. *Tenderness* at thought of the dear ones I shall leave. But though I realize every day that I am so near, I have not the least anxiety or trouble of spirit." He did, however, suffer in body. He said that his head had "been quite bad, so that I can do very little. The least excitement of conversation, no matter how agreeable, affects me *painfully*, or rather, I should say, produces consciousness of brain effect." [27]

Thirteen months later, the final illness commenced. It began in February 1873 as McIlvaine traveled in Italy with Canon and Mrs. Carus. They had taken a steamer from Genoa to Leghorn, then traveled to Pisa and Florence. McIlvaine was reported by Carus to be in excellent health and spirits, and was thoroughly enjoying himself. However, on a Sunday in Florence, while attending the American Episcopal Church, he found the heat to be oppressive. The following morning, while visiting his banker, he "unadvisedly threw off his cloak, and got a severe chill." A doctor was called, "hot applications" administered, and his condition improved. On the two days following, he was languid but active. On the next day, a Thursday, he was less well, and towards evening became exceedingly weak, scarcely able to walk to his bedroom. There followed a disturbed night, with difficulty in breathing, and by Saturday morning, February 22, he was very ill. Two doctors were summoned. After examining the patient and consulting together, they concluded the disorder was pulmonary apoplexy, an inflammation of the lungs characterized by sudden, marked loss of bodily function due to rupture or blockage of a blood vessel. There was, they said, no hope of recovery. On hearing the news, the Caruses were "quite overwhelmed," but McIlvaine "seemed quite prepared for the intelligence, and received it with the most perfect calmness, and prepared at once for his departure to his blessed Saviour." In the hours that followed, his breathing became loud and rapid. "He had," Carus said, "certainly to undergo much suffering from the blisters, which had to be continually placed on his chest, but his patience through the whole trial, and his gentle submission to whatever was prescribed, were very striking and affecting." [28]

As soon as he learned how dire his condition was, McIlvaine began dictating messages to members of his family, especially to his wife, as well as to fellow bishops in America and other friends, clerical and lay. He gave directions concerning his "remains," asking that they be sent to New York to a son-in-law, whence they could be conveyed to Cincinnati, where they would be laid beside his children. He asked that three hymns be read to him. These were "Just as I Am," his favorite; "Rock of Ages" and "Jesu, Lover of My Soul." Between spells of coughing, he spoke to his friends of his "perfect trust in Jesus." He recited Scripture texts, among them Romans 8:32: "He that spared not His own Son, but delivered Him up for us all, how shall He not with Him also freely give us all things?" Carus recalled that he and McIlvaine often spoke of the text as the one which Charles Simeon "considered 'the strongest in Scripture,' calling it 'his sheet-anchor.'" McIlvaine alluded to his early life, and the favor he had found at the hand of the Lord. "He called me," he said, "in my youth in circumstances unfavourable; but He has led me on, and kept me, when I had hardly any to stand with me. He, therefore, who began a good work in me, will certainly carry it on. How can I doubt it?" [29]

McIlvaine's breathing continued loud and labored throughout the day, though he insisted that he felt no pain, only uneasiness after violent spells of coughing. From time to time, he would put his hand to his brow to feel, as he told the Caruses, "whether the cold dew of death was yet upon it." Through it all he remained calm. While the Lord tarried, he prayed without ceasing, asking for strength, pondering the words of the Bible, begging forgiveness for his shortcomings. He alluded to the ministry of angels, a favorite subject. "When the soul is out of its tabernacle," he said, "the angels will convey it to Jesus." [30] At his request, Carus administered Holy Communion to all who were present, a nurse and a courier among them.

To the end, McIlvaine remained a Reformed theologian, clear-headed in his views, agitated still by "Romish" corruptions.

"Horrid doctrine," he exclaimed unexpectedly. Carus was puzzled. A moment later, McIlvaine indicated purgatory was the object of his displeasure. Carus agreed with the assessment, noting that St. Paul "spoke very differently" than the Roman church "when he said, that 'to depart was to be with Christ.'" [31] How happily, they agreed, did the Apostle's words contrast with the Roman teaching, wherein those who were in the grace of God but still expiating their sins suffered the pains of purgation, rather than the pleasures of Christ's company, immediately upon dying.

To everyone's surprise, McIlvaine's condition began to improve. On Wednesday, February 26, a second consultation was held, after which the doctors pronounced the right lung to have been healed. The cough had abated as well, the patient was able to eat nourishing food, and he began sleeping more soundly. When told the doctors had diagnosed his condition as critical on the prior Saturday, he said he had "never *so known* the Lord as he had done *that* day." [32] Concerned that he might have said in his crisis something dishonorable to his savior, tears came into his eyes, and he begged Carus to read to him the words of the hymn, "Crown Him Lord of All." The following morning, he asked for additional hymns to be read, along with Bible passages.

McIlvaine's health improved until Sunday, March 9, at which time it became clear he had been given a reprieve, not a pardon. Growing weaker, he began again to cough incessantly at night. Following a prolonged examination, the doctors declared the situation critical. Though McIlvaine continued in "gentleness and patience" and his mind remained "quite unclouded and his peace perfect," his exhaustion was extreme. Nonetheless, he ate well in the evening, and there appeared to be no immediate danger of his demise. Thus the Caruses went out for a time, leaving the patient in the care of his nurse. Before long they were recalled. "After taking his food," they were told, "a change suddenly came on—he said he had had enough, and after looking very kindly on them [the nurse and the courier] and pressing their hands, he gently laid his head back on the pillow and closed his eyes." The Caruses felt for a pulse and held McIlvaine's hands. "But so quiet and gentle was the end, "Carus said, "that we could not precisely say when the blessed spirit departed." He later put the time at seven o'clock, for at that instant McIlvaine's countenance "lighted up with such an expression of peaceful joy that we felt sure he was even now beholding that dear Lord, whom he had so fervently loved and longed to see. It was indeed a literal falling asleep in Jesus." The small gathering was relieved at his peaceful and painless end, having feared his difficulty in breathing might have resulted in a "severe struggle at the last." [33]

Throughout his life, owing to habits of piety and introspection, McIlvaine had focused on his death, believed it to be imminent, and prayed that he might be ready for it. When it was in fact nigh, by all accounts, he found himself at peace. After a lifetime of joy and service, trial and tumult, he slipped away without a sound.

1. Charles Pettit McIlvaine, editor, *Memoirs of the Life of the Rev. Charles Simeon*, xvi.
2. Lewis O. Saum, *The Popular Mood of Pre-Civil War America*, 23, 99.
3. Quoted in Saum, 24, 97.
4. Mark Twain, *Huckleberry Finn* (Greenwich Unabridged Library Classics, Chatham River Press, New York, 1982), 210.
5. Richard Geldard, *The Spiritual Teachings of Ralph Waldo Emerson* (Lindisfarne Books, Great Barrington, Mass., 2001), 121.
6. Quoted in Edgar Lee Masters, *Lincoln the Man* (Dodd-Mead & Company, New York, 1931), 431.
7. Quoted in William Carus, *Memorials*, 253.
8. Quoted in George Morgan Hills, *A History of the Church in Burlington*, 394, 390, 390-391, 392.
9. Quoted in Carus, 118.
10. Rebecca Lyman, *Early Christian Traditions*, 97.
11. Quoted in Carus, 118.
12. Ibid., 119, 120.
13. Carus, 2.
14. Quoted in Loren Dale Pugh, *Bishop Charles Pettit McIlvaine*, 48.

15. Quoted in Carus, 44-45, 45.
16. Ibid., 47.
17. Anna Pierrepont to George W. DuBois (Kenyon Archives), no. 36-07-04.
18. Quoted in Pugh, 99.
19. Charles Pettit McIlvaine to Mrs. George Washington DuBois (Kenyon Archives), no. 72-11-15-1.
20. Carus, 286-287.
21. McIlvaine, *The Truth and Life: Twenty-Two Sermons*, Sermon XV, "The Believer's Progressive Life in Christ," 344.
22. McIlvaine, *The Evidences of Christianity*, 352, 348, 349, 349-350.
23. Ibid., 351.
24. Quoted in Carus, 289.
25. Ibid.
26. Ibid., 290, 308, 309.
27. Ibid., 318-319, 319.
28. Carus, 343, 344.
29. Quoted in Carus, 344, 344-345, 345.
30. Ibid., 345, 346.
31. Ibid., 348.
32. Ibid., 350.
33. Carus, 351, 352.

AFTERWORD

McIlvaine's Relevance for Today

Episcopalian Evangelicalism, as Charles Pettit McIlvaine would
have understood and endorsed it, was all but extinct by the
beginning of the twentieth century. Within three decades of his
death, the churchmanship to which he had devoted his life had
been reduced to scattered remnants, its few remaining adherents
clinging to the born-again experience and the Reformation-based
theology of the original movement. In large part, the Episcopal
Church had divided its fractious self into two new camps,
consisting of Liberal Catholics and Liberal Evangelicals. Although
members of the latter group continued to use the Evangelical
label, much of the substance of the original had vanished.

The new Evangelicals, of whom many were members of the
cultural elite, were influenced during the latter nineteenth century
by several trends: higher critical views of the Bible from Germany
and Britain; new currents in philosophy; discoveries and theories
in the historical and biological sciences, and new social ideas. The
juggernaut of Darwinism, especially, owing to its radically
different views on both creation and social ethics, altered the
outlook of many Evangelicals. Previous to Darwin, it had been
possible to read the Bible largely at face value. But when the
theory of evolution—as held by many—reduced the creation
accounts to either sublime myth or bad science, it forfeited a

measure of its hold on the educated classes. Ritualists or Anglo-Catholics, who placed less overt emphasis on the Bible and more on tradition and liturgy, were less directly affected.

In need of a new paradigm, Evangelicals accepted the latest theories of natural science and their wider implications, hence devaluing the historicity of Scripture and its concomitant influence on their lives. To use another label, they became Broad Churchmen, close in their views to those of Henry Briston Wilson and the other authors of *Essays and Reviews*, the liberal bombshell of the 1860s. As such, they opposed positive definition in theology and sought to interpret Scripture and church teaching in a broad and liberal sense, always with an eye, as noted, to the latest findings of natural science and critical study of the Bible.

Other factors affected the outlook of Evangelicals as well. The "Gilded Age" itself (so named by Mark Twain), from 1870 until the turn of the century, with its urbanization, industrial expansion, and concentrations of great wealth, left its stamp upon them. In the words of historian Samuel Eliot Morrison, it was "a robust, fearless, generous era, full of gusto and joy of living, affording wide scope to individual energy and material creation." [1] Amidst the optimistic ambience of the period, Evangelicals—alongside men and women of means generally—were more likely to identify joy and fulfillment with the world around them than with an increasingly remote afterlife. The melancholy tone and obsession with death that marked the ante-bellum period receded into the shadows of a newer and brighter world and its seemingly unlimited opportunities. Theological liberalism, with its anti-dogmatic stance and adherence to recent trends in biblical and scientific scholarship, fed on the energies and opportunities of the post-bellum period. During the final years of McIlvaine's life, it had been a struggling minority view. By the closing decades of the century, it had become the dominant trend. According to historian Roger Steer, Liberal Catholics had attained a majority in the Episcopal Church, although "there were also pockets of low-church Liberalism…with varying degrees of orthodoxy….No classical Evangelical party existed from 1900 until the 1960s." [2]

Catholic and Low Church liberals may have differed on matters of worship, but both were deeply marked by the cultural turbulence that was modernizing the church.

For the first half of the twentieth century, High and Low Church Episcopalians quarreled mostly about *adiaphora*, "matters of indifference," aspects of worship perversely guaranteed by their reputed lack of significance to stir factional passions. For their part, Low Churchmen complained of excessive ritual, of "smells and bells" (the burning of incense and the ringing of small bells, particularly during the Eucharist), and of ornately decorated church buildings. In turn, High Churchmen criticized their Low Church brethren for failing to avail themselves of the riches of catholic worship, especially the frequent use of the sacraments. These conflicts were sidelined by less parochial matters in the middle decades of the twentieth century, notably the civil rights and anti-Vietnam War struggles of the 1960s and '70s, in which increasing numbers of clergy and laity participated. Then, in the final quarter of the century, battles erupted over prayer book revision, women's ordination, and the role of homosexuals in the church.

A new—and old—element was added in the early 1960s: the reappearance of the long moribund Evangelical presence in something like its classical form. "In these decades," according to Roger Steer, "Charismatic and Evangelical renewal organizations proliferated, and 'renewed' parishes multiplied." These developments occurred while the Episcopal Church as a whole underwent a dramatic decline in membership. Owing to their passion to evangelize and renew, Evangelicals blunted the decline to some extent by bringing new members into the fold. Yet between 1963 and 1988, the over three-million-member denomination—rocked by innovation, war and protest—lost a million members. [3]

The revival of classical Evangelicalism did not please all Episcopalians. In part, the complaint against it was aimed at the Anglican origin of much of the renewal impulse. "There is an attempt," said historian Urban T. Holmes, "to bring to this country a brand of English Evangelicalism which has never really found much acceptance here before." [4] The remark, patently incorrect, likely represented wishful thinking on the part of a prominent church liberal. For the English influence, as we have seen, had made its imprint once before, and with undeniable success. The vigorous Evangelicalism of the ante-bellum period was clearly marked by English influence, even as Bishop McIlvaine—the undisputed leader of the movement—was an Anglophile to his fingertips, and deeply indebted to the teaching and character of the Anglican saint, Charles Simeon. So too, English influence on the Episcopal renewal of the latter twentieth century was early and profound. According to Roger Steer, the main thrust came from the Charismatic renewal of the 1960s. Dennis Bennett, a transplanted Englishman and Episcopal priest, was a seminal figure in that movement. A powerful leader with some Evangelical roots, he introduced key elements of Charismatic teaching—among them "baptism in the Holy Spirit" and speaking in tongues—into parishes in California, Washington and elsewhere.

In addition, more classical forms of Anglican Evangelicalism took root in the same period. Americans such as Peter Moore, dean from 1996-2004 of the Evangelically-grounded Trinity Episcopal School for Ministry (founded near Pittsburgh in 1976), had studied in England, where he was influenced by Anglican scholars John Stott and J. I. Packer, among others. Additional leaders of the movement, who had also studied in England, joined Moore in founding (in 1963) the American branch of the Evangelical Fellowship of the Anglican Communion. This was another important step in the resurgence of Evangelicalism in the Episcopal Church. Additional influence has been forthcoming from the British scholar Peter Toon, whose "Reformed

Catholicism" has underpinned the efforts of the Prayer Book Society of the U. S. A.

McIlvaine would be perplexed if not dumbfounded by some of the issues that divide the Episcopal Church today. After all, he was a man of his times: the decades of the early Republic, right on through the Civil War. Today, the Republic is an empire of sorts, long since having spread its power and influence in the world. So, too, has the church been altered in far-reaching respects. The victory of something like the Rationalism McIlvaine once opposed, combined with High Church ritual something like the High Church and Tractarian teachings he also opposed, has moved the church, despite the Evangelical revival, in directions that would have distressed him. Yet these developments he would have understood, as they involved issues with which he was conversant. Debates about prayer book revision would have resonated with him as well.

On the other hand, the ordination of women to the priesthood, or of sexually active gay men and lesbians to the priesthood and even the episcopate, would have been beyond his ken. That women should be ordained would not, most likely, have occurred to him, although he was beholden to women's service and appreciated it. He knew well from personal experience the large—and indispensable—role that they played in parish life. Similarly, we assume that homosexuality in the church would have been quite beyond the imagination of a Victorian clergyman of McIlvaine's temper. The beginning of the great shift in sexual attitudes was some decades away at the time of his death, and its apotheosis in the second half of the twentieth century could never have been more than a glimmer in his mind. Homosexuality was the sin without a name.

But McIlvaine *would* have recognized the new breed of Evangelical Episcopalians active in the church today. As with him, they place their emphases on the necessity of conversion, the importance of vicarious atonement, the inspiration of Scripture, and an emotional spirituality. The last had been largely absent from Episcopal worship for many decades, hence reinforcing the church's reputation for staid formalism. To a degree, Evangelicals have countered that reputation by adding a measure of "heart religion" to liturgical worship. Yet despite their emotional style, they appreciate the mind. Like their forebears, they are doctrinally sensitive. There is clarity and rigor in their theology. One need only examine, for instance, the work of Paul F. M. Zahl, former dean of Trinity Episcopal School of Ministry; C. FitzSimmons Allison, retired bishop of South Carolina; any of the contributors to *Can a Bishop be Wrong?* (edited by former Trinity dean, Peter Moore), or any of the many books written by British churchmen such as Michael Green or the aforementioned John Stott, J. I. Packer and Peter Toon.

The resurgence of Evangelicals in the Episcopal Church puts one in mind of the career and character of Charles Pettit McIlvaine. Spirited, principled, unbending, they, like him, have risen up to contend for the faith. Strangely enough, many appear to be unfamiliar with McIlvaine himself, either as writer, revivalist, or Evangelical leader. That this should be the case is puzzling. One would think that historians of the church, Evangelicals most of all, would find him a figure of much interest. As it is, they overlook him, excepting the occasional article or reference in a church journal or historical review. [5] Perhaps this is understandable in the case of church liberals or Anglo-Catholics, neither of whom is likely to trumpet an Evangelical's virtues. Even so, to ignore him is a mistake, for he has much to teach the church. This is true for liberals and Evangelicals both. It is true for liberals because they need an honest portrait of the Evangelical tradition, as represented by an outstanding figure, to correct their tendency towards caricaturing their opponents. It is true for Evangelicals because they are in need of a sense of history to enrich their understanding of themselves and the principles to which they adhere. McIlvaine's theological acumen, leadership ability, personal example, even the way in which he enlisted his weaknesses in the work of faith, are instructive. Aside from theological or party strategy, he would teach them how to peer into their souls, how to come to grips with what it is that has made them who they are.

Whether today's Evangelicals will find a future in the Episcopal Church or disperse into "continuing" Anglican bodies, or even into other denominations, remains unclear. Were McIlvaine present today, he quite likely would remain in the fold, as both a loyal churchman and as a valiant presence ever willing to fight the good fight. He would be present to contend for the faith once given by proclaiming God's word with passion and rigor, by relying on God's strength to counter his weakness, and by praying to God to correct his faults. "Just as I Am," his favorite hymn, would be on his lips. He would be present, just as he was in time past, laboring in grace, by faith, "meaning it" from first to last.

1. Samuel Eliot Morison, *The Oxford History of the American People* (Oxford University Press, New York, 1965), 773.
2. Roger Steer, *Guarding the Holy Fire*, 269.
3. David Hein and Gardiner H. Shattuck Jr., *The Episcopalians*, 133.
4. Steer, 269.
5. Exceptions to the rule are Rebecca Hochstedt Butler and Loren Dale Pugh, who have done valuable research on McIlvaine.

APPENDIX

Charlotte Elliot's "Just as I Am"

Just as I am, without one plea,
But that Thy blood was shed for me,
And that Thou bid'st me come to Thee,
O Lamb of God, I come.

Just as I am, and waiting not
To rid my soul of one dark blot,
To Thee whose blood can cleanse each spot,
O Lamb of God, I come.

Just as I am, though tossed about
With many a conflict, many a doubt;
Fightings and fears within, without,
O Lamb of God, I come.

Just as I am, poor, wretched, blind;
Sight, riches, healing of the mind,
Yea, all I need, in thee to find,
O Lamb of God, I come.

Just as I am: Thou wilt receive;
Wilt welcome, pardon, cleanse, relieve,
Because Thy promise I believe,
O Lamb of God, I come.

275

A Born-Again Episcopalian

Just as I am, Thy love unknown
Has broken every barrier down;
Now to be Thine, yea, Thine alone,
O Lamb of God, I come.

Just as I am, of that free love,
The breadth, length, depth, and height to prove,
Here for a season, then above:
O Lamb of God, I come.

In 1860, Charles Pettit McIlvaine chose "Just as I Am" to be sung at the close of his diocesan convention. It was to be part of evening worship, at which time his clergy would gather to pray, sing, hear the bishop's parting address, and strengthen "bonds of spiritual union." He chose the hymn because it "so beautifully expresses the very essence of the Gospel." He adopted it as his own, and wished to be remembered by it always. [1]

That McIlvaine should be attracted to the hymn is not surprising. The opening alone, "Just as I am, without one plea, but that Thy blood was shed for me," sums up his view of religion as a grace and faith-filled journey, dependent on Christ alone. Additional phrases resonate also. Afflicted by "many a conflict, many a doubt," he trusted Christ for "healing of the mind." Beset by troubles "within, without," he trusted Christ to "pardon, cleanse, relieve." Aware of life's brevity, "here for a season, then above," he trusted Christ to welcome him home. Although a spiritual "invalid" and sometimes a physical one as well, he was strengthened and supported by the Lamb of God:

"Yea, all I need, in Thee to find."

Charlotte Elliott, author of the hymn, was herself an invalid, from early childhood. Born in 1789 in Clapham, now a suburb of London, she led a secluded and rather embittered life for more than thirty years. In 1822, a Swiss minister, Caesar Malan, visited the Elliott household with a view to helping her. By the time he left, his wise words had wrought a change in her heart. In gratitude, she would become a prolific writer of religious verse. Moreover, she would correspond with her newfound friend, Dr. Malan, for the next forty years.

Elliott's famous hymn was written in 1834, at the time her brother, the Reverend H. V. Elliott, was holding a bazaar to aid the building fund of St. Mary's Hall in Brighton. Charlotte had lain awake all night, "tossed about with many a doubt" because of her helplessness while others were preparing for the event. Determined to control her feelings, she penned her confession of an invalid's faith. [2] In the days that followed, the poem was printed and sold across England. The leaflet on which it appeared said: "Sold for the Benefit of St. Mary's Hall, Brighton," followed by Elliott's favorite Gospel verse, "Him that Cometh to Me I Will in No Wise Cast Out." [3] In 1836, her poem was published in both the *Invalid's Hymn Book* and her *Hours of Sorrow Cheered and Comforted.* In the more than 170 years since, it has found a place in hymnals worldwide, and can fairly be called the most famous invitational hymn in history. It is most often set to William B. Bradbury's *Woodworth*, long the popular American setting for the text.

Although she remained an invalid, Elliott edited the *Christian Remembrancer Pocketbook* for twenty-five years. She assisted also in the publication of the *Invalid's Hymn Book* the same year she wrote "Just as I Am." The sixth edition of the book, published in 1854, contained 112 of her original poems. Other compilations were *Hymns for a Week* in 1839 and *Thoughts in Verse on Sacred Subjects* in 1869. She wrote 150 hymns in all, appealing mainly to those in sickness and sorrow. She died in 1871 at Brighton at the age of 82. As her family sifted through her papers, they found over a thousand letters from persons expressing gratitude for the way her famous hymn had touched their lives. [4]

1. Quoted in William Carus, *Memorials,* 199-200.
2. Joint Commission on the Revision of the Hymnal of the Protestant Episcopal Church in the United States of America, *The Hymnal 1940 Companion* (The Plimpton Press, Norwood, Mass., 1967), 259.
3. Robert J. Morgan, *Then Sings My Soul* (Thomas Nelson Inc., Nashville, Tenn., 2003), 113.
4. Ibid.

BIBLIOGRAPHY

Primary Sources

Archives

Bishops of Ohio Records, Episcopal Diocese of Ohio Archives, Cleveland.

Charles P. McIlvaine Collection. Greenslade Special Collections and Archives, Olin and Chalmers Libraries, Kenyon College, Gambier, Ohio.

Christ Church, Georgetown, Maryland, Archives.

Cincinnati, Ohio, Historical Society Library, Rare Book Archive.

Library Company of Burlington, New Jersey.

Spring Grove Cemetery and Arboretum, Cincinnati, Ohio.

William L. Clements Library, University of Michigan, Ann Arbor.

Books, Pamphlets and Other Published Materials
American Tract Society, New York, 1833.

Bodice, William B., *The Kenyon Book* (Theological Seminary of the Protestant Episcopal Church, Diocese of Ohio, 1890).

Carus, William, editor, *Memorials of the Right Reverend Charles Pettit McIlvaine, D. D., D.C.L., Late Bishop of Ohio, in the Protestant Episcopal Church of the United States* (Thomas Whittaker, New York, 1882).

Hills, George M., *History of the Church in Burlington, New Jersey* (Trenton: William S. Sharp, Printer, 1876).

Hodge, A. A., *The Life of Charles Hodge* (Charles Scribner's Sons, New York, 1880).

Jay, John, "Facts Connected with the Presentment of Bishop Onderdonk; A Reply to Parts of the Bishop's Statement" (Stanford and Swords, New York, and George S. Appleton, Philadelphia, 1845).

King, Charles, "A Review of the Trial of the Rt. Rev. Benjamin T. Onderdonk, D. D., by Charles King, editor of the New York American" (Stanford and Swords, New York, 1845).

Lee, Alfred, *In Memoriam: Charles Pettit McIlvaine, Late Bishop of the Diocese of Ohio* (Leader Printing Company, Cleveland, Ohio, 1873).

Lothrop, Thornton Kirkland, *William Henry Seward* (Houghton, Mifflin and Company, Boston and New York, 1896).

McIlvaine, Charles Pettit, *Justification by Faith: A Charge Delivered Before the Clergy of the Protestant Episcopal Church in the Diocese of Ohio, Sept. 13, 1839* (Columbus, Ohio, 1840).

-------- *Oxford Divinity, Compared with that of the Romish and Anglican Churches: with a Special View of the Doctrine of Justification by Faith* (R. B. Seeley and W. Burnside, London, 1841).

-------- "Pastoral Letter, Addressed to the Members of the Protestant Episcopal Church in the Diocese of Ohio" (William B. Thrall, Columbus, Ohio, 1848).

BIBLIOGRAPHY

-------- *"Spiritual Regeneration with Reference to Present Times: A Charge Delivered to the Clergy of the Diocese of Ohio"* (New York, 1851).

-------- editor, *Memoirs of the Life of the Rev. Charles Simeon* (Robert Carter & Brothers, New York, 1852).

-------- *The Evidences of Christianity, in Their External, or Historical, Division: Exhibited in a Course of Lectures* (Smith & English, Philadelphia, 1852).

-------- *The Truth and Life: Twenty-Two Sermons* (Robert Carter and Brothers, New York, 1855).

-------- "Bishop McIlvaine's Address to the Convention of the Diocese of Ohio, on the Revival of Religion" (Cincinnati, 1858).

-------- "The Work of Preaching Christ. A Charge: Delivered to the Clergy of the Diocese of Ohio" (Anson D. F. Randolph, New York, 1864).

-------- *Rationalism, As Exhibited in the Writings of Certain Clergymen of the Church of England, A Letter to the Clergy and Candidates for Holy Orders of the Protestant Episcopal Church, in the United States* (C. F. Bradley, Cincinnati, Ohio, 1865).

McIlvaine, Maria, *Obit Book*, 1873.

"Questions and Counsel for the Students of Nassau-Hall (At Princeton in New-Jersey) Who Hope that a Work of Saving Grace Has Been Wrought Upon Their Hearts" (Concord, 1815), Princeton Weekly Bulletin, May 22, 2000, Vol. 89, No. 28.

Seward, Frederick W., *Seward at Washington, as Senator and Secretary of State: A Memoir of His Life, With Selections from His Letters, 1861-1872* (Derby and Miller, New York, 1891).

Spectator, pseud., "Bishop Onderdonk's Trial. The Verdict Sustained at the Bar of Public Opinion; With Remarks on Laicus and Bishop Doane" (John F. Trow and Company, New York, 1845).

Williams, Isaac, *No. 80*, "On Reserve in Communicating Religious Knowledge," *Tracts for the Times by Members of the University of Oxford*, Vol. IV for 1836-37, New Edition (J. G. & F. Rivington, London, 1839).

Secondary Sources

Books and Articles

Ahlstrom, Sydney E., *A Religious History of the American People* (Yale University Press, 1972).

Armstrong, Karen, *The Battle for God* (Alfred A. Knopf, New York, 2000).

Bell, James B., "Charles P. McIlvaine," *For the Union: Ohio Leaders in the Civil War*, edited by Kenneth W. Wheeler (Ohio State University Press, 1968).

Bloom, Harold, *The American Religion: The Emergence of the Post-Christian Nation* (Simon & Schuster, New York, 1992).

Butler, Diana Hochstedt, *Standing Against the Whirlwind: Evangelical Episcopalians in Nineteenth-Century America* (Oxford University Press, New York, 1995).

Chorley, E. Clowes, *Men and Movements in the American Episcopal Church* (Charles Scribner's Sons, New York, 1950).

Ellis, Ieuan, *Seven Against Christ: A study of 'Essays and Reviews,'* Volume XXIII of *Studies in the History of Christian Thought*, edited by Heiko A. Oberman (E. J. Brill, Leiden, The Netherlands, 1980).

Ferris, Norman B., *The Trent Affair: A Diplomatic Crisis* (The University of Tennessee Press, Knoxville, 1977).

BIBLIOGRAPHY

Geldard, Richard, *The Spiritual Teachings of Ralph Waldo Emerson* (Lindisfarne Books, Great Barrington, Mass., 2001).

Hall, Mark H., "Bishop McIlvaine: The Reluctant Frontiersman," *Historical Magazine of the Protestant Episcopal Church* 44 (1975).

Heick, O. W., with contributions by J. L. Neve, *History of Protestant Theology*, Volume Two of *A History of Christian Thought*, by J. L. Neve (The Muhlenberg Press, Philadelphia, 1946).

Hein, David and Gardiner H. Shattuck Jr., *The Episcopalians* (Praeger, Westport, Connecticut, 2004).

Holifield, E. Brooks, *Theology in America: Christian Thought from the Age of the Puritans to the Civil War* (Yale University Press, New Haven & London, 2003).

James, William, *The Varieties of Religious Experience* (Penguin Books, New York, 1986).

Joint Commission on the Revision of the Hymnal of the Protestant Episcopal Church in the United States of America, *The Hymnal 1940 Companion* (The Plimpton Press, Norwood, Mass., 1967).

Lentz, Perry, *The Anglican Digest*, January, 1997.

Lyman, Rebecca, *Early Christian Traditions*, The New Church's Teaching Series, Volume Six (Cowley Publications, Boston, 1999).

Malone, Dumas, editor, *Dictionary of American Biography*, vol. VII (Charles Scribner's Sons, New York, 1934).

Marsden, George M., *Understanding Fundamentalism and Evangelicalism* (William B. Eerdmans Publishing Company, Grand Rapids, Mich., 1996).

Masters, Edgar Lee, *Lincoln the Man* (Dodd-Mead & Company, New York, 1931).

Morgan, Robert J., *Then Sings My Soul* (Thomas Nelson Inc., Nashville, Tenn., 2003).

Morison, Samuel Eliot, *The Oxford History of the American People* (Oxford University Press, New York, 1965).

Mossner, Ernest Campbell, *The Life of David Hume* (Oxford University Press, 1980).

Niven, John, *Salmon P. Chase: A Biography* (Oxford University Press, New York, 1995).

Noll, Mark, *The Scandal of the Evangelical Mind* (Inter-Varsity Press, Downers Grove, Ill., 1994).

Noll, Mark A., "The Princeton Theology" in *Reformed Theology in America: A History of Its Modern Development*, edited by David F. Wells (Baker Books, Grand Rapids, Mich., 2000).

O'Connell, Marvin R., *The Oxford Conspirators: A History of the Oxford Movement 1833-45* (The MacMillan Company, London, 1969).

Packer, J. I., *The Evangelical Anglican Identity Problem: An Analysis* (Latimer House, Oxford, 1980).

-------- *A Quest for Godliness: The Puritan Vision of the Christian Life* (Crossway Books, Wheaton, Ill., 1990).

Podles, Leon J., *The Church Impotent: The Feminization of Christianity* (Spence Publishing Company, Dallas, 1999).

Rasmussen, Jane, *Musical Taste as a Religious Question in Nineteenth-Century America*, Volume 20 of *Studies in American Religion* (The Edwin Mellen Press, Lewiston, N. Y., and Queenston, Ontario, Canada, 1986).

Saum, Lewis O., *The Popular Mood of Pre-Civil War America* (Greenwood Press, Westport, Connecticut, 1980).

BIBLIOGRAPHY

Smythe, George Franklin, *Kenyon College: Its First Century* (Yale University Press, New Haven, Connecticut).

Steer, Roger, *Guarding the Holy Fire: The Evangelicalism of John R. W. Stott, J. I. Packer, and Alister McGrath* (Baker Books, Grand Rapids, Mich., 1999).

Stephenson, Alan M. G., *The First Lambeth Conference, 1867* (S. P. C. K., London, 1967).

Toon, Peter, *Evangelical Theology, 1833-1856: A Response to Tractarianism* (John Knox Press, Atlanta, Georgia, 1979).

Turner, Frank M., *John Henry Newman: The Challenge to Evangelical Religion* (Yale University Press, New Haven and London, 2002).

Twain, Mark (Samuel Langhorne Clemens), *Huckleberry Finn* (Greenwich Unabridged Library Classics, Chatham River Press, New York, 1982).

Van Deusen, Glyndon G., *William Henry Seward* (Oxford University Press, New York, 1967).

Warfield, Benjamin B., *Studies in Perfectionism* (Presbyterian and Reformed Publishing Company, Phillipsburg, N. J., 1958).

Wells, David F., "Charles Hodge" in *Reformed Theology in America: A History of Its Modern Development,* edited by David F. Wells (Baker Books, Grand Rapids, Mich., 2000).

Welter, Barbara, *Dimity Convictions: The American Woman in the Nineteenth Century* (Ohio State University Press, Athens, 1976).

Dissertations

Pugh, Loren Dale, *Bishop Charles Pettit McIlvaine: The Faithful Evangel* (dissertation, Department of Religion in the Graduate School of Duke University, 1985).

SOME OTHER TITLES BY SOLID GROUND

In addition to *A Born Again Episcopalian*, we are delighted to offer several titles connected with Old Princeton, the school of McIlvaine.

Truth and Life: *22 Christ-Centered Sermons* by Charles Petit McIlvaine is an outstanding example of the powerful preaching ministry of the subject of the biography you hold in your hands.

Notes on Galatians by J. Gresham Machen is a reprint that is long overdue, especially in light of the present-day battle of the doctrine articulated in Galatians.

The Origin of Paul's Religion by J. Gresham Machen penetrates to the heart of the matter and speaks to many of the contemporary attacks upon the purity of the Gospel of Christ.

The Virgin Birth of Christ by J. Gresham Machen is the finest work ever produced to defend the supernatural birth of our Lord

Biblical and Theological Studies by the professors of Princeton Seminary in 1912, at the centenary celebration of the Seminary. Articles are by men like Allis, Vos, Warfield, Machen, Wilson and others.

Theology on Fire: Vols. 1 & 2 by Joseph A. Alexander is the two volumes of sermons by this brilliant scholar from Princeton Seminary.

A Shepherd's Heart by James W. Alexander is a volume of outstanding expository sermons from the pastoral ministry of one of the leading preachers of the 19th century.

Evangelical Truth by Archibald Alexander is a volume of practical sermons intended to be used for Family Worship.

The Lord of Glory by B.B. Warfield is one of the best treatments of the doctrine of the Deity of Christ ever written. Warfield is simply masterful.

The Power of God unto Salvation by B.B. Warfield is the first book of sermons ever published of this master-theologian. Several of these are found nowhere else.

Mourning a Beloved Shepherd by Charles Hodge and John Hall is a little volume containing the funeral addresses for James W. Alexander. Very informative and challenging.

Call us Toll Free at **1-877-666-9469**
Send us an e-mail at **sgcb@charter.net**
Visit us on line at **www.solid-ground-books.com**